TAI CHI AT AUSCHWITZ

An
Unexpected
Reconciliation
Journey

PETER STERNBERG

with MAURA STERNBERG

Tai Chi at Auschwitz
An Unexpected Reconciliation Journey

For information about this title or to order other books and/or electronic media, contact the publisher:

Peter Sternberg
www.peterandmaurabooks.com
peter.maura.books@gmail.com

ISBNs:
979-8-9928841-0-4 (softcover)
979-8-9928841-1-1 (eBook)

Printed in the United States of America

Cover Illustration and Design: Peter Sternberg
Interior Design: 1106 Design

Some of the material in this book was first published in an essay titled: "My Journey to Liberation at Auschwitz" in *Pearls of Ash and Awe (Asche Perlen): Twenty Years of Bearing Witness in Auschwitz with Bernie Glassman and Zen Peacemakers*, Kathleen Battke, Ed. (Berlin, edition-Steinrich, 2015). Used with kind permission.

Peter's Dedication

This work is dedicated to my teachers, my family, and my friends—for your loving faith in me, and to the people who knowingly or unconsciously and unintentionally hurt me, for I could not be *here* without you. And to the creatures and people I knowingly or unintentionally hurt; I so deeply regret my misdeeds, and yet, I find I could not be *here* without those experiences either.

And to all the birds who would not let me be . . .

Maura's Dedication

My contribution to this work is dedicated to the Great Unseen Hands that shape life, move water, grow mountains, and blossom flowers. To the ancestors and wise ones who have kept me on my path, amidst much kicking and screaming.

And to my beloveds, family of blood and spirit, without whom I would have been lost many times.

Author's Note

This book tells stories of my early and recent history. My writing is based on my recollection of that history. The stories are true to what I believe transpired. Others who were present or involved may remember things differently, but ultimately, this is my story as recollected by me.

Names and identifying characteristics of some individuals have been changed. Some dialogue has been recreated. Where dialogue appears, the intention was to recreate the essence of conversations rather than capture them verbatim.

— PETER STERNBERG,
Chicago, Illinois, 2025

Table of Contents

All *Interludes* are authored by Maura.
All **Parts** are authored by Peter.

I *had been comfortable in my life* as a husband and father, loving my work as a psychotherapist, and enjoying my hobbies when I could find the time for them. From out of nowhere in 2013, a sequence began that was so jolting that I felt as if I had been flung off of a catapult. I began a *reconciliation journey* I never planned to undertake—I didn't even know what a *reconciliation journey* was! I was presented with serendipitous events, one after another, that "took me" without me fully understanding what I was getting into. What was consistently required of me was a willingness to say "Yes," which is what I did. The events did their work; challenging me, confronting me, in ways I could not have imagined.

Saying "Yes" took me to countries I never thought I'd travel to (Germany, Poland) and to encounters at places that held history with wrenching, gutting stories: Auschwitz, Buchenwald, a Lakota Sioux Reservation, and the American triad of Black-enslavement history in Selma, Birmingham, and Montgomery, Alabama—to name some. As those encounters unfolded, I was thrown back into my personal history, forced to leave the comfort of my identity as a Jewish victim of persecution, and face my capacities as a perpetrator.

From the beginning of this journey, I knew to keep a journal. Those passages chronicled the reworking of my identity and the development of the relationship between *reckoning* and *reconciliation*. My journal entries became the basis for this book.

I was plodding along with my writing when my daughter Maura (who was, at the time, a celebrated English teacher) volunteered to get involved and guide the process. Again, the unforeseen. . . . Doing the project together opened a completely unexpected dimension of the journey for me and for us. I had always known that my purpose in writing the book was to convey a unique and interesting story: from the outset, I knew the title was going to be *Tai Chi at Auschwitz*. But it turns out there was a second, deeper purpose for writing the book that revealed itself only as Maura and I came to the end of the writing.

I take you with me, dear reader, into some tortured places in the world, some tortured history, and some tortured places in my past—into moments of a *dark night of the soul*. But the story does not end in pain and lostness. The reworking I was undergoing produced unsought—yet amazing outcomes for me *and* for my daughter.

So, welcome. Do come in. . . .

— PETER STERNBERG
Chicago, Illinois, 2025

Maura

Interlude #1

Parallel Tracks

Some six summers ago, before my life fell apart, my dad asked
me to read a few essays he'd authored. It was as though he had,
in his words, been unknowingly launched off of some invisible
catapult that had been waiting underneath him to fling him into
the unknown of transformation. He found himself meditating
at sites of atrocity, such as Nazi death camps, Museums of the
American Enslavement of Africans, and Native American res-
ervations, and had put pen to paper to capture the vibe.

I'm a writer and a teacher. I learned how to edit (ironically
enough) with a militant *German fierceness*, from my mother—whose
heritage is Irish. In an effort to preserve their marriage, she had
passed on the project of turning Dad's self-proclaimed "literary

dribble" into publication-worthy text. So, one summer night, my father and I sat outside, underneath buzzing moths and the cherry-stained pergola. And I, with no small measure of trepidation, took my first peek into my father's head.

It was like swimming through reedy pond water, dense and mysterious. The thick summer air coated our keyboards, and I had the familiar feeling of falling into something karmically important. I was like Alice shrinking into Wonderland, or Aladdin rubbing the lamp. And for many pages of skimmed and distracted reading, I had no clue what I was falling into—or what I was waking up.

Until I read "Track 17."

"Track 17" is the familiar nomenclature my father and I use to refer to a story he tells about a strange encounter he had standing on the platform of the *Track 17 Holocaust Memorial* in Berlin. I tried to keep my cool out under the pergola, but reading it, shrinking like Alice, and expanding like the Genie, all I could think was, *I have to help get his sorry ass published.*

The piece begins with a series of "coincidences":

I set my red carry-on case on the empty platform of the Track 17 Memorial, the point of deportation of Berlin's Jews. Because our car broke down and we could not get a replacement until the next day; because then I had to schlep all of the video-recording equipment I had with me in the red carry-on case; because, for a few minutes, Daniel and I were the only people walking around Track 17; as I walked reading the inlaid metal memorial plates, I set my red case on the platform of the Track 17 Memorial.

The Memorial, as my father tells it, is a site of in-between, a further step in the transformation from "German citizen" to "human fodder," as Jews were consumed by the Nazi regime. He describes it today as looking "poetic," nestled in between brush at either end of the platform; railroad tracks that, now, lead to nowhere.

My father is a Virgo, a licensed psychotherapist, and a pragmatist. He has deep access to the world of spirit and the divine but is Jewishly wary and reluctant about the whole thing. When birds visit him to deliver messages, he often raises his hands up and shrugs. So he didn't say it in so many words, but, to put it plainly, Track 17 is full of ghosts, brimming with "what has been," caught and hooked in the anguished fury of the past.

In "Track 17," my dad writes of the heartbreak throbbing around the red suitcase he'd left waiting on the empty platform. He says he turned back, saw it, and knew he had to take a photograph. In the midst of the snapshot, as though the red case and the snapshot were drawing him into the scene, a young German man on a bicycle approached, and their exchange buzzed with the heartbreak that the red suitcase captured in the first place: waiting, full of feeling, for tracks that lead to nowhere.

The young man began speaking excitedly and pressured in German. I made it clear I didn't speak German. He pressed on in broken English: "Did your father fight in the war? Your grandfather? Were your people killed? I'm so sorry for . . . I'm sorry to . . ." He couldn't find the English words to adequately express his distress. At this point, I made a grave mistake. I mistook him to be apologizing for interrupting me on the platform. Through our troubled communication, I kept saying, "No, it's alright, I'm just touring, visiting—you are not interrupting." On he went with still more emotion: "If I had been alive then I would have done something! I would have unlocked the doors of the train; I would have shot myself!"

By this time Daniel, my guide and translator, was standing with us, but even his fluency in German could not penetrate the misunderstanding I had begun. Although I knew that he was talking about the war and the Holocaust, for some reason I could not grasp that he was apologizing to me in such a driven way for it. Picking up on my misunderstanding, Daniel, too, thought he was apologetic for interrupting what we were doing on the Platform of Track 17. The German man finished his desperate and emotional monologue, got back on his bike, and rode off.

My father was possessed by a hatred for Germans and for Christianity all his life—he considered them his enemies. And, he's well versed in dramatic irony, because he married an Irish Catholic woman and spends as much time as he can these days doing Taoist practices.

In his writing, he admits to rage-fueled retribution fantasies of wiping Germany off the face of the Earth for committing the mind-bending atrocity of the Holocaust. Like a vengeful, war-lusty god, his dream of finally getting a chance at payback would not abate.

So, in this *in-between place*, with the red suitcase waiting like heartbreak on the platform, with my Jewish father in unknowing holy communion with ghosts and grief and rage and love, a German man arrives to openly apologize for his people's crimes. And my father, so reluctantly reverent and bone-headed, misses it. Completely. Two men, souls touching, hearts racing, with minds and tongues riding opposite trains, on parallel tracks that led to nowhere.

Within minutes, my father realized too late what the German man was trying to communicate. He honors this man in retrospect, wishing he could tell him that he need suffer no guilt for his ancestors' behavior, that the young man's acknowledgment is heard and fully received. And after all, America's colonizing and racist crimes are ongoing, and, how good are *we* at taking responsibility over here? Not great.

Out under the pergola, my father laments "In my imaginary redo, that German man and I would have realized the ways in which we are brothers in our respective and yet very similar soul-struggles. I would have gotten his name and contact information. Perhaps we'd have become friends."

Perhaps we'd have become friends.

The line rings loud in my ears, swirling with the moths under the pergola, a clamoring I can't ignore. Souls seeking friendship that so quickly slips through fingers, swirling down the drain of time and space—it strikes me as one of the most heartbreakingly beautiful things I've ever seen. And I tell him so.

My father, actively inquiring after his own ego demolition, and a bit browbeaten at the whole process, looks at me incredulously.

"Really?" he asks with his eyes wide.

"Yes," I say. "People need to hear this story."

Time freezes, out there under the pergola, and the distinctions between perspectives (father/daughter, teacher/student, victim/perpetrator) dissolve. They swirl like moths in the hot summer air. Suddenly, I see my father as though he's a student of mine, who—for the first time—can maybe see himself through my eyes.

"I don't think I've ever heard anything more divinely beautiful than this, Dad."

I know I'm reaching with the word *divine* here, but the impact of the piece and the hot summer air has me feeling brave. He seems nonplussed.

"It's a very painful experience for me, Maurz. I missed it—I missed the whole thing." He shakes his head with despair.

I realize that he can't see the medicine of his stories with quite enough clarity. He can only feel the grief of the miss and can't yet see the beauty of his heartbreak. For a fleeting moment, I worry that the power of this story could be lost. That amidst the intensity of his experiences and the burden of all the transformation, no one else might know about this *great wild thing* that was happening to him.

As the clamoring in my head quiets long enough for me to catch a glimpse of *what could be*, I sigh and respond:

"I'll help you write the book, Dad. We're gonna write you a book."

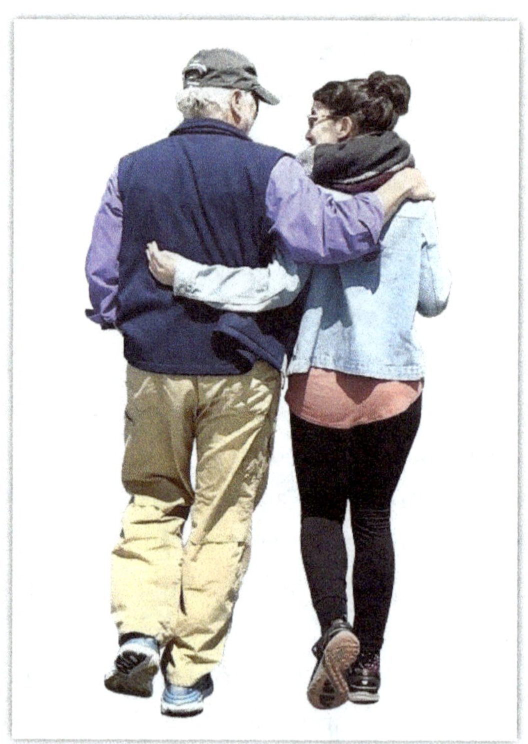

"On the Path"
Photo Credit: Ellianna Sternberg.

Peter

The Catapult

The Catapult:
I Could Be Him

can recall the excitement in my home in 1960, when I was ten years old, when Adolph Eichmann, a member of Adolf Hitler's SS and major organizer of the Holocaust, was captured by the Israelis and taken from Argentina to Jerusalem. He was put on trial for crimes against the Jewish people. Soon thereafter, I encountered and read the book and then saw the movie *Exodus*, by Leon Uris, telling the story of the Holocaust, the Jewish refugees and the birth of the State of Israel. The sense of excitement at Eichmann's arrest gave way to shock, horror, rage, and a sense of deep betrayal as I got my first glimpse of what his trial was about. The introduction to the material of the Holocaust through the book, the movie, and the trial had a profound and lasting impact on me. Fifty-three years later, without having ever planned to, I revisited the impact—of being afraid to be what I was . . . Jewish.

At Eichmann's trial, a man named Yehiel De-Nur (also "DiNoor"), who wrote under the pen name of "Ka-Tzetnik (Camp

Inmate) 135633" (the number tattooed on his arm), was called to testify. At one point during his testimony, De-Nur became agitated in the witness box. He stood up, stepped out, flailed about, and was told to sit down. He could not comply; he flailed about some more and then passed out—crashing to the floor. He was attended to and taken out of the courtroom on a stretcher. It was assumed that he was overcome giving testimony about his experiences as an inmate at Auschwitz.

Years later, when De-Nur was interviewed on the news program *60 Minutes*, he was asked if that was, in fact, why he'd fainted. "No," he said, "it was because when I looked at Eichmann, I did not see a monster. I saw an ordinary man. And I realized I could be him. That is why I fainted."[1]

And now, only now, after an intense encounter with history, sites of atrocity, groups of people I rejected, and my own history—now, after years of immersion in all of that, when I contemplate these two men, Eichmann and De-Nur, am I able to join De-Nur and see two ordinary men.

And now I realize I could be either—or both—of them.

---

1 Wikipedia, August 19, 2024, *Yehiel De-Nur,* September 2016, {*https://en.wikipedia .org/wiki/Yehiel De-Nur*}

The Catapult:
Paranoia

In *my early twenties,* I bought gold coins
—Jews should own gold before they need it.

I own a shotgun, a rifle, a pistol, and ammunition
—Jews should own guns before they need them.

There are no fewer than five combat staffs placed in various rooms
in my house and "throwing stars" in a drawer.

I have a third-degree Black Belt in one martial art and training
in three others.

I know how to subdue, maim, and kill with and without weapons.
    My family's passports are always up to date.
Eat everything. *Do Not Ever Leave or Waste Food. Ever.*

One day in late 2013, for the first time, I wondered: *Why would a person have this particular inventory of items, skills, and admonitions?*

For my entire adult life, I never thought anything about this. It seemed normal.

But it isn't, really.

———

The Catapult:
Germany

never purchased anything that was made in Germany. Or Poland. Or Austria. Or Russia. I avoided products made in France, Spain, or Eastern Europe. When I traveled abroad, I avoided Eastern Europe. My big moral compromise was to go to restaurants that served those cuisines. It was a case of food-induced hypocrisy—a weakness I must own. Hearing Beethoven's Symphony No. 9 with chorale rising to the crescendo of joy—in all of its soaring, uplifting beauty, making the German language sound sublime, created a cognitive dissonance in me that was staggering.

I did not have many people in my life from these countries. The cleaning-service personnel were from Poland. I was pleasant toward them as they were toward me. I was aware of a subtle vibration between us that has to do with the unease of a Polish canard: the "wealthy Jew taking advantage of us poor Polish." In that instant, I am connected to the aftermath of World War II, in which Poles were very wary of the rare surviving Jew returning to reclaim their homes, possessions, and businesses, which had been expropriated by their Polish neighbors. In almost all cases, the Jewish person's possessions were not returned or paid for. And, as though my unease needed any more fuel, I came home one evening and interrupted some of the cleaning crew robbing me.

And then there is Monika, who was, hands down, bar none, the best massage therapist I ever encountered. She was an infant and young child in Germany during the war. She said her father, conscripted into the German Army, died in Hitler's ill-conceived assault on Russia in winter. She hates Hitler for killing her father. In my fantasy of delivering blistering vengeance upon the population of Germany as a World War II bombardier, I would have annihilated Monika. And then, the terrible price of vengeance: I would have wrecked my pinnacle massage experience!

I would have gone on this way, I suppose—low-key hateful and quietly paranoid—except for an unexpected occurrence. I attended a professional conference on Post Traumatic Stress Disorder in Joshua Tree, California, in the fall of 2013, led by Edward Tick, Ph.D., who wrote *War and the Soul.* In the book and the conference, Tick pointed to reconciliation as central to healing Post Traumatic Stress Disorder. He saw the profound impact of reconciliation accompanying American soldiers who had served there, back to Vietnam. I was blown away to learn of the reception the Vets received in Vietnam—how they were greeted by their former enemies with warmth, openness, and forgiveness. They discussed battles they fought against each other and visited orphanages and villages that had been decimated in the war. The Vets went from being frightened and wary of entering the country to feeling comfortable and feeling some healing from the visit. Tick noted that reconciliation with the enemy and with the deeds one has done is a core aspect of healing, of forgiveness, of moderating Post Traumatic Stress Disorder and the *Moral Wounding* that so often accompanies it. Tick calls PTSD *Post Traumatic **Soul** Disorder* to account for the profound and lasting impact of a Moral Injury. *Moral Injury (Moral Wounding)* occurs in two ways: when one experiences the betrayal of the authority whose position and pledge was to act on one's behalf, and when one is compelled to do things that go against their moral code.[2]

At that conference, I was blithely taking notes, finding the material of great interest. And when Ed Tick said, "Reconciliation is necessary for healing PTSD," I became airborne.

It was as though all this time I had been sitting on a loaded catapult without knowing it. At the instant of Tick's saying, "reconciliation," the catapult released. I was stunned to notice that I was hurtling through the air. It was my first brush with being in two worlds simultaneously. One version of me was still at the seminar. Airborne-me heard Ed Tick's voice fading as I went through a life review. Five nanoseconds later, I was hit with these two utterly bewildering thoughts: *I have Post Traumatic Stress Disorder* and *I have to go to Germany.*

---

2 Tick, Edward, Ph.D., *War and the Soul* (Wheaton: Quest Books, 2005), 236–237.

The Catapult:
Home

I *grew up in a Jewish home* in the 1950s and '60s in Chicago. As the oldest of three, I was the object of a lot of attention by my parents and extended family. My parents were, by any objective macro measure, successful; they lived the *American Dream* of homeownership, vacations, world travel, and financial success from their hard work, creativity, and my father's entrepreneurial drive. They were moral people who provided for their children. The home had a daily structure, values, overbearing rules and limits, and rigid, *Old World* discipline. I absorbed my parents' love of music, art, theater, comedy, travel, books, good food, and learning. But these gifts and modeling, along with the "homey" cultural norms of the early 1950s did not obviate this observable fact: my childhood left me emotionally damaged.

My father was a veteran who spoke a total of a short paragraph about his World War II experience: he was a radar tech in the Navy and saw the ships limping back to safe harbor for repair after battle and to have the bodies taken off. That was pretty much it. A pragmatic go-getter, he attended the University of Hawaii while stationed at Pearl Harbor and left the service with a degree, all the while cultivating a side-hustle of selling decks of playing cards to servicemen.

His parents were émigrés who'd made it out of the old country in the early 1900s. My paternal grandfather's people were from Austria, and my grandmother's were from a town in Poland/Ukraine that, despite a search for it and enlisting the help of my guide in Poland, seems to have gone out of existence. My grandparents kept an observant Orthodox home. My father's younger sister once described how, as things became more dire in Europe in the late 1930s, there was a sense of desperation that came over their father and her brother (my father). My aunt stated that her mother was in complete denial about what was occurring there. She simply could not take in the reality of annihilation being visited upon her family and community even when the letters she sent to her parents and siblings kept coming back "undelivered."

My mother grew up in a secular home; there was some celebration of major holidays—but little else. Her father's people had come from Hungary, and her mother's from Ukraine. My great-grandparents were the émigrés, and there was never any reference to family left behind in the old country.

By the time I came along, my father had "converted" to Reform Judaism. I went to Sunday School leading to confirmation at age sixteen and to Hebrew School until my Bar Mitzvah at age thirteen. There was nothing inherently appealing to me about these experiences—it was pure obligation. Any sense of spirituality was largely lost due to the *steady erosion of trust* in a benevolent divine power.

When it came to being Jewish, I absorbed what was in the environment of my home, overhearing comments adults made in conversation. The Holocaust came up in our house only tangentially. Much like my father's refusal to buy a Ford product (he never explained why, but I later learned of Henry Ford's famous, vicious antisemitism), there were other economic sanctions in place in the house: no German cars, no German products. My parents, who loved classical music and frequently attended the symphony, opera, and ballet, were deeply conflicted about attending a concert of Wagner's music.

I absorbed from my environment that Christianity was our enemy because we were perceived by *them* as *their* enemy. We were and are the outsiders. Although I do not recall my parents consciously linking Church-sanctioned antisemitism to the Holocaust, that came into full focus when I understood more history as an adolescent. By my young adulthood, this is what I had come to understand: antisemitism was the pernicious hate-child of the Holy Church and was nurtured as such over the centuries. The Reformation did nothing to interrupt or modify the hateful, twisted dogma that Jewish recalcitrance was preventing salvation on Earth. Both Protestant and Catholic dogma were fertile ground for Adolf Hitler's madness.

Clearly, the fertile ground was not just in Germany, nor was a demagogue like Hitler needed to unleash the average Joe's and Josephine's savagery-in-the-name-of-Jesus. (Anyone reading this who might be unclear about Christianity's historic theological position of hatred toward the Jews, I refer to *Constantine's Sword* by James Carroll.)

When, as a ten-/eleven-year-old, I read *Exodus* by Leon Uris, a story about the Holocaust and the birth of the nation of Israel, there was no monitoring from my parents, no intervention to help me digest that material. Seeing the movie *Exodus* only made it worse. Up until that moment, I had desperately clung to the idea of a loving God with whom I could connect and who would protect me. I had been told he was there. *Exodus* was the official end to a "loving God." The sense of betrayal and abandonment was visceral and profound—my effort at trying to soothe my bedtime anxiety by reading prayer books in my bedroom in order to face sleep had ended. That Big Lie was now exposed—my situation was as bad as I feared; I was alone and huntable. Then came the anger: this was the end of my affiliation with the religious practices of Judaism. I was fiercely ethnically Jewish, but I viewed theology, all theology, with contempt.

But there was another, related Big Lie in my life—that I was safe in my home. I was not.

I have memories of feeling taunted and humiliated to varying degrees by both of my parents. One of my aunts validated a memory of mine. She witnessed me at the bathroom sink as a little boy, with my poor, troubled father behind me. While washing my face before dinner, on more than one occasion, he would intentionally rub soap directly into my eyes, which I later came to understand as an expression of his unknown, unacknowledged, hateful feelings toward me. I became quite afraid of him.

In my home, discipline included corporal punishment, administered by my father, which was not uncommon in the 1950s. I also experienced odd moments of "play" with my father, and that play becoming torture. As an example, my father would tickle me to the point where I desperately tried to squirm away, somehow managing to yell "Stop!" But he pinned me and continued, denying that he was hurting me because, as he pointed out, I was laughing. I recall this torment occurring in front of my smiling mother. Once, while we "played" in a pool, he dunked me underwater and held me there while I thrashed to break free, desperate for air. Finally coming to the surface and gasping for air, I encountered his laughter. It was clear that my father enjoyed seeing me in torment and fear.

Despite that, desperate as I was for a relationship with him, I could be seduced by him into an interaction. In these moments, he would delight in utterly dominating me in a game of ping pong or tennis. But being trounced by him (the foregone outcome) wasn't the end of it, for he would celebrate his *victory* by forcing me to: "Tell your mother who won and by how much!" The Queen, seeming oblivious to what was happening to me and the distress on my face and in my voice, smiled sweetly about the wonderful outcome of her guidance, having impressed upon her husband the need for father-son time. I never heard my father and mother say these words out loud, but through and through, I experienced this to my core: Him: "You were right hon—we had a great time. I got to crush him and then humiliate him in front of you." And her, smiling at how things were finally on the right track, saying with a sweet lilt in her voice: "Seeee?" The crowning moment would occur after I'd fled to my room. My mother followed close behind and responded to the hot tears of humiliation on my face by telling me that she was "so concerned" about me. This was my cue to take care of her by not being upset.

Growing up in my home felt so oppressive, so terrible, that, once I was able, I did anything I could to avoid being there. During my freshman year of high school, after work (at the local golf course, or cutting grass or shoveling snow—later the grocery store), to avoid dinner time, I'd wander the streets in the vicinity of my house, looking into homes from the sidewalk to catch a glimpse of or imagine what other families looked and felt like. I needed to know that there was another way to be, and simply seeing people move easily from room to room in their homes seemed hopeful to me.

If I had enough pocket money from my work, I'd walk to the local cafe for dinner. I was usually one of three or four patrons. My dinner conversation was a response to "What are you having?" The loneliness of that meal did not compare with the relentless tension of sitting around a table with my parents, being grilled about my school day. When I could not stay out any longer, I steeled myself for reentry into the house. From one or both of my parents came the usual questions: "Where were you? What were you doing?" that I fended off with vague answers or lying (which had become second nature to me). I made my escape saying I had homework, and then, once alone in my room, I felt a respite—although generally, I did not do my homework. I escaped into reading and fantasy. I was bright and argumentative, which led adults to remark I could have a good career as a lawyer. I was accused of being sullen when, in fact, I was very depressed. This was not some teenage angst—it was a depression that had been building from the beginning of my life.

It wasn't until I was working with my fourth therapist in my thirties (my first foray into treatment was at age nineteen), that I was able to see my early life clearly. In this respect, I was lucky; I had access to good data for filling in the story of how I ended up so depressed, scared, and angry. As the first child in this family and the first grandchild in my mother's family, there was a considerable amount of eight-millimeter silent-movie film shot capturing *The Wonder of Peter*. Without intending to, my parents captured moments that, years later, when I was in my thirties, allowed me to comprehend what had happened to me.

To my fourth therapist (the previous three could not figure out what was wrong with me and handled that problem by letting me ramble on about some angsty complaint and otherwise endorsed me as being well), I said, "There are home videos." She said, "Bring them in."

I hauled a video player and a small TV to her office. I watched her intently as the video played. And it was seeing the shock on her face, the tears coming into her eyes, and hearing her audibly gasp that allowed me, finally, to see what had been captured on film. Up to that moment, my eyes could not and would not register what they had seen watching those movies. When I saw the movies through *her* eyes, pain and sadness finally made their way into my consciousness.

The highchair I was seated in was not a good place to be. In one movie, I'm sitting there being pelted with rolls of toilet paper, which clearly scared me and made me cry. I wondered if my poor, troubled parents were trying to get my attention, so I would look at the camera. But the thing is, I had already been looking at the camera and smiling at that! In another segment, I am propped up on pillows on a couch and have a bottle lying on me—I was too young to hold it. I am an infant, and, even in that grainy eight-millimeter film, I look lost. Lost with a bottle I cannot hold. . . .

Our viewing continued. I was again in the highchair with my very young mother smiling for the camera as she alternately spooned food into my mouth and gave me the bottle. After a bit, it was clear that I was finished. Despite my head turning and my little body squirming, I was unable to escape the spoon—the spoon that was loaded with the food I had just spit out. My mother chased me with that spoon, waited for a chance to pounce and jammed the food back into my mouth. No matter my infant's protest, on it went until all the food that had been set out ended up in me, capped off with the bottle thrust so deeply into my mouth, my head jerked back. There was no escape, no reprieve.

It looked like I was simultaneously being nurtured, assaulted, and neglected. Oblivious to me, my poor, smiling, troubled, very young mother fed me every bit of the food she prepared for every feeding. It seemed that getting all of the food inside me was, for her, the measure of her competence as a mother. Throughout my life (*even as an adult!—"Why aren't you eating the chicken?"*), I not only lived this experience but also observed this *steamroller approach* to others, nowhere made more clear than in her interactions with her infant grandchildren. As an uncle and then as a father, I refused to cooperate with her directions for bottle-feeding a child (who had made it clear they did not want the bottle): "You forcefully insert the nipple deep into the infant's mouth. Deep." Her admonition to do this "correctly" versus being attuned to and respecting the signals from the child, helped me know that I did not imagine or exaggerate my childhood experience. It helped me to know it wasn't my fault.

As a thirty-four-year-old, I tested for my Black Belt in *Budo Aikido*. Up to this point in my life, I had eschewed any graduation and never wanted my parents present or involved in any aspect of my life. But that fourth therapist of mine, knowing what the martial-arts study meant to me, raised the idea of me inviting my family to observe this test. It felt like a bold step for me to take, but I saw the potential impact of the event, and I invited them to attend. My mother and brother couldn't make it, so it was my father, sister, and my brother-in-law (who kindly recorded the event) in attendance. Intense and demanding as the test was, my Sensei and I both knew the outcome before it began—I put on a show for the board, the school, and everyone else there. Afterward, with my Black Belt in hand, I found my family outside the training hall. Congratulations were offered, as were comments about my competence. And then my poor father gave me this unexpected precious gift by saying: "Well, I guess I can't give you a lickin' anymore." With a wry smile on my face and intently looking him in the eye, I slowly said, "Not without dire consequences." No response.

Right then, I saw it—the end of his intimidation, injury, and humiliations without my having to lay a hand on him, sending him to the hospital and me to jail. And he also saw it: that, by observing my skill and feeling my resolve to use it, his disturbed aura of power and access to me had been broken.

And finally, I bring this story forward for two reasons: because it contains an image that strangely reappeared later in my life and is in a story in this book, but more importantly, it sealed the experience I'd lived from infancy in ways subtle and overt—*of being emotionally and physically abandoned*. More than any other story, it reveals a picture of deep psychological and moral injury, and it helps me understand why I have been quietly paranoid. I have clear and distinct memories of this story from 1958. It was early Christmas break; I was eight years old, and my sister was five and a half. My brother was not yet born. My father came home from work and announced he needed a break from the wintry weather and "Let's all go (on our first family vacation) to Florida!" My parents swung into action, and the next day my grandparents were dropping us off at Union Station in Chicago for the train to Miami. I can picture all of us in the train station and the excitement my sister and I felt to be around the bustle and these huge trains. I can recall the interior of the train car, the physical discomfort of that long train ride and the novelty of the dining car. The train pulled into Miami, and, before long, it was apparent to my parents that our luggage had not made it onto the train in Chicago. This turned into a ten-minutes-until-closing sprinting shopping trip at a nearby department store for some clothing and supplies for the next few days and then a check-in to the motel on Miami Beach. The shopping was so helter-skelter that my father bought a shirt for me that, ten years later, was still three sizes too big.

The next morning, after breakfast, my sister and I were checked into a daycare center on the grounds of the motel we were seeing in daylight for the first time. We were led to a fenced outdoor play area, where my parents told us that they needed to do some shopping and would not be gone for long. We were to stay in the daycare and have a good time playing. In a strange place, in the care of people I did not know, I was immediately seized with terror and loudly protested their plan. They made their way to the exit of the play area. I tried to follow and was prevented by the grabbing hands of the adults working there. I repeatedly yelled, "**No! No! Don't Go!**" My parents never turned around. I grabbed the chain-link fencing *screaming*, "**DON'T GO! NO! WAIT!**" My poor sister was scared and tried to soothe me. The adults there at first spoke gently to me, trying to reassure me while attempting to pry me off the fence. They finally gave up. I was watching as my mother and father walked on and then left the property. The terror had me *shrieking*, "**NO! DON'T LEAVE ME!**" Even after they were out of sight, I did not stop. My shrieking and screaming continued until I slunk to the concrete, leaning against the fence in exhaustion, in tears, and having entered a despair that would last for decades. (There is a look a child has when their world irrevocably shifts: the head almost imperceptibly pulls back, there is distrust in the eyes, and the voice is quiet or gone because the child has given up. This was me now.)

When they returned, they were all smiles and ready to enjoy the day in the pool. The impact of their leaving did not register (and plainly, neither did I). For them, the crisis (being embarrassed by my screams and shrieks) had passed. We were in Miami, after all, and it was *time for me to soldier on* being their broken, shiny little boy.

My poor parents . . . my poor sister . . . my poor me. . . .

––––––––––

As the much-needed exploration unfolded, it was plain to my fourth therapist and me how I had ended up so secretly paranoid and feeling so adrift in the universe. We marveled at my spirit, which had not been extinguished, the spirit that would not stop searching until my body, heart, mind, and soul had been reclaimed from disturbed authorities and from the abandonment, depression, and rage that, at times, had me suicidal.

In my successful treatment, I had spoken of my experiences of personal, familial, and collective antisemitism. But lurking in the shadows, an invisible energy had formed as those experiences fused with the paranoia and insecurity of my childhood home. I was proud of the level of tranquility and stability I had achieved through my successful treatment. I had spoken openly in psychotherapy of the breach of faith I'd experienced with any spirituality or creator—but it turned out I had not cleared that rubble. Unrecognized by me, the history of Jewish persecution was still lurking. I simply had not identified it as a problem! My paranoia was taken by me and others as normal-for-me and was entertaining as a source of comedic material! I was simply the guy who had weapons strategically placed around his house. Certainly, no reason for concern there. . . .

While the marks left by the injuries from my youth were not visible to the untrained eye, the broken conditions of my childhood had created the Big Lie. "We love you" and "We are worried about you" from my parents left me feeling alone, confused, and enraged. Hence, the Big Lie in my home, taken together with the Big Lie of a loving God, meant that Trust was broken, Faith was broken, and being vulnerable in the world was a *very, very bad thing*—to always be fiercely avoided. From my childhood on into my adulthood, being vulnerable lived like this: I could take help if it was offered, but I would never ask for it.

It was going to take many years and a serendipity of events to illuminate the Two Big-Lie Mess and set me on a journey to clear it.

When, in 2013, at the conference on PTSD, I said the words, "I have PTSD" and "I have to go to Germany," I set off a reconciliation journey that unfolded itself as a wild ride I had gotten on and could not get off. The beginning was a study of German-Jewish reconciliation, and I hadn't even known this was possible.

The Catapult:
Fantasy

"*Thus saith the Lord of hosts. . . .* Now go and smite Amalek, and utterly destroy all that they have, and spare them not; but slay both man and woman, infant and suckling, ox and sheep, camel and ass." (1 Samuel 15:2–3 of the Hebrew Bible.[3])

At the age of eleven, my personal "Jewish Problem" (being Jewish in an already unfriendly world) deepened and intensified the morass of loneliness and rage I was already in. I longed for strength, power, and capacity, and took refuge in a revenge fantasy that goes like this: I am in the air service during World War II and get to firebomb not only Dresden, Pforzheim, and Hamburg, but every German city, town, village, hamlet, and farm. I magically get to influence the military decision-makers into adopting this war strategy: turn Germany into a sheet of glass. Concentrate on annihilating the place, the bad people, the indifferent people,

____

3 Chabad.org, 2024, *The Complete Jewish Bible*, Chabad, September 2016, {https://www.chabad.org/library/bible_cdo/aid/15844/jewish/Chapter-15.htm}

and the good people (sorry, collateral damage). Leave nothing. Nothing. I'm your volunteer. I'll run mission after mission. Once that is achieved, annihilate the German troops. In my fantasy, there is no surrender. I imagine German officers trying to surrender after noticing their country is disappearing. We send them over to the Russians because the Russians . . . how to put this, "know what to do." When I am finished, *There Is No Germany.* We say to the Russians, "Go ahead, take it; the only useful thing is the charcoal."

My fantasies are, of course, an effort at cruel justice in its crudest, most primitive form: an eye for an eye. Even in my fantasy, I am keenly aware that with every torturous, murderous act on my part, I kill off another of the remaining cells of pity in my body. So be it. I see myself as mechanical, methodical, and unstoppable.

Who do I sound like? Why, I sound like Adolf Hitler, or the Lord in 1 Samuel. I have a certified enemy who requires extermination. The truth about me? The very afraid and lonely child, the quixotic, young-adult war protestor, the "slightly" paranoid husband and father? *I have an Inner Hitler.* So far, I haven't killed, maimed, or seriously harmed a human in this life. I would consider it a grace to get to the end of my life without doing so. Unlike poor Adolf, I feel revulsion at my capacities.

I feel bad for Adolf, subsumed as he was as a child—the victim of child abuse and neglect, raised in an alcoholic, violent home. And then, on top of that mess came PTSD from serving in World War I. Adolf, the great force for change over a scant fifty-year period in the latter 20th century—change that advanced humanism, human rights, and the concept of equality virtually across the globe through the grotesque perversion he propagated. No one in history that I am aware of, as much as Adolf Hitler, has been a *singular force* to:

- advance gender equality

- advance acceptance of human sexuality in all its manifestations

- advance inroads toward ending racial discrimination

- shift the values of the species, e.g., there are now "crimes against humanity," the disabled are valued as humans, genocide is named as a crime, and it has become commonly held as unacceptable to abuse children

- make slavery unacceptable

- make colonialism unacceptable

- guilt modern Catholicism into Vatican II, which, at long last, made inroads to debunk the theology that Jews are in opposition to Christ and responsible for his death

- guilt Christianity into owning its *sponsored abuses of all kinds* (racial, colonial, and sexual, to name three)

- advance democracy throughout the world

- advance medicine, communication, education, and technology throughout the world, and

- acknowledge the homeland of a dispersed, often despised, outcast religious minority (Israel).

That poor bastard accomplished a lot! And does he get credit? He does from me. I picture Adolf meeting The Almighty looking weary and troubled. I picture The Almighty saying, "You've done enough—go rest. Don't worry—you're in the witness-protection program."

How to make sense of Adolf and the madness he brought to blossom in the German people? *This is how things get done.* It is simple and ridiculous: **This Is How Things Get Done**. In the *Bhagavad Gita*, Lord Krishna tells Arjuna to do his duty, unconcerned about the morality of the slaughter he is about to perpetrate. It's Lord Krishna's business, not Arjuna's. A Creator, **unconcerned with morality**, is how things get done. With that I re-confront the notion of a loving Creator presented to me throughout my youth . . . "Really?" I want to say retrospectively, "This is as good as *loving-God* gets?"

I am left with the disorientation and unease of the data—that this is, in fact, how things get done. In the book *Pearls of Ash and Awe* (a compilation of testimonies of attendees of twenty years of Zen Peacemaking at Auschwitz), I came across a line from a poem attributed to a man who died in the Lodz ghetto: "God, change yourself!"[4]

----

4 Battke, Kathleen, Ed. *Pearls of Ash and Awe: 20 Years of Bearing Witness in Auschwitz, with Bernie Glassman and Zen Peacemakers* (Berlin: edition-Steinrich, 2015), 64.

Catapult: Rebuttal

After my catapult launching at the conference in 2013, I spent the next thirteen months deep in the study of twentieth-century German history, Holocaust history, postwar Germany history, and German-Jewish reconciliation. I was aware that some Germans have grown weary of feeling bad about what their predecessors did two generations back, and that they now resist bearing the yoke of feeling bad about their ancestors. I have heard that spoken to Americans specifically as: "Everyone continues to point to us and say, 'Germans should feel guilty about what our ancestors did—what about what Americans did to the Native Americans? What about slavery? What about Vietnam? What about Americans owning their guilt instead of focusing on ours!'"

I was in the first draft lottery in 1969 for compulsory military service during the Vietnam War. My birthday drew a high enough number that I was not called. As a younger teen, I was enthusiastically supportive of the war—after all, we had to fight communism, and I had visions of gallantry in the service of my country. I had been inculcated into the macho-John-Wayne image of a "patriot" lock, stock, and barrel. Heroism was available to me. As a gallant, brave, heroic warrior for my country, I believed I could slay the dragon of my inferiority. Hero-warrior-me would equal, if not exceed, my father's service, *and* I would be able to impress the ladies. The whole fantasy was pure romance—nothing but male romance. My heroic fantasy was supercharged by the absence of any healthy, grounding rite of initiation into the society as a male, as a *healthy* warrior, or as a youth-emerging-into-adulthood. (You will soon read about initiation gone awry for me in college.)

So, yes, whether as an overeager volunteer or a conscript, I could have been in Vietnam, undergoing the character-deforming moral wounding that haunts many Vietnam Vets—if I had survived at all. And why? Because I would have been following orders.

I didn't have to *imagine* that—I had already *done* it! I recall a protest my parents were part of when the community objected to a sanitation substation being built nearby. As a malleable adolescent, eager to be a good soldier, I was a ready participant. So, when a cement truck tried to enter the construction zone that was the scene of the protest, I responded to my elders' shouts of "Stop that truck" by jumping in front of it. Yes. I jumped in front of a cement truck, got knocked down, and carted off to the hospital for X-rays with one of those caring elders bent over me, saying, and I quote: "Don't worry—you'll be all right. You won't have to pay for it—I'm a lawyer." I find that quite funny—and instructive: a) people will use other people to achieve their purposes, and b) people will appear to care as long as it suits their purposes.

It is possible to undo character, as Jonathan Shay tells us in his groundbreaking work on Post Traumatic Stress Disorder, *Achilles in Vietnam*—basic training is designed to do just that.[5] After the "break-and-rework" of the recruit in basic training, any of us could find ourselves doing things we could not otherwise have imagined doing. Understand: fitting in with our fellow recruits or cadets can have us doing things we would not have imagined doing. Yes. That could easily have been me in Vietnam. I was so driven, with such powerful father-hunger that I would have been great fodder. Under the influence of "leaders" who could exploit my vulnerability, they would have unleashed a monster. And I know in my bones this is true: if I had been the adolescent I was, in Germany in the 1920s, '30s, or early '40s—I would have found a home for my yearning for status and belonging with the Brownshirts. I could easily have been not just a conscript—I could have been, would likely have been, a striving-for-recognition Nazi.

To drive this point home, anyone who thinks men are not romantic does not understand the word "romance" or has not seen men in action. When warriors say there is no love like the love between fellow warriors, they are not exaggerating. When any group of men care about one another, once you've made it into the club, you are loved and cared about and cared for. You may not be *liked*, but *when the shrapnel is flying*, you are loved. Now consider the impact of adding testosterone, *especially* with someone who is in a psychologically diminished state, however that occurs: disadvantage, abuse, prejudice, violent subjugation, economic depression, parents with their own weak egos, being a bully, being bullied—the mechanism doesn't matter. You have a *tinderbox of need ready for "bro-romance."* Look out.

After learning more history as an older adolescent, I was able to move beyond the myopic view of "my country right or

____

5 Shay, Jonathan, M.D. *Achilles in Vietnam: Combat Trauma and the Undoing of Character* (New York: Scribner, 1994), 151

wrong." I realized that what took place in Vietnam was a travesty. The people of my country had their fears played to achieve some political posturing. Those in the government in a position to know, *by 1965* knew the war was unwinnable, any *glory* lost. They put their views in writing! The pursuit of an unwinnable war had three purposes: to make money for the industrialists that supplied it, to allow military officers to advance their careers by having "their war," and by engaging in fantasy to preserve the egos of the instigators of this cynical folly. Once I came to my senses, I was able to sidestep what had been a powerful seduction: the *John Wayne caricature* of manly glory, instead seeing it for what it was—a bastardization of masculine humanity and self-serving greed. I came to appreciate what warriors went through and how they were forever changed by being warriors and being used. In the case of Vietnam, they were often sacrificed for the aggrandizement and enrichment of a superior officer, always for government power brokers, and always for the industrialists.

I did not enlist and instead worked for peace as part of the protest movement. Even after I was "safe"—with a high draft-lottery number—I continued to work for peace. I took responsibility as a citizen of this country for the actions of the country. I felt (and still feel) great guilt and shame at what my government perpetrated in Vietnam, how my country wasted and deformed the precious lives of its citizens and the precious lives of the Vietnamese in the falseness of the whole enterprise.

And I am aware of the full scope of my country's perfidy. This wasn't a one-off; we keep on going with our arrogance, corruption, and abuse of power. What the white man did to the native population in this country and in this hemisphere is genocide— plain and simple. It was cruel murder and theft. It was, and in places still *is*, eradication-colonialism. It was, and still is, racism.

The natives living here suffered horrendously. Native people living on the mainland and on offshore United States Territories suffer racial disenfranchisement to this day. The genocide of the American Indian is being acknowledged in fits and starts and remains uncompensated. Treaties are violated by the American government to this day.

I am sickened by the ongoing abuses. I stand for correction. I cried when I watched the video of the United States Army veterans who showed up to support the Standing Rock Sioux protesting the Dakota Access Pipeline at Standing Rock in the Dakotas. The vets approached the Elders *on their knees* to acknowledge profound wrongs done by our military to their people over the decades and to ask for forgiveness—which was given.[6]

The United States of America was built on slavery. My immediate ancestors were not here for that. Jews certainly were, and some were active participants in the slave trade, colonization, and plantation life, which included owning slaves. I have lived with every advantage of the freedom, possibility, and largess this country can offer—and all of that is ultimately connected to this country having been built, in large part, on the backs of slaves. I realize the true founding of this country was/is a process; it required a civil war and an elongated civil rights movement to address profound wrongs. That correcting process is far from over as of this writing. I feel a responsibility to acknowledge that what was taken from the slaves in America enriched the rest of us, and further, a responsibility to acknowledge the ravages of slavery on the descendants of slaves, on the Black race (and on the White race as well).

---

6 TYT Politics, Dec 5, 2016, *Veterans Ask Native Americans For Forgiveness At Standing Rock*, December 2016, {https://www.youtube.com/watch?v=YtvZXvDN03w}

And, as if those origin facts were not appalling enough, what the White man did here became the template Germany turned to in the 1930s and '40s! The American "Wild West" was literally the basis for the German "Wild East."[7] For Germans, settling the "Wild East" envisioned the eradication of most of the Slavic populations of Poland, Ukraine, the Baltic States, and White Russia! Those *cleansed lands* were to be inhabited by "Colonial Germans" (see the books of Carroll Kakel).[8]

When you point out that I have not turned my house over to the Potawatomi Tribe, upon whose appropriated land that house sits, I agree—I have not, which is uncomfortable in its hypocrisy.

Throughout my adulthood, I noticed this about myself: I strived for consciousness about who I am. I ponder my hubris and karma. I became vigilant for my false entitlement in all its subtle manifestations. I try to put my money where my mouth is and strive not to deny guilt or responsibility personally, ethnically, or as a community, race, or country. I strive to see my country in its promise, along with its significant inconsistencies and flaws. I strive to see the whole. And I found, in 2013, that seeing the whole of me meant accepting my capacity to be a perpetrator, a bombardier, a researcher, an accomplice, a hypocrite—a "regular guy," if you will. Going to Poland or going to Germany, where I could have traveled comfortably in the role of "victim" was instead going to *put my face in it*, the "it" being me.

––––––––––

7 Kakel, III, Carroll, Ph.D., *The Holocaust as Colonial Genocide: Hitler's 'Indian Wars' in the 'Wild East'"* (New York: Palgrave McMillian, 2013), 51
8 Kakel, III, Carroll, Ph.D. *The American West and the Nazi East: A Comparative and Interpretive Perspective* (New York: Palgrave McMillian, 2011), 2, 17, 30, 45.

The Catapult:
It's Me

Early in January of 2014, I met Harold, an academic who had
published material on his own Jewish-German reconciliation
journey, to begin a face-to-face conversation about reconciliation.
He wrote an email, offering advice for exploring ". . . the German
part of your heritage." *What the fuck?* This man just came out and
said, ". . . the German part of your heritage." I wanted to scream,
"What are you talking about? I'm Jewish—there is no German,
there is no Polish, there is no Russian, there is no Hungarian
heritage. Those were places where Jews lived. I am not them, not
from there, not part of them, not identified with them, not them,
not them!" For the longest time, I wished for most of Europe to be
swallowed up by a sinkhole. It makes me dizzy to consider what
he said. And my wife has mentioned it, too, casually, matter-of-
factly, in conversation: ". . . and you're German. . . ."

Sternberg—from the German; *Stern*—"star," *Berg*—"mountain."
Also the name of a small village in Mecklenburg-Western

Pomerania. Plum Kuchen. Rigid, harsh child-rearing practices and many other familiar features of "homelife."

Contemplating this apparent component of my heritage stimulates a bizarre fantasy: I go to Germany. I get past the initial fear that I will be pounced upon and move on to my next fear, which is that *I* will pounce on someone. I get past that fear and move on to my next fear, which is that I will walk out of the airport and promptly go insane with images, sounds, smells. I get past that fear and see myself walking out of the airport and beginning to weep or scream—unable to stop. I get past *that* fear and find I am afraid that I will find the language oddly familiar, see the people as oddly familiar to me, find myself attracted to the women, find myself enjoying the food, their hospitality—I am afraid that I could, that I would, feel comfortable there. Son-of-a-bitch—at home in Germany! Son-of-a-bitch! It feels like the most perverse and insidious co-opting. I'm being co-opted into the normalcy of Germany.

And of course, Germany *is* normal. Germany is a mirror for us. Germany is the poster child for humanity! I see it as a travel poster with the outline of the country and the tagline; "*Willkommen!* Come. Visit. Take a long, hard look. You could have been here. This could have been you. You could be us." In its descent to the extreme of vulgarity and obscenity, Germany was normal. As are all the other God-fearing/God-loving sadists, murderers, torturers, rapists, thieves, and bystanders that populate human history.

"Harold (I imagine explaining to him as a way of warning), I have been a relatively well-balanced individual for some time now. No joke—I function well as a therapist, husband, and father. I am well regarded in the community. I have even developed a spiritual self along the way—no small feat from where I started.

And now I feel like I have entered an un-fun funhouse. Like the United States Holocaust Museum, the floor here is uneven; the lines are disorienting. I'm not sure I should continue."

Within one week of discussing my "Germanness" with Harold, I got two new psychotherapy referrals of people whose family-trauma history lies in the Holocaust: one, a child of Holocaust survivors, and the other a grandchild of an SS officer. Are you *kidding* me? What is going on here? (Is the Universe slapping its knee in hysterical laughter?) I picked up *The Sunflower* again, Simon Wiesenthal's rendering of the bizarre experience he had as a concentration-camp prisoner near the end of the war. Wiesenthal was randomly picked out of a work crew by a nurse to come to the bedside of a young, dying SS officer who insisted she do that, because he was desperate to confess his crimes to a Jew and be granted forgiveness. As I read, I identified with Karl, the dying SS officer riddled with guilt, confessing his complicity in atrocity, and begging a Jew for forgiveness before dying. As I reflect on a life filled with fantasies of sadism returned to the Germans (so easily triggered in me by a movie or a book), I can see myself as poor Karl, suddenly outside of the spell and beyond self-sickened at what my actions have wrought. And I identified with Simon Wiesenthal. Like him, I can't, won't, couldn't forgive. I am a walking, talking, self-contained definition of conflict.[9]

I am a seasoned therapist. I am a veteran of my own treatment. I am a third-degree Black Belt. I am drawn to this material. It feels dangerous. I—am—afraid. And now, my German heritage? I am already disgusted by the demonic monster that reveals itself in

---

9 Wiesenthal, Simon, *The Sunflower: On the Possibilities and Limits of Forgiveness* (New York: Schocken Books, 1976), 29–30

my fantasies. Now I feel shoved closer to my horrific self through a connection with Germans.

God damn it! I know the only way to manage the Beast is to encounter him. Know him. Stay close to him. I do this every day in my work with my patients; I did it in my own treatment. However, I managed to sequester this small, almost inconsequential piece of business. . . .

My German heritage? From the distance of being born in America, my inner-Hitlerness is an abstract and caricatured fantasy. I suppose I could act on those feelings and lusts, but I haven't. *I have not been tested.* But set foot in Germany? That is the place where it was all real. There, Hitlerness happened. I believe this is why I am so shaken and frightened. "When I go *back* to Germany" (I misspoke that line *repeatedly*, for I had not ever traveled there), "the Beast awaits me."

Not in the Germans.

In *me.*

Just there, instead of "me," I wanted to say, "God help me—it's *me.*" But then I remembered *1 Samuel.* This is the worst of it—the loss of the child's illusion that the Creator is the God that would help us, help me, when the Creator is also Shiva, who Destroys—Hitlerness, if you will. As in Adolf. As in ME.

Although these words make sense to me, they boggle my mind. My words and the truth they speak alarm me, agitate me; I sense my capacity for vengeance; I sense my rage activated and the wish to destroy.

In my basement, I listen to *The Water* and *The Bad in Each Other* by Feist, while I do Tai Chi sets—to try to find some calm. And the Tai Chi does just that. I can lose myself within the slowness and precision of the movements. The movement and the flow of a slow energy inside me reorients and steadies me.

Harold told me about a group called The Zen Peacemakers, founded by a Zen Roshi named Bernie Glassman, who'd founded a socially engaged Buddhist practice. By 2013, they had done their eighteenth annual five-day Bearing Witness Retreat at Auschwitz based on Bernie's Three Tenets of *Not Knowing*, *Bearing Witness*, and *Compassionate* (Loving) *Action*. His idea was to show up and allow places of atrocity to teach. To do this, one sheds their pre-conceptions and understandings so they can have the openness that comes with Not Knowing. Bearing Witness allows the participant to take in all without judgment. Compassionate Action arises naturally from the first two.[10]

Upon hearing this, I knew I had to defer getting to Germany, to first encounter Poland and Auschwitz with the Zen Peacemakers. That night, I discovered Auschwitz has a website where one can take a virtual tour. For about ten minutes, I "looked around" the entrance area of Auschwitz I—the Main Camp. As I had been at my computer for a while, I decided it was enough for one night. I went upstairs to get ready for bed. I was standing at the sink when a sudden pain struck both of my arms. The pain was a powerful muscle ache—as if I were being crushed. It wasn't a sharp pain; there wasn't pain in my head, neck, face, belly, or legs. Then, my chest hurt with the same powerful muscle-being-squeezed ache. It hurt to breathe. My hands were weak, too weak to operate the cuticle nipper I was holding when the pain struck. I literally forced my hands to work just to see if I could make them work. I could. I sat down. I knew I wasn't

---

10 The Zen Peacemakers Order, 2023: *What Is Z.P.O.?* The Zen Peacemakers Order, December 2023 {https://zenpeacemakers.org/about/zen-peacemaker-order/}

having a heart attack. I tried to meditate. After approximately eight minutes, the pain began to subside, and then, it quickly disappeared. I struggled for words to describe what had just happened. All I could come up with was that I had spent the last eight minutes being crushed. I had not ever had an experience like that before—it blew my mind. I had no doubt it sprang from "visiting Auschwitz" ten minutes earlier.

When I told him about the experience, my closest friend, Louie, said, "Oh, this is preparation for you; it's training; it's inoculation." "Yes," I said, "that is it precisely."

I shared these experiences with Harold, who looked aghast and wondered why I would consider going to the camps after that! Good question. This led us directly into the discussion of his question to me: "What do you mean by 'reconciliation'?"

I said, "I don't think you can reconcile with something that you don't know."

My purpose in going to the camps was, first, to physically memorialize what had occurred there. Second, to feel the place, touch the ground, smell it, let the vibration in. It is the exact same purpose I have for wanting to visit Dresden. Exactly the same. In one instance, me, feeling the Jewish victim, and in the other, me, feeling the Bombardier. These places are the externalization of what is internal. I avoid them at my peril. Harold responded by saying that a woman he knows who attended the retreat there speaks of Auschwitz as a place of love.

I heard that and immediately said, "I can imagine what she means. The sinister, the insidious, the monstrous, the obscene, sit vacant. What is vile did not, could not endure. The hideousness of the derangement that overtook Germany—with all its awful power, in the end, could not prevail." Prevail over what? Lincoln might have called it "the better angels of our nature." Perhaps one might call it love.

Yes, perhaps from a certain, weird angle, Auschwitz is a mind-boggling, hideous testimony to . . . love.

———————

Peter

Descent

Descent:

Ah, Sweet Home Poland

A*h, Sweet Home Poland*, where, in 2018, a law was enacted making it a crime to implicate Poland in the crimes of the Holocaust. I've continued my study of history and recent efforts at reconciliation between Poles and Jews. I got reacquainted with material I knew well: the virulent and centuries-old antisemitism many Polish people supported, aided, and abetted—administered through the teachings of the Polish Church (See *Poland's Threatening Other* by Joanna Beata Michlic).[11] These two stories are snapshots of Polish complicity in the Holocaust. *After* the war, the few Jews who slipped through the Nazi net came back to their homes and searched for relatives. In the town of Kielce on July 4, 1946, the "blood libel" accusation (that Jews needed a Christian child's blood to make matzo) was resurfaced by the Poles living there to justify a pogrom in which forty-two Jews

____

11 Beata Michlic, Joanna, *Poland's Threatening Other: The Image of the Jew from 1880 to the Present* (Lincoln: University of Nebraska, 2006), 122–123.

were murdered, including a newborn baby and a woman who was six months pregnant. Another forty were injured.[12] In July 1941, in a massacre in Jedwabne, Poles slaughtered their Jewish neighbors by herding them into a house that was then burned to the ground. After the blaze, the Jews' former Polish neighbors "appropriated" the now "abandoned" Jewish farms. (Who lets fine farmland sit idle??) The perpetrators ascribed the disappearance of the Jews to Nazi deportation, and, for years, the community maintained that lie.[13]

I'm doing my preparatory study and having a hard time reading about Jews funding the new museum in Warsaw, dedicated to the one-thousand-year history of Jews in Poland. It strikes me as an effort to capture and appreciate a piece of Polish and Jewish history, without the nastiness of Poles having to live next to "the disgusting Jews." "Hey, Jews, now that you're not here, we really appreciate you! You are good for business!" And Jews donated money to build this museum? Are you kidding? And now I am going there!? Why did I agree to go to Poland? *God damn it! I have made a big mistake.*

But. But . . .

A loud and striking problem for me is how many Poles, including some clergy, risked their lives and their family's lives by hiding Jews. Many paid for that humanity with their lives and the lives of their families. Most of the memorial trees planted at Yad Vashem (the museum and memorial to the Holocaust in Israel) honoring *The Righteous Among the Nations* (Gentiles who rescued Jews during the Holocaust), were planted there for Poles.

---

12 The United States Holocaust Memorial Museum, Opened in 1993, The Holocaust Encyclopedia, *Kielce Pogrom*, January 2013 {https://encyclopedia.ushmm.org/content/en/timeline-event/holocaust/after-1945/kielce-pogrom}
13 Gross, Jan, Ph.D., *Neighbors: The Destruction of the Jewish Community in Jedwabne, Poland*, (Princeton: Princeton University Press, 2001) 106–110

God damn it! Again, I am deprived of the simplicity of hate.

I am going to Auschwitz, a place that embodies the collapse of trust, the collapse of relationship, the collapse of humanity, and the collapse of benign authority. In Poland, will the law protect me? Will the Church authorities protect me? How about the police? How about the friendly people on the street? How about the Rabbis? God? Can I protect myself there?

Is it possible to have remembrance without hate? Without rage? Without fear? This is hard business.

Descent:
Crucified

It was winter 2014. My plans were coming together for travel to Poland in November. One day, for no apparent reason, my shoulders and neck began to ache. They ached a lot. It was quite delineated: from the back of my neck, radiating down and out along my shoulders. I thought I must have done something in a workout. Then an oval formed on the back of my neck running from my hairline to my upper spine. This patch of skin was cold. It felt cold internally, and it was cold to the touch. It felt like there was a hole in my body, and the heat of my body was pouring out of this spot. It was this weird: when I was working out, sweating, I had a sweatshirt wrapped around my neck because that spot was so cold. I had to put a heating pad on my neck when I was sitting down to counter the heat loss. This went on for several days. I mentioned it to my meditation master, who asked if I'd ever had an injury to this area.

"No," I said. And then a thought came into my mind. "Actually, yes . . . of a sort," I corrected.

By the end of my freshman year in high school, I was flunking out. My parents identified a military school that seemed like a possible option to "straighten me out" (of my severe depression). So, I became a fifteen-year-old "new-boy" cadet at a military high school. I did not object to going. Although I was homesick, I was also very glad to be away from home. For the first time in my life, I realized I could learn and be academically successful.

I was, along with the rest of the new-boys, subjected to hazing as a rite of initiation into the corps (culminating after four grueling months, in becoming an "old-boy"). Hazing was officially forbidden but was understood and accepted as a tradition. It was frightening, intimidating, humiliating, and physically and emotionally hard. Generally, it did not cross the line of physical beatings, although that intervention was always implied and sometimes occurred. For a Jew, hazing took on additional dimensions. There were a few "old-boy" cadets who took advantage of their position to pursue their antisemitic inclinations.

My recollections of antisemitic treatment are of three interactions; one was a daily occurrence, another was limited to Jewish holidays, and the last one occurred only once.

Every day the Corps attended Chapel. This was mandatory. The school was affiliated with the Episcopal Church. Praying (or looking like it: mouthing the words and kneeling) was required, or one would incur great wrath for failing to participate, especially if one was a Jew.

The very few Jewish cadets in the Corps were offered opportunities to be in the homes of local Jewish families to celebrate the High Holy Days and Passover. On those days, a number of old-boys in my company formed a line to whip my Jewish roommate and me with their belts as we exited our room and moved down the hall to leave. We had to *walk* down this line. We were whipped.

And finally: in each cadet's room, there was a "picture rail" approximately five feet off the floor, running the length of the walls. The picture rail was a piece of molding on which one could place pictures, banners, etc. It also had hooks from which one could hang a rifle or saber if you were an officer. On one occasion, four or five old-boys entered my room, and, while I stood at attention, they took a broom pole and ran it down the buttoned sleeves of my shirt. The ends of the pole extended from my outstretched arms and shirt cuffs. Then they picked me up by the broom pole and used it to hang me on the hooks. I was hanging on the wall, several feet off the floor. I had been threatened not to call out.

"You are crucified!" they announced. (I want to keep writing, but I pause now to force myself to breathe deeply . . . to take a few breaths and to be in remembrance . . .)

"You are crucified! You are crucified!" they joyously taunted.

I hung there. Soundless. They went on congratulating each other while mocking me.

I was thoroughly conscious of my condition and circumstances. Other than screaming for help (which I did not do), I knew I couldn't remedy my situation. I cannot recall, all these years later, how long it went on. And I cannot recall the physical pain (although, all these years later, my body remembered very clearly). I remember my tormentors laughing and jeering at me. Their delight intensified my adolescent humiliation. I know I tried to keep myself calm as a way of denying them the satisfaction of breaking me down. I know I looked them in the eye. That tactic was a basic survival mechanism for me: the "Fuck You" look in my eye would draw fire, but it usually also earned me some grudging respect.

I have no memory of being taken off the wall, of having the pole removed from my shirt, of being threatened if I spoke, of them leaving my room, or of what I did next. They did not do this to me again.

After I told this story to my meditation master, it took several more days before the pain in my shoulders and the patch of cold dissipated and then disappeared.

Reflecting now, I don't know what to make of my membership in the club of "the crucified." I imagine most don't survive it, but I did. The pain my body was in tells me I have carried this experience throughout my life. In a sense, my tormentors did me a favor—they made real and physical what had been a vibration humming in the background of my life. Being a Jew means living with the uncertainty of peril that is certainly coming: random deadly attacks pop up in the environment. A further favor to me was how the experience steeled me for the rest of my new-boy experience and life after military school, with a commitment to honing psychological and physical defenses (the physical capacities would have to wait for another fifteen years before I could begin that training).

In the aftermath of attending military school, I saw myself with a capacity to survive, and that brought an ironic semblance of pride to me. To my fifteen-year-old mind, there was no one else to depend on. I do not recall these thoughts being part of my calculus about whether I would scream for help or not. I knew—in a way I could not have articulated—that my life would ultimately go better by enduring it, surviving it. Of course, confirming my belief that there was no one in the world I could depend on was not good for me; it took years for me to come to trust others. But, in the short term, trusting no one looked and felt like reality. In a strange way, it kept me in the game.

And then there is this: I recall very clearly the great pride I felt during the ceremony where I was inducted into the company as an "old boy," made sweeter by the fact that I was recognized as a marksman and put on my company's riflery competition squad.

The antisemitic persecution? *Fugget about it.* At the end of the academic year, I was informed that I was slated for rank next year. I was all in. The romance was on.

———

Descent:
Josef Mengele of Monkeys

After a year of academic success at military school, my parents decided I had received "the cure," or, in my father's words, I "had matured," and they pulled me out of there. Surviving military school was a boost to my broken ego. Once back home, I got a part-time job, resumed a couple of friendships, did well in some classes and limped along in others, and somehow figured out how to date. But being back home landed me, once again, in the heavy strife of the dysfunction in my family.

My significant accomplishments in high school I graded thusly: during one particularly awful parental interaction, I put down the kitchen knife that I had picked up, and so my father lived—"A" for the effort to pick it up and also to put it down, followed immediately by me ingesting all of the prednisone (a steroid medication my pediatrician prescribed for my shaking hands) remaining in the three-quarter full bottle. I then ran through my mother and sister's frantic efforts to stop me, and out of the house. It turned out to not be lethal, so I lived as well—"A" for the effort and an "I" for incomplete. After some time passed and it was clear to me that the pills were not going to have much of an effect, I returned home. My effort to end my life was met by my poor parents and my physician with silence, *as though nothing had happened.*

I did well enough in high school to get accepted at an out-of-state college, packed myself up, and off I went. I did well academically and less well socially; I was again relieved to be away from home yet, strangely, living with a desperate unease about being away from home at the same time. I worked over the summer before heading back for my sophomore year. But my poor, damaged father (and in my mind, by extension, my mother) insisted that by the end of the summer break I repay him all the money he had laid out for my freshman year. That was not possible. So I got a student loan to pay him off and to cover my tuition at a commuter university in Chicago. My sophomore year of working and going to college was doable. Living at home was untenable. By age nineteen, I was on my own, sharing a carriage-house apartment with a roommate, working, commuting to school, and protesting the Vietnam War.

When I was twenty-one, I was a senior in college and extremely interested in physiological psychology (as neuroscience was called at the time). I approached my professor about a phenomenon I'd stumbled upon in my studies. I wondered if it could become an independent study. It is this: when both hemispheres of the motor cortex are removed from an animal's brain, that animal will lose all voluntary movement and never recover it. But, if one hemisphere is removed, and, after a few weeks, the other hemisphere is removed, there is a mysterious transfer of function of some voluntary motor control to other regions of the brain. For my sterling research questions (*How does this occur?*

Where are those other regions of the brain?), I was referred by my professor to the University Medical Center research labs and a possible sponsor who, it turned out, was intrigued by the questions and took a liking to me. He helped me develop a research design and then gave me three of his monkeys to do the project. He pitched the idea of this project being a stepping-off point for my Ph.D. He was going to teach me the neurosurgery, the care and testing of the animals, and he would guide my writeup. I was *ecstatic.* Receiving attention and an endorsement from "an elder" was intoxicating. Plus, an undergraduate getting a research opportunity like this was absolutely unheard of. Most undergraduate and graduate students did their research on rodents. To work on primates was simply an unimaginable, extraordinary opportunity! Can you sense the egoic inflation that rippled through me when I told family, friends, and peers of this academic recognition and status? Me, doing research with primates at the medical center— after growing up hearing that I would amount to nothing? The recognition I felt! Right? (Recall I was flunking out of high school six years earlier!)

But here's the thing: as I strapped on the heavy leather gloves to pry those monkeys out of their cages and take them to their doom (recall me clinging to chain-link fence screaming to not be left), I became Josef Mengele to them—Mengele, the "infamous doctor of death" of Auschwitz, who calmly walked the selection platform at Birkenau as the trains disgorged their broken inhabit- ants, on the prowl for "subjects" (preferring child twins), upon whom to perform grotesque "medical" experiments in order to "advance medical knowledge."

The details of my work in the laboratory are revolting and sickening to me. The monkeys were, of course, terrified of my approach. To serve my research (understand that as: to prop up the shambles of my ego and be accepted into the club), I pried them off the bars of their cage. (*Oh, God damn . . .*)

I learned and then did the neurosurgery. It is excruciating to write these words, but the truth is performing that surgery felt like *a trip*. I had so impressed myself—to be opening a primate cranium, revealing a living brain so much like our own, there for me to explore and manipulate! (*Oh, God damn me!*)

I took care of them afterwards. It was in caring for them through their recovery and then testing them that the horror of my actions fully penetrated, and the whole enterprise became a living hell I inhabited with those poor creatures. Through their remaining godawful days, they followed me with their eyes. (I am sick. Sick.) I felt I was living Dostoyevsky's plot in *Crime and Punishment*—Raskolnikov's damning guilt. . . . And no way out of it.

I lost all interest in the science and wanted it to end just to end the monkeys' (and my own) suffering. I saw the project through, out of a commitment to the animals—since I had utterly devastated their lives, at least I was going to not waste them. In the end, I *harvested* (killed) them to examine their brains so I could confirm the experimental results. I was relieved to put them out of their horrific misery. I analyzed the data I had collected, wrote a paper, and, to the dismay of my sponsor, ran out of the lab, completely revolted by what I had done to those poor creatures, never to return.

And thus began my begging. I begged, I begged, I begged them for their forgiveness. I tell those three monkeys now: "I got a close-up view of power over another creature, the ego inflation of it. I got a hefty dose of *glory*—being singled out to 'advance science,' to 'understand the secrets,' to see what creatures look and feel like when it seems they are there simply to be used, ***how***

they don't look like 'beings' when you are in your glory—*in your self-righteous, self-serving, ego-inflating, 'God-given' glory."*

So, yes. I have an up-close, intimate view of how one becomes a bad actor, a "doctor of death." It isn't hard at all. I tell you truly; it isn't hard at all to be, or to become, bad—and all the while believe you are fine. Fine, and recognized for the contribution you are making.

There is a crucial interaction that never occurred. Neither the researcher at the medical center, nor my professor, *nor my analyst* (who had been treating me for depression for two years) asked me how I felt about my intended actions toward those animals. No one pointed out that we reveal our deepest self-perception through our behavior and that I was about to render three help-less creatures incapable of movement and entirely dependent on me. No one said, "Wait a minute Peter, **does that mean anything to you?"**

And whenever I think of it, I beg those monkeys for their forgiveness.

Mercifully, that is not the entire story. Although the project was meant to advance neuroscience, what it did was advance my trajectory into what has become my life's work of healing through encounter, reckoning, responsibility-taking, and reconciliation. Those monkeys' lives were made horrific by my actions, but, truly, their suffering has not been forgotten or neglected. Their lives and mine became and remain entwined.

I remember them and remember how easy it is . . . for a quietly damaged person who is a reasonably good guy, to, quite unconsciously, go bad.

———

Descent:
I Killed Who?

My wife, Maggie, has made this observation to me more than once: "What is it with you and priests? In a crowded room of Catholics, you are in the corner conversing with the one priest for hours!"

By the grace of the Trickster-God, this sequence happened. In 1980, I met Louie at a conference (well, actually, it was on the ski slopes) at Park City, Utah. He was a California boy, some years older than me, but we became instant friends. We skied together once a year, and we made warm-weather trips to get together in California and Illinois here and there over the years. We spoke weekly and were by each other's side through life's challenges for thirty-six years. We were each other's *Person*. And Louie was *The Irritating Monk* in my life . . . often causing me to want to pull my hair out in frustration, but, invariably, he was saying or doing something that proved to be of incalculable value to me.

In 2013, he lived in California, near Yosemite National Park, with his wife, Judy, who insisted, one day, that she needed to spend some time in residence on the coast. That became a fact. And now in a new location, Louie did what Louie always did, saunter and meander, taking in everything and everyone he encountered during any movement from point A to point B. (This attribute strained our relationship—always.) In his new town, he came across a number of men gathered outside of a building, greeted them, and asked what they were up to. "We volunteer for the veterans treatment court (a program of treatment, mentorship, and rehabilitation, meant to provide an alternate path for veterans who get into trouble with the law). What do you do?" "I'm a retired therapist." "We need you—get in here." Later that year, the volunteers attended a conference in Joshua Tree, California, for training in Post Traumatic Stress Disorder. Louie suggested this conference would be right up my alley. "I can't possibly," I said, having just returned from a trip. No worries, he said and sent Dr. Edward Tick's book (*War and the Soul*) to me. After reading the first chapter, I called him: "I'm coming." It was at that conference in October of 2013 that the catapult released, and it was also there I met the Veterans Court volunteer chaplain, Fr. Michael Cicinato. And apropos of my wife's observation about "something with me and priests," Mike and I hit it off over the five days of that conference and became fast friends.

Within two months of my return from the conference (December 2013), I had heard about the Zen Peacemakers annual *Bearing Witness Retreats at Auschwitz*, and I signed up for November 2014. My reconciliation study commenced as soon as I returned from the conference at the end of October. By early January of 2014, that immersive study had brought me back to a particular work: *Constantine's Sword* by James Carroll. *Constantine's Sword* begins with Carroll (a historian and former Paulist priest) standing at Auschwitz and asking, "How could this happen?" In answering his question, he describes and details the two-thousand-year history of the sordid treatment of Jews by Christianity. The catalogue of persecution is a collection of foul crimes ranging from (at the mild end) disenfranchisement, sequestering, getting roughed up, and the removal of citizenship rights to (at the heinous end) forced conversions through torture, eviction, removal, rape, beatings, theft, and murder—not infrequently by burning. All of that was policy and behavior that was blessed by, promulgated by, and benefiting the Catholic and later, the Protestant Church.[14]

I owned the book for thirteen years, but despite making several attempts, I had not been able to get through it. When I tried, I became overwhelmed with such rage and grief that I could not go on. I could not even listen to a series of lectures I had purchased on the work. I tried again and, this time, with great difficulty, was able to complete it.

I was at a loss. I knew my goal was reconciliation, but how to handle the torrent of grief, rage, betrayal, helplessness, fear, and exclusion that was the legacy of my people, which was also my family legacy of relatives murdered and history buried, which was my personal history with antisemitic brutality, which was my legacy experience of simply being born a Jew? I could not imagine an encounter with any church authority about these matters. Yet, without that encounter, reconciliation seemed impossible.

When I finished *Constantine's Sword*, I had a long discussion with Louie about this material. He made some pertinent and challenging observations. Louie also remarked on my "search for a Christian cleric" with whom to go over my history and

---

14 Carroll, James, *Constantine's Sword: The Church and the Jews—A History* (Boston, Mariner Books, 2001) 134

my reaction to Jewish/Christian history. "You already know someone—Fr. Mike!" I saw the possibility and took the plunge. I wrote to Mike and told him the wrenching and ugly encounters I was having with Jewish-Christian history. I asked if he might be willing, as a person of authority in the Catholic Church, to process this ugly business with me. He said:

Hi Peter,

I would be glad to do that.

Our Church has a lot to atone for with Judaism, but it has also, on occasion, done well. I would never make excuses for the Church. It needs to own its shit just like the rest of us. If we can't break open the pain with each other, we can never heal. I have not read *Constantine's Sword* but would be happy to hear from you about it. When Constantine converted and the Church became politically acceptable, it entered a period of decline and became involved with power and politics. Some of those politics, drawing from things from John's gospel, began to demonize the Jews. Unfortunately, while we have condemned that, there are still some who do it in the name of the Church. They don't recognize that Jesus, Mary, and all the apostles were good Jews, who never left that belief. Anyway, feel free to contact me so we can set up a time to talk.

Love and blessings,
Mike

I worked out what to say, what to ask, what to go over with him. I am aware of the subtlety of some of the material: Mike says: "Jesus, Mary, and all the apostles were good Jews . . ." And right there, I'm into *good* and *bad*. Why insert the word "good"? What is a "good Jew"? Ask an observant Jew, and she or he will tell you a good Jew is, like them, observant of the religious laws. (They would likely describe me as a bad Jew.) Ask a German during the madness and they would say that the good Jew was the one they knew personally, the one who was a childhood friend, the one who wasn't offensive, the one who helped them out at a time of need and because of these extenuating factors, ought not be treated as vermin.

The alternative is this: Jesus, Mary, and the apostles were all Jews. They would not have conceived of identifying themselves any other way. And they would likely be appalled to be used as instruments of persecution of their (or of anyone's) people.

In conversation with Louie about this, quite unconsciously and speaking out of the culturally accepted norm, he said, "Well, the Jews killed Jesus." Which instantly brought this correction from me: "No, my friend, *the Jews* didn't." As the late Ron Miller, Ph.D. (former Chair of the Department of Religion at Lake Forest College), pointed out, "the Jews killed Jesus" is as ridiculous as saying "the Americans killed Lincoln." Dr. Miller went on to explain that the Jews did not have a problem with Joshua (Jesus's actual name) as the Messiah; they'd already had a history of encounters with others who claimed to be Messiahs, one was crucified by the Romans about forty years before Joshua. To the Jews at the time, a Messiah was understood as one who would lead them to freedom against their oppressors, such as the Romans.[15]

Dr. Miller pointed out that any serious scholar of Roman history will likely tell you that it would be decidedly un-Roman of the Romans to let any potential grassroots leader go free. They

---

15 Miller, Ron, Ph.D., *recorded lecture series on* Constantine's Sword *presented at Common Ground, Deerfield, Illinois, in September/October 2001*

crucified any and every potential leader whenever they surfaced. The guy who always gets a pass in the Jesus-ends-up-dead story is Pontius Pilate, known for his excessive cruelty—so much so that he was removed from his post because of it three years after poor Josh's death.[16]

James Carroll makes it clear that the *deicide charge* (the Jews killed Jesus) is actually subtle, quite subtle. The Jews became "bad" because they did not join in the movement. They did not accept Jesus as the Son of God. That is how and why they "killed him" and "kill him" to this day. The Jews are a thorn in the side of Gospel theology by the fact that Jews continue to exist and continue under the mantle of having a covenant with God. They are, we are, the miserable sibling that just will not go away, yet must give way in order to validate the newly anointed sibling.[17]

This was a hard moment with Louie. I felt a distance between me and my dear friend that, other than the aggravation of trying to walk down a street to a destination, with him stopping to talk to someone or investigate a storefront every six feet, I was unaccustomed to feeling. I had not experienced my being Jewish and his being Christian as a disconnect before this moment. What was so potent was that I spontaneously challenged and refuted his utterance in that difficult moment, and I suppose I would say I trusted that we'd end up okay with each other.

Louie was appalled at the impact his words had had on me. He truly had not realized what he said—it was that automatic. I accepted his apology and appreciated his willingness to learn some history and to be sensitive to how this canard about Jews operates in his thinking going forward.

---

16 Miller, *Constantine's Sword* lecture series
17 Carroll, *Constantine's Sword*, 58–59

We got past it. He was a loving and true friend to me, nowhere more so than in his unwavering support through thirteen months of my dark-night-of-the-soul plunge after the 2013 conference and in his insistence that I write this book. Since his passing I miss him fiercely—even walking down the bloody street. . . . The night he died (seventeen hundred miles away), I was awakened at one in the morning by a restlessness in my body I had never felt before. I was twisting and turning in bed—it felt as though I was shedding my skin. Finally gyrating awake, I blurted out loud: "What's it like to be dead, Louie?" I heard him laugh and say, "Well, I don't know—it just happened." Still out loud, I said, "That's okay. I'll find out soon enough." Five minutes later, I got a text from his wife saying he had just died.

Mike and I met days later in January of 2014, and did this over the phone, no less. We faced the moment we had both agreed to, momentous in ways we couldn't have anticipated, and, scared as I was to reveal my pain, I drew a breath and began. Out came the previously unshared Jewish/family legacies and my personal experiences of religious persecution in detail. From Mike, I heard a steady voice speaking from the depths of his heart: "I am *so* very sorry for what my Church did to you. I am *so* very sorry for what my Church did to your people. We have so much to repent for. The Church lost its way," he said. "It became corrupted by power and became political with Constantine. The Church lost its teaching. I am *so* sorry for the anguish we have caused." Mike repeated these statements over and over as our conversation went on. Something was happening here. I felt connected to our conversation and to Mike, and the emotion became more accessible for me to share.

Although this was over the phone, I felt Mike's presence intensely. I felt his sincerity, his openness. I told him how touched

I was by how he received and responded to all the vile, rageful feelings pouring out of me. He told me he was touched that I was bringing this to him. I said, "I've never had an experience like this before and could not have envisioned it." He said he, too, had never had an experience like this before and could not have imagined it. We discussed my experiences at military school. We discussed the history and Carroll's three main points to explain the central distortions in the two-thousand-year history between us: 1) "Jews as Christianity's negative other; 2) Christianity's derogatory "replacement theology" (known as *supersessionism*), in which the Jews' covenant with God is now taken over by God's covenant with Christianity; and 3) because the Jews refused to yield to that claim, the Church defined itself as the enemy of Judaism."[18]

I believe the *Chosen People* business was *the* setup from the start. And since then, thank you Trickster-God, we have all been caught in an archaic sibling rivalry! It has nothing to do with the core values we all claim we hold dear. I have an idea—let's never bring up "Chosen" again. We won't, you don't. Of course, I'll have to run this past my co-religionists. I don't anticipate a problem with them relinquishing that mantle (but sadly, that is true only in a parallel universe). Put another way, Jews' attachment to being *The Chosen* will ensure that we will be the target of a not inconsequential amount of vicious jealousy—forever.

Another two thoughts before I leave this . . . The two necessary ingredients for *redemptive suffering* (what Christians believe Jesus did for humankind) are *someone* and *suffering*. As I understand the story, Jesus knew what was going to happen to him, and, out of

---

18 Carroll, *Constantine's Sword*, 58–59

his love for humankind, he consented to a prolonged, torturous death. On that point alone, blaming the Jews for killing Christ is absurd. As the story is told, Jesus knew better than anyone that he needed to die a suffering death to complete his destiny. Jesus needed Judas and the Pharisees to do exactly what they did, *and Jesus loved them in spite of it.* The people around him, including the Romans, did exactly what was necessary for the redemption story to unfold. One more time: without his being set up, betrayed, and suffering a heinous death, there would be no Easter! He did not hate the people who played their part in his story. So, why would anyone else? The second point is this: does anyone who understands his behavior and his teachings believe that Jesus would endorse the hatred and persecution of his people, his relatives—or the persecution of *any* people? Would Mary endorse the persecution of her people, her relatives—or the persecution of *any* people? We have evidence to the contrary. Jesus loved his people, including the man who betrayed him as well as the colonizers (Romans) who were his torturers/killers. I'm unaware of any scripture in which Jesus says, *Hunt down and kill the Jew and the heathens also.* Other people said things like that (in direct contradiction to his teachings) **but not him**.

The pain, rage, and paranoia I had carried were fully described to Mike. I made clear to him how my (at that point) thirty-five-year history of study of the martial arts was, in part, an effort to live with the legacies I carried. I did not believe that "Never Again" for the Jews was likely—history points to repeating cycles of persecution.

The standout experience of my encounter with Mike was his unhesitant responsibility-taking. Without any defensiveness, allowing the facts and my story to, in his words, *"penetrate my body,"* with full acknowledgment of the harm done, without excuses, he, as a representative of the Catholic Church, spoke for that Church, took responsibility, and was deeply affected by all his Church had done. He told me he'd been affected viscerally—he heard from me the history he already knew—but, this time, through me and my words. This time, he didn't just know it factually—he *felt* it. He said he felt the "blows of your words in my body." When he said that, I knew I had been received, I knew his apology was real, and I knew I was I hearing him unhesitantly taking responsibility.

An authentic reckoning had occurred.

My breathing deepened. I noticed the anger beginning to dissipate. I took in the reality of all that had occurred in my life and the historic legacy of the Jews over the last two thousand years. I felt visible. I felt validated and respected. And then I felt lighter.

As a psychotherapist, I knew the power of taking responsibility in healing troubled relationships. Whenever someone takes responsibility, the possibilities for healing even very deep and repeated wounds are great. No amount of understanding, explanation, or prayer can heal the hurt individual as much as having the harmer see and hear them, acknowledge the reality of what was done, take responsibility, and then open the door to reconciliation. That makes "interactive forgiveness" possible and powerful for the harmed and the harmer.

Mike made it clear that I was bringing a deep teaching to him and helping him with his personal and spiritual development. He thanked me deeply for bringing this experience to him. His words could not have been more meaningful to me.

Our conversation deepened over the next two months as I continued my preparation for travel to Poland. Mike asked to read my journals, which were filled with notes from my study and my own multigenerational suffering and rage. He said the dark-night-of-the-soul struggle I was going through was the very material he needed to access for the veterans retreat he was building. He asked if I would collaborate with him on that project, contributing my (umm) *unique approach* to facing extreme moral injury. I said I would join the effort, and, together, we built and launched the *Elderwarrior Healing Journey.*[19] Mike and I co-facilitated Elderwarrior healing retreats for many years, helping veterans and civilians ease the burden of moral wounding—work born out of our serendipitous meeting and the necessary reckoning work I had to do with the Church.

That is simply amazing.

---

19 Elderwarriors, 2015, *Welcome to Elderwarriors: Transformation Happens,* Michael Cicinato and Peter Sternberg, 2024 {*https://www.elderwarriors.org/*}

Descent:
Expect to Be Sickened

think about the things I am ashamed of or feel guilty about—my poor monkeys are a proper example. I think of how unbearably awful it would be if those things/moments were on display, visited, and made into a teaching point for how not to be a human. Then I imagine myself as a German. I imagine that the deepest shame of my people, committers of the most heinous depravity amongst the pantheon of human perversion over the ages, is a stain because I come from them. And then there is the fact that the actual places where the perversions transpired are now museums. And I wonder how I could bear knowing that these places exist and that, in the eyes of the appalled visitors, I would see my people (and, by extension, me) reviled. I have heard German people speak exactly like this. Pity that the rest of us aren't in the same straits as the Germans. Pity. Perhaps we can all do with a dose of feeling our shame. Hell, just acknowledging that we and our ancestors likely stood on other people's backs to "advance ourselves" would be a fine start!

I am acutely sensitive to those wounded by shame and guilt, having been so wounded myself. And I feel compassion for them, even if shame and guilt are correct responses to heinous wrongs. (I hardly sound like Peter-the-Bombardier right now, do I?) This leaves me remembering this scene in the film *The Railway Man*: the torture victim's inability to pull the trigger in revenge when the opportunity is finally presented. Instead, there is reconciliation between the victim and the torturer when the torturer opens himself to the truth of his deeds and becomes profoundly repentant.

It isn't the diabolical, the insensate, the dissociative, the madness, and the monstrous in human experience that is a wonder to me. I believe it is naïve to not expect this from ourselves individually or as a collective. My understanding about our species is . . . *expect to be sickened*.

The wonder is that there is love at all, that a scintilla of a soul can emerge from annihilation, as though it were a small shred of a seed that somehow gets blown out of the incinerator, lands in soil, germinates, and grows. This is the wonder. This is what is miraculous.

Lest you think I am speaking of the small shred of victim soul, I am not. I am speaking of shreds of all: victim soul, perpetrator soul, indifferent observer soul, defiler soul, pious soul, eager onlooker soul, collaborator soul, fighter soul, anguished resister soul, duplicitous soul, rescuer soul, guilt-ridden survivor soul. That any shred of any soul emerges, finds soil, connects to the life-force and thrives in some incarnation of "human" is so wondrous to me that it is almost beyond comprehension. We humans make these descents into "the hell realm," and we come back up. Something in us knows to take another step.

What to call this? The life-force? The flowering of soul on Earth? That people were going to show up at the Auschwitz retreat in November 2014 in states of anger, guilt, ignorance, fear, shame, defensiveness, openness, peace, or love was almost irrelevant—they showed up. The collective resilience is a stunning thing for me to behold.

In the face of that, what to do? I say this to myself and to my children: "Grow yourself so you can love. Grow yourself so you can protect your soul and protect life. Your assertion in all of its manifestations (creativity, love, sex, intuition, heart, ambition) is a gift to the universe—do not hold it back. Develop yourself so you do not fear death. That is all."

———

Entering the Alternate State

Entering the Alternate State:
Untested

Recently, I revisited *Peter-the-Bombardier* by reading about DIN (three Hebrew letters: Dalet, Yod, Nun, meaning *Judgment*) in the book *Forged in Fury* by Michael Elkins. DIN was a small group that formed at the end of the war from remnants of the Jewish Resistance Movement. They operated amidst the chaos in Europe immediately after the war. They administered extralegal justice by murdering SS men when they encountered them. Frequently, these SS men appeared to have accidents or to have committed suicide. (Bombardier–Peter feels drawn to this work.)

In the immediate aftermath of the war, Jews waited expectantly to see the world administer justice to the perpetrators of evil. By a large margin (there were more than 13 million possible indictments that could have been handed down in the American Sector of Germany alone), any sense of justice was sacrificed for want of money, time, energy, and the growing need to fight the Cold War. So DIN continued to operate in Europe and traveled to North and South America to track down and kill the SS who had escaped with the support of a well-developed network of international industrialists, bankers, governments, and the Vatican's *Ratline* (a network established for the purpose of getting perpetrators safely out of reach of prosecution).[20]

I could easily envision myself with DIN. It is quite an experience to coldly contemplate murder—even from this distance. What they did feels like taking out the trash. In another way, it sends a very important message. The message is vital in content and in language. One cannot reason with people who are beyond reason. One cannot touch a heart that has become untouchable. But even people beyond reason and beyond humanity are capable of understanding a certain language—it is the language of violence: *Hmmm. If I proceed, I will pay an exorbitant price.*

While the law is functioning, there is the hope of a nonviolent remedy within the courts for those who threaten others. This is how the Southern Poverty Law Center takes on the Nazi Party, the Ku Klux Klan, and the other White Supremacist groups in the United States—the SPLC sues these groups, seeking to financially cripple them. When the law and the courts don't work, there is a risk of descent into retaliation and revenge.

I ask myself if I was a coward for failing to turn in my tormentors at military school. With either the beatings or the "crucifixion," I could have had the whole lot of them busted and thrown out. I didn't even consider it. Was that me being a *Shtetl Jew* (one who meekly took it)? Was that me bowing to fear of reprisal? Was that me agreeing with my lot? Was that me *taking pride in enduring and elevating myself above them*? This much I know: When they took me off the wall, I did not turn them in, I did not hit one of

---

20 Elkins, Michael, *Forged in Fury* (London: Piatkus Books, 1996)

them in the face. They left. I went about my business as though nothing had happened. I told no one about the event. It was never brought up during my tenure at military school. If I weren't a coward, would I have hunted those guys down and broken their arms by now? I survived military school. I actually *thrived* there. I was relieved to be in a place where I wasn't confused, where I knew the score, where no one was telling me that they loved me. I felt pride in my accomplishments: academically successful for the first time in my life and personally successful at having endured my new-boy year and being accepted into my Company. And now I'm wondering if I ought to be ashamed of my complicity.

As a highly sensitive child with an acute sense of empathy for frightened, injured, and persecuted people, I felt helpless to stop the bullies. I was a small child, always one of the youngest among my classmates. I had occasions long before military school to experience the social blows of my inadequacies. Very simply, I longed to be effective against the bullies of the world, so it was not surprising that I took up the study of martial arts as an adult. I recall my first class vividly. I felt I had finally arrived where I had needed to be all along. I felt at home. The movements all seemed natural. I drank them in and practiced relentlessly. Quietly and calmly, my proficiency revealed itself to me and to my instructors. I noticed a strange feeling within my body and my psyche—it was *confidence.* Sadness and relief came when this sentence formed in my mind: "That's what's been missing." I was studying Budo Aikido, a blend of Aikido, Judo, Jujitsu, and Karate. The head of the school spoke an insightful word of guidance to me, which was some of the lack I was addressing—"Poise." As I earned multiple Black Belts, the compensatory bravado of my teens and young adulthood was being replaced with poise, with confidence. This study gave my anger, accumulated from the blows of inadequacy, fear, and injury, a safe and effective outlet. "Oh, this is what it's like . . . to not feel so scared."

My thirst for proficiency and skill took me to the study of Samurai Sword, Pressure Point Fighting, and then, under the influence of my daughter Leah, to Tai Chi. Tai Chi (translated from the Chinese as "Supreme Ultimate Fist") is an art form consisting of patterns of movements originating in China approximately 700 A.D. or earlier—possibly as much as 2500 years ago. The Yin/Yang symbol captures Tai Chi's oneness and dualistic principles. Yin (dark) and Yang (light) operate in balance and, together, capture oneness. Tai Chi's movements are executed slowly, gracefully, looking dance-like, often performed by groups of people in a natural setting.

Tai Chi is distinct from the martial art *Tai Chi Chuan*. Tai Chi, the gentle, slow, relaxing forms that balance energy, have been well-researched and found to promote healing, wellness, and strength. These soft movements, emulating flowing water, transform into combat (Tai Chi Chuan) through a change in intention and application. My Tai Chi practice was supported by studying Qigong, one of the Chinese *internal arts*, a distinct set of movements and postures for refining energy. Over the centuries, Chinese Taoist masters have developed numerous schools of Qigong.

I began my study of Tai Chi when my then ten-year-old youngest daughter expressed interest in studying a martial art. Rather than automatically guide her into one, I suggested we explore some classes together. One of those was Tai Chi. We were both intrigued. The instructor said she could take the class if I would take the class with her. I agreed. After we learned the twenty-four-step basic form, guess who dropped Tai Chi and who kept going? (She said she had homework to do. Besides, her work of delivering me to this art form had been completed.)

This was the beginning of an immensely powerful transformation in my identity as a martial artist who had prepared himself to deal with the threats of the world. It was the beginning of what my meditation and Qigong master called developing "tranquility." Those movements, whether for healing, balancing, wellness, strengthening, or self-defense—all of it—calmed and grounded me. I was going to need every bit of calming and grounding for what lay just ahead in my life—taking excursions to places of atrocity I had become compelled to explore.

I wish to be a person who lives in the world of the law. I wish to be just. I wish for reconciliation where there is hatred, misunderstanding, or ignorance. I wish for forgiveness as the highest evolution of us: as one who becomes fully capable of asking for forgiveness and one who becomes fully capable of receiving true apology and giving forgiveness. I wish for empathy. I wish for love. But when those things fail, I wish to be able to respond—including with violence, if that is the only way to protect life and address evil . . . if that is what is necessary. I have experienced the application of necessary violence while working on an adult inpatient psychiatric unit. There were times on the unit and elsewhere in the hospital when patients had to be subdued because they were physically out of control, dangerous, and injuring others. I used my training to develop and teach the staff a humane take-down protocol and *Moves of Last Resort* for those times when healthcare workers had to save themselves or others from violent attacks. But behind all those words, what I was teaching was an ethical, humane, well-controlled application of violence in response to dangerous, out-of-control violence.

Tai Chi helped me find the courage to look deeper into the perpetrator experience and discover the universal capacity for evil—the ever-hungry, demanding, "insatiable" ego that vexes us. It helped me identify how my hungry ego can turn evil. As a martial art, Tai Chi Chuan is a vital, healing statement, a pledge, and my prayer: "I am here, a Jew, a person who will face evil, name it—even in its subtlety—to change it or condemn it. I know how to show up; I know how to resist and, if necessary, fight. And I am not the only one.

———

Entering the Alternate State: Smiling at the Devil

When *Adolph Eichmann was on trial* in Jerusalem, Hannah Arendt (a German-American historian and philosopher who escaped the clutches of the Nazis after being detained in a camp and fled to the United States in 1941) covered Eichmann's trial for *The New Yorker*. What emerged from her reporting was a profound insight about the *Shoah*, evil, or any genocide—her concept of "the banality of evil."[21] She took us there: to the ordinariness of the actors, the matter-of-factness with which evil is accepted and perpetrated, set against the victims' nonsensical and mangled existence. In my words: **grotesque evil is within the realm of the ordinary**. That juxtaposition is almost mystical. The far reaches of human capacities are so beyond comprehension that they are, to me, mystical.

---

21 Arendt, Hannah, Ph.D., *Eichmann on Trial: A Report on the Banality of Evil*, 2006, New York, Penguin Group, Page 252

We feel and know the ground around us. We think we are grounded. The ground is solid, and so are we. *Oh, yeah?* Talk to the trees in rot when torrential rains wash away half of a mountainside. We hold ourselves as sane and civil. *Oh, yeah?* But how easily we go insane. The far reaches of human and cosmic grotesqueness and depravity alongside the moments of being grounded and loving—this is us.

In the 2012 biographical film *Hannah Arendt,* Hannah is depicted giving a speech to students and colleagues in defense of her articles in *The New Yorker* (which became her book *Eichmann in Jerusalem: A Report on the Banality of Evil*). In the film, she is answering her rabid critics who accuse her of being a *self-hating Jew, an arrogant* (snobbish) *German intellectual,* and generally unfeeling in finding Eichmann to be a mediocre, unthinking bureaucrat and not a monster at all. In the film, she responds to Eichmann's defense that he was only obeying orders by countering that "the greatest evil in the world is the evil committed by 'nobodies.'"[22] The ensuing controversy that dogged her to the end of her life was that she was seen as **normalizing and thereby minimizing** what most people took to be monstrous acts. I do not believe she was doing that. I believe she was pointing out our "normal" human capacities to do monstrous things. That is precisely my understanding of myself and of us all.

Such moral and intellectual courage from this woman, shunned by her colleagues, friends, and remaining family, and threatened by members of the Jewish community! She was so incisive in penetrating through the intense and fierce emotion Eichmann's presence triggered. She saw him, really saw him, *as De-Nur saw him,* "not a monster" at all but a functionary, a bureaucrat, a

---

22 *Hannah Arendt,* Directed by Margarethe von Trotta (2012; Toronto, Canada: Zeitgeist Films (US), 2013, Motion Picture

technician. Eichmann was extraordinarily common and, as such, was and is an immense threat to common folks everywhere.

Eichmann says he personally never harmed a Jew or anyone else. He says he personally had no enmity for Jews. Let's imagine that is so. What begs to be made plain is the moral and hence legal obligation of the citizen to retain authority over their actions and the actions of their society. Arendt leads us to it: it is a crime to stop thinking, it is a crime to "split oneself" (the exact words Eichmann used to describe how he managed his conscience), and to act out of that split when one is doing harm. Following orders was repudiated as a defense since it was a means of not taking responsibility.

From the book *Operation Paperclip* comes a quote from the Nazi planner and architect Albert Speer: "One seldom recognizes when the devil puts his hand on your shoulder."[23] Oh, Albert, that is so true. And then, what do we do in those moments when the devil *does* put his hand on our shoulder and we have that queasy feeling or the ever-so-slight retraction of the body? We give a questioning glance that involuntarily passes across our eyes; we look away in the moment(s) of silence. We discover the difficulty of returning the devil's smile, such that we make all those little signals of our distress go away. Yes, it takes just a moment or two before they pass. When our unease passes, we *do* smile back at the devil, we do laugh along with him, we do nod in agreement, or we simply say "Yes," because after all—we don't want to offend . . . we certainly don't want to offend the devil. And why is that? What capacity is missing in us just then? Hannah Arendt's *capacity to think*? Judgment? Courage? Conviction? Strength? Common sense?

---

23 Jacobsen, Annie, *Operation Paperclip*, 2014, New York, Little, Brown and Company, page 423

I think of myself as a teen or as a young man or as a middle-aged man—in a group. It doesn't matter if it is at work or a social group. Someone proposed an idea—one that did not appeal to me but grabbed the attention of the group. "Oh, come on!" I heard, and more like that, until what? Until there I was, doing a thing I did not intend or want to do. I may have done the thing halfheartedly or wholeheartedly—it doesn't matter. Belonging trumped judgment; it trumped critical thinking; it trumped my values; it trumped common sense, significantly; it even trumped my fear.

What will we all do to belong? If a person was secure in their sense of belonging—by that, I mean in their *original* need to belong—then would they retain (not *develop* but *retain*) the capacity to feel themselves, to feel the other (with empathy)? Would they retain the capacity to think their own thoughts? Would they retain the agency to execute or not—based on *their* judgment—and then endure the rejection, snubbing, or shunning of their peers? What do you think?

I reflected on the times in the primate lab, where I was doing my research, that I saw my then friend, an employee there, do things to torment the primates warehoused there. Two examples are 1) he would stand in front of their cage and taunt them with aggressive facial gestures, and 2) use a stream of water from a hose aimed at a wheel of their cage to make their cage vibrate. It was, simply put, sadistic. I did nothing to stop or curtail his behavior. To my everlasting shame, I "did not offend my friend." I laughed with him at the distress of the animals. It sickens me to recall it and to claim it as true about me. It is deeply humbling to me—I have a grotesquely vivid picture of my vulnerability to the primary human drive to fit in, to belong. I have hard and awful evidence of what one will do to achieve this.

I realize that sadism, evil, or atrocity is not distant, not out of reach at all. It is simple and complex at the same time. It is social psychology; it is in our gene-driven struggle for dominance and hierarchy which we, handily, call the *instinct for survival*; it is a "demonic spirit"; it is testosterone run amok; it is the will of the Lord; it is receiving sadistic child-rearing or horrific trauma redux; it is a "weak and faltering" ego; it is a sermon we hear. Any one or some mélange of forces can transform us from our better selves to monstrosity. Perhaps there are some who are immune to such a transformation. If you are, I don't believe I know you. You are blessed.

And from Bernie Glassman:

All karma ever committed by me since of old,
Due to my beginningless greed, hatred, and delusion.
Born of my actions, speech, and thought.
Now I atone for it all.[24]

—————

24 Glassman, Bernie, *Bearing Witness: A Zen Master's Lessons in Making Peace* (New York: Bell Tower, 1998), p. 214

Entering the Alternate Space: Ready?

I *was looking at places to stay in Krakow.* TripAdvisor was suggesting I look at vacation apartments that can be rented cheaply.
"These nicely refurbished and decorated apartments are located
right in the Old Jewish Quarter of the city!" I started looking
at them and thinking about staying in one but wait a minute—
these were Jewish homes. Where are the people who lived here,
the people who owned these homes? Most killed. Any survivors
were later likely chased out. And I'm going to stay in their home?
I'm going to enrich the "replacement owners" of those homes?
It was sickening to contemplate.

I'd been searching for the correct word to capture my state of
mind. It wasn't *anxiety.* It turned out to be *dread.* This morning,
I again had the quantum experience of being in two places at
once. I knew I would have a good trip, an exciting and possibly
life-changing set of experiences, meet interesting people, and
meet nice Polish people.

Yet, in my mind's eye, I saw the plane; the door open for boarding, and I saw an overlay of a boxcar with the door open. It was the nose, tail, and wings of a plane with the body of a boxcar. The simultaneous thresholds awaited me. I was *anxious*. No. I had *dread*.

I was propelled by the dread. "Have I got everything? It's seven weeks before I leave. Seven weeks. How did that happen?" I went over my lists. Yup, I'd been going about this very well. Very organized. Flights set since January. The hotels in Warsaw, Lublin, and Krakow were paid for, the retreat paid for; I got my single room and the add-on excursions. I got things squared away with the guide; got the itinerary. I'd gone over the guidance from Zen Peacemakers several times; I bought two sets of waterproof boots and warm socks. I purchased a new waterproof winter jacket. I'd read the books on the prep list and gone way beyond that. I was in good physical shape. I had my pack list prepared; I'd shown it to my wife to double-check. I had enough medication to open a small pharmacy and layers of clothes for the cold. The family pictures were on my phone; I had my music. I had my: earbuds, computer, chargers, pens, writing material—all the personal items I would need to . . . , to . . . , to . . . **to what . . . *to what?!*** To be "comfortable"? To "survive"? ***What?!***

Not only did I have everything, but I'd also done everything I could imagine to prepare. Forging my Qi as I had been by doing Tai Chi, the Standing Qigong, the Flying Phoenix Qigong, the standing and sitting meditation, journaling, the uncharacteristic sharing, the study of books and documentaries, the immersion, the support, the talking, the uncharacteristic receptivity to input and guidance . . . son-of-a-bitch!

How could I not be *Ready*? I'm right where I thought and hoped I'd be in my preparations seven weeks out—how could I not be *Ready*?

I mulled all this over one morning as I was getting ready for work, and the sobbing started. All my carefully planned clothing, all my accoutrements, "my papers" (always to be kept on my person), all those necessary items, the ones on my back and the ones I'll keep within easy reach in my carry-on—all those are suddenly gone, and I am naked.

There is nothing. No possessions, no papers, no pictures, no memory, no practice, nothing keeps me from the nakedness of the quantum state, the-being-in-the-other-place, the alternate place, the parallel reality, which scares me to my core, while it appears I'm getting on an airplane in 2014.

I am naked. Just like they were. . . .

Entering the Alternate Space:
Birds

t is time to write of the strange bird encounters I had been having for eighteen months or so, beginning in early 2013. A yellow finch (a bird I had not previously seen in downtown Chicago) entered my downtown office through the overlapping space between the two windows when I had the lower window open a mere two inches; birds buzzed my house, on one occasion hitting the front door of my house in the dark of the evening as I did Tai Chi in my basement; two birds hanging out beside me while I hiked a trail in the Black Hills, taking turns advancing alongside me in twenty-five yard spurts; birds dashed back and forth in front of the window I faced as I meditated. And on like that. I kept wondering what was going on. Of course, the little bastards ignored my demands for more straightforward communication.

And then this: two months before departure, I traveled to Colorado to spend some time with Louie. While I was hiking,

Louie roamed around town, as was his custom. When I met up with him, he handed me the numerous brochures he had picked up during his walkabout and said excitedly that he noticed in one of them that the Polish artist Witold-K had just returned to his studio in Denver after mounting an installation of his work in Krakow. He told me he called Witold-K and described that he had a friend about to travel to Krakow and asked if he would meet with us. Louie excitedly told me Witold was awaiting a call from me. "What?! Louie, you just called the guy up? We're supposed to leave tomorrow." "Just call him." With a familiar roll of my eyes and a sigh, I took out my phone and rang Witold. Yes, he said, we could meet him briefly the next day as we made our way to the airport.

The next day we arrived at Witold-K's studio in Denver and introduced ourselves. My introduction included the reason I was traveling to Krakow in the first place. Witold invited us to look around the studio and said he was very busy working on a commissioned piece. Louie and I looked around, and then Witold reengaged us in conversation. He described being a child during the occupation of Warsaw by the Nazis. He explained that his father had been a psychiatrist who ran a psychiatric sanitarium. And he told me that his father hid Jews there during the occupation. I asked how that could be since the first places the Nazis emptied were the sanitariums. He explained that his father had *information* on the Nazi in charge of Warsaw, and that kept him at bay. He saw the disbelief in my face and said to look it up. He recalled how the poor psychotic patients could not understand their reduced rations and screamed they were being killed. He then dismissed us saying he had to return to his work. We thanked him for meeting us, and, as we reached the door, he called us back and reengaged us in conversation. More about his life and work and stories about him and the very famous people he had known. Then an abrupt, "I must work." Okay, thanks again, and again, another approach to the door only to be called back.

This time he fully stopped what he was doing and looked at me. He said (verbatim), "When you go to Poland, you will be like a bird. On one wing you will discover the destruction of your people, and on the other, you will discover their rebirth. Now I must work."

Louie knew about the bird encounters I had been having. We stood there briefly, completely stunned by what we had just heard. I murmured another *Thanks*, and, this time, Louie and I made it to the street, where I turned to him and said, "Did you hear what that guy just said about a bird?" "Yes, I did. Yes, I did." "What the hell, Louie?! What the *hell*!" He just smiled. And with that, we walked in head-shaking silence back to the car and made our way to the airport.

———

The day before I was to leave for Poland, it was time to finish packing. In my basement office, I gathered all the stuff I was going to pack. My arms were filled with clothes as I came up from the basement to the first floor and was about to walk upstairs to my suitcase when movement from the picture window caught my eye. In the stand of bare birch trees twenty feet from the window, I saw something I'd not seen before. There was a "cyclone of birds" (I am estimating something on the order of fifty plus) flying rapidly around and around the trees. Around and around they went, flying fast, from near the base of the trees to the top, indistinct as individual birds, they became a bird-blur, a dark cone that surrounded the stand of trees.

I stood in awe for a couple of minutes and then put the clothes down to open the front door so I could be face-to-face with them.

The front door opening, of course, disturbed them, and off they went. *What was this?!* I knew I had just witnessed something unique (I had never seen birds in a cyclone before or since). There I was, not able to understand it, somewhat overwhelmed by it, perhaps even a bit frightened, moved and touched by it, and mystified because something undeniable was going on between me and birds.

The need to finish packing pulled me back from the ethereal. For all the angst and turmoil I had been through, I was strangely calm as I finished packing—could that calm have possibly come from them?? I was glad to feel calm; I was glad to feel that what I was about to do was right-action.

I had prepared myself as well as I could to encounter the knowns and the unknowns of Poland and places of extreme atrocity. My life insurance was paid up; whatever was to come next . . . so be it.

———

Maura

Interlude #2

Hummingbirds

My grandfather visits me as a hummingbird.

He died one summer, years ago, while my sisters and I were away at camp. Leah and Ellie cried out of shock, disoriented about having to attend their first funeral, but I—I was old enough to be relieved: *thank God he's finally gone.*

I had watched the man who "raised" my father into "manhood" slowly decline into old age. He lost his memory, forgot his words. By the end, he was a docile old man; the dementia rendered him soft and sweet. But I was old enough to remember his hardness and observant enough to notice my father's wariness around him. So his decline felt like a blessing.

I felt small waves of grief at his death, both for my extended family's sadness and for the loss of a relationship that would never have been fruitful anyway. But there was a new spaciousness in the family, for my father and his wife, and for me and my sisters. The three of us sisters had felt whiffs of tension at our grandparents' dinner table, but up until recently, we had not been told the full story of why it was such a relief when Grandpa died.

I can't even quite recall how my sisters and I came to know that my grandfather sent the hummingbirds. Or how we managed to convince our mother of the same.

Maybe it was that we saw hummingbirds all day during his funeral. Or it could've been that whenever we spoke of him or walked his favorite gardens, a hummingbird would buzz by and hold our gaze.

Hummingbird sightings aren't all that common in the little Midwestern suburb I grew up in. On the rare occasion Grandpa became the topic of conversation though, sure enough, a hummingbird would swing by to watch. So, however we came to know it, for my sisters and my mother, it was codified as truth.

When my sisters and I told our father the meaning behind the hummingbirds, he exclaimed, "But why a hummingbird? What does it mean? And for that matter, why the hell is he coming around now? He thinks we can be buddies now that he's dead?" And in other moments of pain and no small amount of anger, "Fuck 'em, fuck the birds, and fuck him. I'm done with his bullshit."

My dad was, and sometimes still is, not all that interested in seeing the Divine in the everyday, so our grandfather-hummingbird theory was a far reach for him. And in Peter's defense, my grandfather was a real asshole to him.

Eventually, we learned to keep the hummingbird sightings quiet. We'd waggle our eyebrows at each other, silently talking in our minds, like sisters do. *There's another one*, we'd think to each other, smiling quietly into our laps. We learned an important lesson about our father and about the world: you can't show a man the Divine before he's ready.

But, ready or not, the birds came for my father: cardinals, sparrows, robins, bluejays, crows, hawks, and even the yellow finches. What began as grandfather-inspired hummingbird sightings expanded until it seemed that All the Birds of the Midwest descended upon him, doggedly trying to deliver a message. And in an ultimate cosmic joke, they inevitably found Peter standing with his hands over his ears, deaf to their significance, wed to his disbelief.

He'd bring news of the bewildering sightings to family dinners. "There was another one today, Maurz. . . . I just . . . I just can't figure out what they're trying to say!" He was curious to hear my interpretation of the signs, but pretty reluctant to accept the divinity right in front of him.

The subtle hypocrisy of his behavior drove me nuts. The man talks to the trees in the backyard. He has studied Taoist energetic practices like meditation, Tai Chi, and Qigong. He's learned in what many would consider "spiritual arts." And yet—when his witch of a daughter tells him the birds are trying to tell him something, he just shrugs his shoulders and says, "Eh—if they wanted me to understand their message, they would've learned to speak English."

My father thinks he is very funny.

Over and over the stories arrived: a yellow finch in his eleventh-floor office through a barely open window, bluejays accompanying him on his evening strolls, cardinals taking up residence summer after summer in every branch of his favorite tree in the backyard, Robins hopping around on the windowsill of his home office in below-zero temperatures! The birds refused to leave him in peace.

Honestly, my sisters and I were slightly perturbed. We would have been glad to have the birds come visit us, chirping near our shoulders as we played, or swirling around us as we walked in the garden. But the birds had chosen him. Or, perhaps, he had chosen the birds. Regardless, their symbolism, their meaning, the message they were trying so hard to impart remained "Return to Sender: *Undelivered.*"

That is, until my Dad was preparing for his big trip to Poland. At the beginning of the wide arc of transformation he had been launched into, the birds finally . . . delivered.

One night at dusk, as Peter was packing his suitcase and buzzing about the house in "about-to-visit-Auschwitz" anxiety, a wild flurry of movement descended into our front yard.

My sisters and I sensed something going on outside of the big front windows. Hovering around the birch trees was a swirling cyclone of . . . something?

We had never seen anything like it before.

My mother joined us; her jaw dropped in disbelief, and she called for my dad: "Uhhhh, Peter? You're going to want to see this!"

More than fifty, probably a hundred, delicate gray-brown sparrows were swarming and flying laps of perfect circles in the air around the birch trees in our front yard. There were so many of them we could sense the moving air through the windows. It felt like an odd wind, but it was just the force of the birds coming to visit, with the weight of their message demanding to be received.

My father walked into the front room, dumbstruck. He dropped the pile of clothes meant for his suitcase and stared solemnly out the window. In that moment, the awe was too large to dismiss.

He looked over at us with his eyes wide, "What the . . . ? Are you guys seeing this? What . . . what's happening here?"

His three daughters smiled quietly, as had become our custom. We nodded and exclaimed softly, *"Oh, how beautiful,"* and *"Wow, it's amazing,"* as we watched the birds fly their loops.

My mother put her hand on his shoulder and said gently, "Seems like they're here to wish you safe travels, Peter."

He did his usual scoff in disbelief, but then returned her wry smile. "I—well—you might be right, Margaret."

I was prepared to be politely silent about the cyclone of birds in the front yard. But on my way out of the front room, I caught a glimpse of my father, mesmerized, gazing out that window. I could see both the awe and the pain etched in his face. I couldn't help myself—I murmured, "Something big is happening here."

And here, the trouble was upon him:

My father has this recurring joke about "the spiritual teacher who smokes way too much weed." He thinks they point out the beauty and purpose in all things, just to ignore that the world is a bloody mess. He can't trust their penchant for syrupy "meant-to-be-ness." So, when we, his family, look to understand what the birds are trying to tell him, we sound like a caricature of an archetype he can't possibly trust.

We stood for a moment, the front room full and still. The birds broke from their cyclone when he opened the front door to get closer, but still many of them remained poking around the front yard. I decided, *To hell with sounding stoned or fearing his dismissal—I'd rather look the fool than miss the moment.*

And besides, my father was leaving, beginning some large and unfathomable quest into the great unknown of Auschwitz to heal himself and his unknown *other people.* I wasn't quite sure who he was going to be when he got back. If there was ever a time to speak, it was now.

"You're looking pretty lucky, Dad," I said pointedly. "You're being sent off with a blessing."

I nodded my chin toward the window and took a step toward him.

"A blessing, Dad, from *him*, from all of them."

I couldn't bring myself to name my grandfather, but he was in the room with us, just as obvious as the hummingbirds in the backyard, or the sparrows whirling around those trees. My father looked at me and then turned back to consider what he had just been shown.

The tension was palpable. Was he prepared to receive a blessing, a wish for safe travels, from the man and family who had tormented him as a child? Was this wild and sacred thing, somewhat obvious to his daughters, available to him?

Is it possible to reconcile with the dead?

He turned toward me and cracked a half-smile. He looked at me differently; then he looked into the front yard. Like he was seeing something new.

"A blessing, huh?" he said, his eyes narrow and uncertain. Turning, he reached for the clothes piled haphazardly on the floor to finish packing. "I guess I'll take it."

And the next day, he went off to meditate.

At Auschwitz.

———

Peter

Auschwitz

Auschwitz:
I Can Smell the Place

In November 2014, Swiss Air brought me to Warsaw.

I landed at three in the afternoon, collected my bag, and met George, my "non-Jewish, more Jewish than Jewish" tour guide (as described by the Jewish owner of the Polish tour company) for the next five days. I quickly noticed that I was not overcome with emotion as I stood in Warsaw, Poland. The unbelievable was happening. No drama, no near-stroke, no breakdown, just constant orientation: *I am in Poland, this is George, the encounter is happening, I am walking on ground where people were herded out to the street and shot down. Picture that, Peter! Picture what you know!*

It took a year's worth of preparation for me to get to Poland. It was harder still to have my mind there simultaneously in both 2014 and 1939—the "quantum" experience I have previously described. "Being in two different decades" was essential to my reason for being there. That awareness and that effort were constant throughout this reckoning and reconciliation journey. It wasn't that I couldn't have a relaxed meal or sleep in the car while George drove through the countryside to our next destination. But once we arrived, walking through a village or forest or extermination camp—I was working.

George understood my interest in taking advantage of every minute, so we went immediately to two sites in the late afternoon of that first day. I was taken to the Korszak Orphanage. When the German death machinery followed the German military into Warsaw within days of invading Poland, they delivered on their well-thought-out plan for those who were to be immediately exterminated, including people living in hospitals, sanitariums, and orphanages. Janusz Korszak was a Jewish pediatrician who devoted himself to an orphanage in Warsaw and, beyond that, to children's rights. He was also an author of children's books. Korszak, along with other caregivers, was provided with multiple opportunities for escape; instead, they sacrificed their lives by staying, thereby not abandoning the children in their care. He is quoted as saying: "You do not leave a sick child in the night, and you do not leave children at a time like this." Korszak and the other caregivers willingly accompanied the children to all of their deaths at the Treblinka gas chambers, keeping them calm as they were rounded up. I cried when I heard the stories of his love and devotion to them.

Then, in the waning light of the day, we arrived at the old Jewish Cemetery in Warsaw, the site of a bloody slaughter and a mass grave. I learned from George the history of the slaughter of Poles as well as Jews. It was dusk and unusually warm for early November. The old cemetery is on a hill, and the scene is eerily beautiful, enhanced by the smell of leaves. No one else was there. I found an area next to the mass grave and did the first of many Tai Chi sets in Poland. The scene, the smells, the mild weather, the fading light—all combined in the moment to make it strangely peaceful. George asked me what I was doing. I explained the art form of Tai Chi and said that, for me, it was a ceremony, in this case, of remembrance and honoring.

Before their advance into Poland, the Germans had identified the government officials, the professors, the intellectuals, and the religious leaders. Those people were quickly rounded up and imprisoned to be tortured, killed, or sent to camps. This wasn't just occupation; this was the initial effort at *Slavic eradication.* Pawiak Prison, the Gestapo prison in Warsaw, is one of the most chilling places I have ever approached. It is physically ominous—an iron gate barring the passageway which sloped down to the entrance of the building. The feeling evoked when walking into this place was, "You will not be leaving here alive, and you will want your life to end as quickly as possible."

I saw some remaining sections of the Warsaw Ghetto wall, the *Umschlagplatz* concentration point—the roundup area for deportation. Nearby were Nazi office buildings and memorials to those who left from this spot. *Surreal* was the descriptor that kept coming to mind as I struggled with the normality of walking down the street without fear: pedestrians and traffic moving about as though there was nothing special about places like *Mila 18* (the headquarters of the Jewish Resistance). Each time George brought me to another site of Jewish history, I was wobbly from the magnitude of what had occurred *right there.* The work was remembering my study, not just relying on George's tour-guide explanations, but remembering what I absorbed about the Ghetto: the enormity of the suffering, the dying in the streets, the children wailing in hunger and fear, the children's dead bodies, and their dying, broken parents.

Picture what you know! I insisted to myself—the firsthand descriptions I'd read and heard spoken in documentaries of the sounds of yelling and wailing and the superhuman efforts at maintaining complete silence while hiding during another roundup; the smells of unwashed bodies, the rotting corpses, the garbage, and sights of terror, degradation, and depravity alongside resolve, faith, and intrepid acts of courage brought on by starvation, disease, selection for extermination, and helplessness.

I walked on, as though in a movie; I felt I was literally walking out of 1943 and within a few steps, into 2014, such that, in 2014, I was comfortable in Warsaw, I slept well, and I enjoyed the food. What other word can there be than *surreal*? At breakfast in the hotel restaurant one morning, a young German boy crawled on the bench away from his parents and toward me. We "interacted" through eye contact—completely natural, while to me, it was utterly *surreal*.

After touring Warsaw, George took me to the Treblinka Extermination Camp, from there to the city of Lublin and the Majdanek Concentration Camp, and then on to Lancut, Tarnov, and finally Krakow. I saw and touched the remnants of the Ghettos. I was awed to see the places I had read so much about. I no longer had to imagine them. I did have to imagine the people. There is the work again: to be in a place, know what occurred there and, in the moment, use my imagination and put individuals, couples, families, and children there. And put the perpetrators there. And in doing the work of imagining the people and what they are going through, my thoughts turned again and again to the source . . .

With *luckier than Hitler* in mind, I moved around Poland with George, who took me to some places I hadn't known to ask to visit. He was deeply invested in my experience. At times, I found myself aware of being slightly distracted by his reaction to where we were and the history he was giving me. A deep sigh and other sounds signaling emotional distress from him would leave me wondering—was this a real reaction or being done for effect? I pushed past my cynicism and concluded that George (seasoned, well-educated tour guide that he was) was being real in the moment. He gave me access to a Polish Gentile's reaction to the material I was encountering. If I accept that, then I am left with how uncomfortable that made me—which I find very interesting. Why did I need to distance myself from how George held the injuries that riddled his land and his people? George and his open emotion confronted my emotional dismissal of Poles. I could not justify my invulnerability while in the presence of his vulnerability. It was a missed opportunity to connect with a real person in a real way. My being ashamed of my prejudice kept me from discussing this with him, and I deeply regret that.

Poland is a graveyard. Jews, Poles, moral life is buried everywhere, in mounds, in memorials, in depressions in the earth, within ghetto walls. Everywhere I went, something or someone had been slain and was burned or buried. The Polish people are riddled with intergenerational trauma, having been invaded (again), occupied (again), and brutalized (again), and, in 1939, had their annihilation initiated. That was always the German plan.

And, amid all that terror, hunger, dread, and death—some Poles rescued their neighbors. Some did it for money; some didn't, and some saved Jews who were utter strangers. That sentence makes me go "Huh!" and then shut up at the wonder of that fact.

Poland is restoring its historic towns and architecture; it is presenting its culture, its food, its beauty, and the resilience of its people. One of the most beautiful places I saw was a medieval synagogue in Lancut. The Jewish population had been exterminated. After the war, a local took it upon himself to comb through the artifacts strewn around the ruined building and the grounds to restore the building. He transformed the rubble into a museum. It is his relationship with the place that added an unexpected dimension to the visit. George knew the fellow, so we were given admittance. I also had a chance to hear the caretaker's story. He, very simply, felt compelled to do this work. Only after he had done a significant portion of the restoration himself did a Jewish religious organization get involved to help support the effort.

At the two death camps I had put on the itinerary, I encountered what had been a hideous assembly line, constructed by gifted design technicians who demonstrated a deep understanding of primal mass psychology. What the Germans constructed at Treblinka was elegant. Not a wasted motion, not a pause in the movement of objects through the line. The design touches at Treblinka: a clock at the disembarkation point, train tracks curving into the terminus so no one could see the end before they were there— are all designed to create confusion, foster denial, and maintain promise and hope. The just-right installation of terror; not too soon or too much—since that would have evoked hysteria and panic. Once yards away from the tucked-away, flame-disgorging crematoria, people were in such a state of shock, mental and physical degradation, and terror that they could be "processed" with very few guards—a tribute to the level of design, psychological engineering, and "psychological splitting" mastered by the master race. Most of the guards were Ukrainians; the Germans shielded themselves whenever possible from "the dirty end of the business" by hiding in oversight roles. Elegant. This was all very clearly thought out with great precision and attention to detail. There were even adjustments made to deal with the signs and symptoms of psychological stress the SS exhibited from time to time, from tweaks in staffing to rest and relaxation.

Majdanek (My-dan-ick) does not have any of these elegant design touches. It is straight ahead in its design, much like Auschwitz. Majdanek is also distinguished by a unique memorial: a huge, round, open mausoleum with a dome holding mounded human ashes. On the grounds is an original barracks that has been turned into a museum of clothing and personal items. Row after row, bin after bin; it is a warehouse that is a museum. It is startling in its effect—made more powerful by one other feature . . . it has a smell. The barrack smelled like old organic matter. It is the smell that made the place so powerful and real to me.

Of course, smells bring reality to a place—it is our most primitive sense. Smells can hint at what occurred there. An example would be the smell in the beautifully restored synagogue in Lancut, which has a smell of disuse that says *You are in a relic.* In Lancut and Majdanek, that subtle, primal, olfactory sensory experience held the vibration of a cataclysmic event in a way words and vision cannot.

It was right that I was in these places. It took me this long to accomplish it. I was not staggered as some folks report when they visit these places. I had studied well—deeply exposing myself; therefore, I was not shocked at what I was seeing, touching, and smelling. Yet, there is no substitute for the ground, for the mounds of ashes, for the deformations of earth that reveal where bodies or ash lie, for the remnants of the buildings, artifacts, and objects taken, and objects left behind.

I visited four mass graves, one in a forest and the others in cemeteries. At each ghetto and site of murder, I placed a small rock that I had brought with me from home. Doing that was another part of the ceremony that connected me to each site. My words were: "I am here; you are not forgotten."

I did Tai Chi in these most unlikely places; by the waning light of day at the mass grave in the cemetery in Warsaw dating from the 14th century, in a corner of a field at Treblinka, watched by a group of Israeli youths on tour, off to the side of the entrance to Majdanek (where the video George took shows a speck in the sky approaching us, that revealed itself to be a bird, that flew directly over me as I did the form).

And one of those places of Tai Chi was in a forest near Tarnov that I didn't know was on the itinerary. We were on a two-lane road to Krakow, with forests on either side. The sun had set, so the forests were dark and featureless. George suddenly pulled over and positioned the car so the headlights shone into the forest. He pointed into the forest and said, "There is a mass grave in there. Walk in, and you will find the clearing that marks it. I am going to stay with the car."

I was too stunned and fearful to appreciate the brilliance of how he set this up as my solo journey into the dark. The way into the forest was illuminated by the headlights of the car. Light illuminating death. I began walking in and immediately registered the "live earth" smell of the damp forest. Soon, the illumination of the headlights was well behind me, and I had to inch my way into the dark. The night was moonless. I felt more than saw my way in, feeling and probing with my senses for the open area of a mass grave. Leaving the light from the car behind meant overcoming my fear of the darkness of this place and my fear of the act I was moving toward. Sweating with fear and exertion, I pressed on around trees and through brush until I found an open area that was the mass grave with its memorial markers.

Standing at the clearing of the grave and looking back toward the road, the headlights had become two distant, small, diffuse beams that indicated the way out, the way back to 2014. The light of those beams was eerie. The trees, silhouetted by the headlights, became a singular, tangled entity like a drawing from a frightening fairy tale. There was a light breeze, not enough to make a sound through the trees. The forest was utter stillness, utter quiet. It occurred to me what a contrast this soundless space was compared to the sounds of the massacre.

The mass grave was powerful. After the Germans converted the forest into a pit, a moving line of local townspeople, including children, took their turn coming up to the edge and were shot into it. I took deep breaths to steady myself with that scene. After I felt settled standing there, I did something I had not ever done before or since: a Tai Chi form in darkness by feeling the ground. Doing the form was otherworldly as the darkness slowed me way down and focused my concentration. With each step, my feet had to find their bearings on the uneven soil of the clearing. What a metaphor.

I completed the form, which was the first part of my ceremony. Then I did the second part. Taking a small rock from my pocket, I placed it in the clearing, saying, "You are not forgotten." After a long pause, I felt it was time to leave, and leaving these places was always poignant for me. I took some deep breaths and fully noticed the intoxicating, rich aroma of the damp forest. Then slowly, I made my way back toward the headlights in the distance, continuing to smell the forest and feel the ground for purchase.

I was glad George had stayed with the car. It was brilliant. Although I never asked him why he did that, I imagine he knew that the approach to this grave needed to be a solitary journey. Having to find the place in the dark and being there in dark silence held the encounter just right. I felt more connected to this place than any I had visited because it required walking into an uncertain darkness and having to feel my way in and out. The aliveness of the forest made the history contained there feel real and palpable. All these things made the place vibrate in a way I can still feel. I can hear the quiet of the forest, and I can, in my memory, smell it—right now.

———

Auschwitz: Dysentery and Love

George got me to Krakow, where we parted. I thanked him deeply—he wished me well for my upcoming encounter. Only in retrospect have I been able to appreciate how he contributed to my experience in Poland. He was what the tour operator told me he was: "More Jewish than Jewish" although it took some time for me to trust his sincerity, his compassion, and his responsiveness. He was, in all those ways, a corrective experience for me. His sensitivity continually came through, nowhere more so than the surprise stop at the forest in the dark when he sent me in on my own.

I think of my "Fuck Poland" rants and my derisive: "Dead Jews are good for business in Poland" as I contemplate my time with George. George may indeed make a nice living taking Jewish tourists around his country, but my encounter with him forced a reckoning upon me: the ease with which I become derisive. George did not deserve that from me (as perhaps is true for many,

many other Polish people who work in the tourist industry, or Polish people in general). I appreciate him as a professional and as a person of integrity, which forced me to take responsibility for my prejudice—a huge, unplanned benefit to the Encounter-with-Atrocity I had embarked upon.

And then, this:

I linked up with the Zen Peacemakers at a hotel in the old city of Krakow, which was their base of operations. I had signed up for some touring around Krakow prior to the retreat, which afforded me a chance to see the stunning city and meet a few of my fellow retreatants. Before leaving Krakow the Sunday morning of our departure for Auschwitz, I took one last walk through Kazmircz—the old Jewish quarter. There were the shops, the homes (with plaques on the outer wall saying the family name of its former residents and the years they had inhabited that location—for some, it was from the 1600s), the Synagogue, the open square. I was told it looks much the same now as it did when last inhabited by Jews. Walking the plaza, one is even invited to come in for "authentic Jewish cooking and authentic Klezmer music!!" That's right, Kazmircz is a tourist trap! I was taken aback by this co-option. My head spun as I realized the area that ought to be vacant was not vacant and was being preserved at least in part, for the dead-Jew-tourist-trade. "Yes! Come on in, we are authentic, in almost every way . . . Heck, you might not even be able to tell the difference." It seems the dead-Jew-tourist-trade is a very good business in Poland. And in two seconds, here I am, in derision *again*! Is it prejudice? Or truth? Or both?

It was time to go to Auschwitz, the one hundred of us from Germany, Poland, Italy, England, Australia, Ireland, Israel, Palestine,

Native Americans, the United States, France, Switzerland, and Austria. I came to learn that at least half the participants had been there multiple times. The coaches taking us to Auschwitz could not maneuver Krakow's old-city streets. They were parked a half mile away, requiring us to walk from the hotel staging area to them. A line of one hundred people dragged their luggage over narrow paving stones sidewalks. Single file. Hushed. Dragging luggage that didn't easily move over paving stones. People on the street stared at us—we were an odd-looking formation, snaking our way out of the old city on our way to Auschwitz.

"Oh," a voice said within me, "this is what it could have looked like then." And just then, it became a little hard to breathe.

The modern and comfortable coach was a respite from "the walk." This induced the next mind-bending experience: being in comfort on the way to Auschwitz! This level of switching between different states in time and circumstance created deep cognitive dissonance within me. *Bearing Witness* and *Not Knowing* were well underway. I was looking out of the window, twenty minutes into the drive, and I knew that, after one of these turns. *I am going to be there.* How to describe knowing you are approaching the Gates of Hell? Anxiety? Anxiety seems far too mundane. And then I settled again on *dread* to capture this; around one of these curves, I will be at the Gates of Hell.

Going to Auschwitz had a very different feel from my visits to the Treblinka or Majdanek camps, for several reasons. Auschwitz is far more an icon of the evil of the *Shoah*, much larger and a more "complete camp": slave labor, murder, torture, medical experimentation—whereas Treblinka was exclusively for murder, and Majdanek was a combination of slave labor and murder. The other distinguishing feature was that my time at Auschwitz was going to be far more immersive, and I was going to be staying on the grounds. And the encounter I was going to have at Auschwitz was going to be with Germans, Poles, Austrians, *et al.*, many of whom I had assiduously avoided up to this point in my life!

Not yet, not yet. And then, the coach pulled into a large parking lot, one you would expect to see at any tourist attraction. Off the bus, I am standing at the entrance to Auschwitz I, the Main Camp. And, although it is as crazy for me to write this as it was to live it, it was time for lunch, which we obtained in the cafeteria right there at the entrance. It's a bit of a struggle to find adequate descriptors for this truly bizarre moment!

- Truth: I am at the spot where starving, desperately thirsty people staggered through the gates of a hell-realm.

- Truth: I am hungry.

- Truth: There is a cafeteria, and our lunch is distributed to us.

- Truth: Right after eating, we moved to an auditorium and watched the raw-footage film taken by the Russian Army as they entered Auschwitz: the walking skeletons, the dying and the stacked dead, the bulldozer moving piles of bodies into a mass grave . . .

- Truth: I am watching this, having just eaten.

- Truth: I am wearing good clothes and am not cold.

- Truth: I am on the grounds and in the buildings where, in a quantum sort of way, this section of land became its own planet, where the rules of *human relational physics*—of interpersonal life as we know it and expect it, as those people knew it and expected it—no longer applied.

- Truth: In 2014, in Auschwitz I, if, for an instant, I lost track of where I was and just looked around, the buildings do not look ominous; the trees are pleasing; the paths are clean; it looks like it could be a little neighborhood in a village.

- Truth: In the building next door to the movie theater, we viewed the "standing cells" where there is only enough room for a standing body—where the people put inside stood for days.

- Truth: We walk on to the building where horrific "medical" experiments were performed. We viewed the rooms and equipment.

- Truth: We knelt at the execution wall, the place where, after being tortured, some prisoners were stood up and shot. We knelt in silence, reflection, and prayer.

Head-swirling, heart-swirling disorientation, some part of me in shock, some part of me observing. Annnd, now it's time to get on the comfy coach and drive to the retreat center just down the block. I whirled in and out of realities as I took my luggage from the bus, having this very thought, which I convey to you *verbatim*: "This time, I don't leave it in a pile for the prisoners to sort through for distribution in Germany." Where did *that* come from? I do not know.

I ponder how to convey encountering the planet named Auschwitz. Only here and there did the human contracts we make in life as a matter of course hold marginal sway for the prisoners. All was unpredictable and mostly random. *Luck, somehow making a friend,* and *wits* seemed to matter more than anything else in affecting the course of one's experience while in the grasp of the hell-realm. Conveying the fullness of the place requires an immersion that cannot be achieved in film or books. So, I've chosen to convey these five underrepresented experiences to help you conjure the sensations that were endemic to the place.

Lice: They had the run of the body, so much so that they burrowed under the skin and had "highways for travel" about the body.

Dysentery: It eroded any sense of dignity; it clung to lower-body garments, stained, reeking, and chafing. The body was described as "an open tube in which whatever entered the mouth was almost simultaneously discharged as a foul, watery mess."

Smells: They were inescapable; they singed the nose and the brain, and they blurred the boundaries between one's now-foul body and the foul bodies (often dying or dead bodies) in the surroundings.

Forced Marches: Either to work, to another camp, or to move on from the advancing allies, during which another minute's survival depended upon the body functioning beyond its limits, beyond its endurance, without fuel, without rest, without protection from the elements, a body inexplicably operating at all—spirit-infusing-brain to block the perception of pain and reason.

And, if you can believe this, within day-to-day life on what the camp survivor and author Yehiel De-Nur, aka Ka-Tzetnik 135633, at the Eichmann trial called *Planet Auschwitz*, there was: making art, the care of children, music, acts of friendship, resistance, acts of sabotage, faith, worship, and kindness. And falling in love.

Auschwitz:
Names

The retreat included a daily sitting meditation on the selection
platform at Birkenau (Auschwitz II), where Nazi doctors determined who would die immediately after arrival and who would
be worked/diseased/starved or later gassed to death. I worked to
hold close the study I had done of how the men and women of
Germany who went into the healing professions were a necessary ingredient for the slaughter. I worked to remember those
perpetrators who retained some aspect of their character, and
those who turned to alcohol and drugs, and those for whom it
seemed natural to kill, and those who found that the stars had
aligned and their savage sadism finally had a sanctioned outlet.

The one hundred Zen Peacemakers meditated daily on the
Selection Platform at Birkenau, right where trains-from-hell
disgorged their battered, starving, thirsty, and terrified contents.
Walking through the infamous gate to Birkenau with *"Arbeit
Macht Frei"* ("Work makes you free") mocking every poor soul

deposited there, we showed up every morning. It was November, and, although the weather was mild for this time of year, it was still cold. Some of us carried benches, others carried chairs, others, cushions. The one hundred of us set ourselves up on the selection platform in a large oval. I faced the west,—looking at the chimneys of numerous now-missing barracks with the beautiful birch forest in the distance serving as an out-of-place, beautiful, and serene backdrop to this bizarre landscape. A leader spoke an introduction, and then we were in silent meditation. At designated times, taking turns, four of us stood at the cardinal points of the oval and read out loud the names of victims from a prepared list. To that list, we were free to add names of family or a friend's family that we had brought with us. That was our practice each day except for the last day. On the last day, with all one hundred of us standing, the group simultaneously spoke out loud two pages of names. That was deeply powerful. It felt that our combined voices were placing a different vibration into that defiled ground.

I spoke the names that some relatives and friends had provided to me. I spoke the Zliser family name (my paternal grandmother's family), and, in a moment of grace, I spoke the names I had given to my poor monkeys. I also referenced all the other animals I performed experiments upon and the animals whose torment I failed to stop so many years ago. I could not have anticipated what remembering them *at that place* and *in that context* would lead to—I had no idea it would become a moment of liberation. Taking my turn, reading the names on the list handed to me, reading the names I'd brought with me to Poland, and in speaking the names of the animals I had responsibility for, something I hadn't consciously realized that was on me lifted off me. I was lighter. I felt physically lighter, and I found myself reflecting on the peculiar phrase I encountered at the beginning of this odyssey, "Auschwitz is a place of love."

I can say, openly taking responsibility for my actions with those animals, facing the shame of inflating my ego on their poor, broken bodies and their suffering, speaking of them with respect and with a profound remorse as I was, allowed the weight of them to lift. Was it forgiveness that came to me as my voice merged with ninety-nine others in a chorus of affirmation? I can't say the animals forgave me. Did I forgive myself? That is a very murky question. I do have empathy for that boy (for that is what I was at twenty-one). I feel sorrow for that boy, a boy desperately trying to find a way to be a man. I was bright, inquisitive, willing to be daring—needing good guidance from a true elder and a path into manhood. I feel sorrow for what that boy did not receive. I am so grateful for his revulsion at his deeds. I am proud that his values and ethics ultimately shone through the indoctrination he had been given. The man I am today, knowing his deep remorse and responsibility-taking, can and does forgive that twenty-one-year-old boy. So, I've refined the question to: Can that boy forgive himself?

The closest I can come is to imagine this scene: the man I am now walking beside the boy I was to an encounter with those animals. The man stays by the twenty-one-year-old boy's side, kneeling with him as he kneels before them. Then, with my arm on his shoulder, the boy, from his entire being, asks for their forgiveness and explains how he lost his way. The boy will know in that moment that the grown man forgives him and that the animals know that there is repentance and restitution from the two of us.

And that will have to do because . . . the stain is the stain.

———

Auschwitz: Wedding

The one hundred of us were assigned to a *Council* group of ten people who met each morning to process our experiences. It turns out, I was the only Jew in my group. I had a German woman on my left and one on my right. One co-leader was Swiss and the other Polish. I joked to myself: *So many opportunities for me to "play nice in the sandbox and make friends."* The first morning on the grounds was our first time meeting, and it was my turn to introduce myself. That moment struck me as: "Tell the truth, or go home." So, I began by telling the group about Peter-the-Bombardier and my revenge fantasy of turning Germany into a sheet of glass. They listened to my rage. I told them of my awareness of my inner-Hitler, and they nodded. I told them about being beaten and "crucified"—they gasped and moaned. I told them what I did to animals in the lab. They felt and held my anguish.

After each person spoke, Council ended for the day, and we walked to breakfast. A woman from my group who spoke only

Polish was walking beside me. The Polish Council leader had been translating our statements for her during the group. We walked alongside each other and then, in an instant, she took her shawl and swirled it over my head and shoulders, as though it was a babushka. We smiled at each other deeply. We walked on wordlessly, with tears in our eyes, her shawl covering me, giving me shelter. What a moment. What a breath-taking, world-altering moment—Peter, receiving and accepting loving shelter from a Pole.

Over the next days of Council, there were such touching, often tearful moments that flowed from our revealing ourselves and our reactions to this place, to the *Shoah*, to our ancestries, to shame carried, pain carried, rage carried, terror carried, secrets carried. Any and all could be spoken of—all received and accepted with no judgment, no criticism, no analysis. Just acceptance.

At the end of the first day in Auschwitz I, after checking in to the dormitory, while waiting in a long line to purchase some tea, a woman just behind me tapped me on the shoulder. I turned, feeling surprised, and then I smiled. In German-accented English, she blurted out to me that she had to tell someone this fact: she was the granddaughter of a major Nazi who served many years in prison after the war. She was so ashamed of her lineage that she could not bear to live in Germany. She asked me if she belonged at this place and belonged in our presence. (Pause here.) A stranger whom I habitually fantasized about obliterating along with her family and community had just sought me out and shared her struggle of being a German, the granddaughter of a perpetrator, and being present here at Auschwitz. I had let the shock of her outreach pass through me and instantly realized I felt compassion for her and her struggle with profound shame—with *the stain*. I offered genuine support for her presence and her courage in speaking herself in such a vulnerable way. I told her I was glad she was there. She was visibly relieved and said so. She was touched. And then, I was touched. Smiling, she asked why I was there. I said, "Because, for most of my life, I could not shake the feeling that I wanted to annihilate you and your people." Her smile deepened as she slowly nodded in understanding. We sat down and had tea together. We are friends to this day.

Another German woman from my Council group told us she did not feel entitled to be at the retreat because of her ancestry—as though her presence was profaning a sacred place. I met Germans split off from their families (in three cases, Germans unable to continue living in Germany) because their families would not accept German and familial history. I heard rage carried for a lifetime. I heard awareness of our common capacities for madness. What I noticed is that without effort, I felt deeply touched by these people and their stories. People were touched when I spoke, and they told me so. Each with our unique pasts and our unique reasons for being present there were seen and deeply received, so that, together, we could sink into, see, feel, and perceive *Planet Auschwitz*.

One evening, as a group, we toured a nearby Franciscan Monastery that contains the artwork of Marian Kołodziej. Marian, a political prisoner, was one of the first prisoners at Auschwitz. He survived the war at Auschwitz, married, and never spoke of his experience. After a serious stroke in 1993, he began his rehabilitation by spontaneously making pen-and-ink drawings. In drawing after drawing, he depicted the experiences he and others had endured in the concentration camp. These drawings capture the horrors and the profound humanity of Auschwitz. In 2006, Marian met Bernie Glassman and attended the annual *Bearing Witness Retreat*. They formed a friendship which continued until Marian's death in 2009. His art installation—*The Labyrinth*—is a permanent stop for the in-depth touring of the Retreat, and does what all art does: bypasses the cognitive mind and penetrates.

Day after day, we went deep into the camp. Together we sat still in meditation, we walked the women's, men's, and children's barracks, we stood where the poor prisoners stood for roll calls in all weather (which could go on for an hour, or hours, for a day or days—where failing to stand at attention meant being beaten to death), stood in the guard tower, saw art done by prisoners during and after the war, saw where "medical" experiments were done and the bodies "harvested," saw where the clothing and other possessions were processed, saw where the musicians played to accompany the work details leaving and returning every day, saw the field where the women from Hungary were left in the open to die of exposure and starvation because there were too many Jews to "process," saw the rooms and equipment for torture, walked into a gas chamber—saw the scratch-marks on the concrete walls made by the fingernails of the dying. We touched the ovens. It was in the barracks—dingy, dark, and holding the vibration of despair that one can still smell the place: old, worn wood, and a hard-to-place smell of "organic matter" in states of decay.

Every day after returning to our rooms at The Center for Dialogue, formerly a barracks for the SS, I went outside and did Tai Chi on the lawn. My practice did its magic, allowing me to find a calm center and to feel a buoy in the midst of a museum that vibrated with depravity. It was my daily ritual for the witnessing I was doing: of myself, my fellow retreatants, the details and vastness of the enterprise of evil,—including the profound deformation of the perpetrators.

———————

(I share with you now my remembrance of an event that took place on one regular day of the retreat.)

The mother of one of the women on the retreat had survived Auschwitz. Her father was also a camp survivor. The woman was on the retreat with her fiancé. Their wedding was to take place shortly after their return to the United States. On this day, we were touring one of the intact Women's Barracks, when the man spontaneously approached his fiancée and said, "Let's get married right here, right now. There are rabbis with us—let's ask one if they would marry us right now!"

In the moments of considering it, I saw her move through the bizarreness of what he had just pitched and land in the utter rightness of it.

She said, "Yes."

They approached and asked one of the rabbis, who said yes, he could do the ceremony, but asked in kindness and concern, "Are you very sure you want to do that in *this* place?!"

The two of them said that, without a doubt, marrying right then and there was the exact right-action. And with that, it was decided that the ceremony would take place just outside the barracks where we were standing. Outside, the ninety-seven of us gathered around them and the rabbi in the open space between two barracks—a space where back in the day, anything green got instantly eaten, leaving perpetual mud in its place; a place where the women stood in the weather for roll call at least twice each day. By 2014, the grass had long since returned.

The sun was radiant in the beautiful blue sky. The weather could not have been more compatible with an outdoor wedding in November. The light, the warmth, and the energy of one hundred people Bearing Witness to the heart-mending experience of survival and love made what we were witnessing seem natural while we were all simultaneously blown away by the juxtaposition of this ceremony outside this barracks.

Four people held a shawl over the couple, creating a *chuppah*. The couple faced each other, and the rabbi began. Tears flowed freely amongst us as we held space for them between the barracks. They held hands as the rabbi spoke of the spontaneity of the moment—what that meant to them, what it meant to us, and what it likely meant to the souls that might still be lingering in the ether. They spoke their vows, and then they kissed.

We sang songs in celebration and danced around them. It was as mind-bending as you can imagine. It was the ultimate act of reclamation, the triumph of beauty over depravity, an infusion of humanity into ground that had been so profaned. The ceremony was for the people who perished and the people who managed to survive. It was a wedding for the ages, a spontaneous union, an affirmation of life, on the same poor soil that had absorbed years of sadistic roll calls.

What a wedding!

———

Auschwitz:
Naked Again

Back on the selection platform to meditate, I was "naked" again.
I was everyone, everyone who was ever on that platform.
I faced the faded red boxcar that sits on the siding,
feeling porous.

From the broken beings stumbling, falling out of the boxcars to
the officers of destruction,
to the prisoners, to the Ukrainian guards.
To enter Poland is to walk among the many hands that emerge
from the soil,
each vying for acknowledgment and a response to their pain,
along with the quiet remembrance of selfless giving.

Tai Chi steadies me.
I can acknowledge the grabbing hands
without being grabbed.

Their need—so hungry for soothing,
is calmed, as I am,
for having walked among them.

I see the hands relax as they absorb dignity,
and recede back into the earth—able to rest,
able to *be at rest*.

———————

It is strange to consider a factory of death, where null-humanity was revealed in its full madness, or Poland for that matter, one big cemetery to Jews, Poles, Gypsies, and many others, turns out to be a place of calm, of quiet, deep reflection, and connection. But it was. It was very healing for me to be there. It was healing to do my practice there. Being there, as I was able to be there, was liberating. When the retreat ended, it was hard to leave.

Yes, that's right; it was hard to leave Auschwitz.

It was hard to leave the people I had connected with so deeply. It is strange to travel to a place that, for a lifetime, has been a beacon of terror and instead find love there. But I did. The barriers I spent my life behind had come down. I watched a lifetime of hate and paranoia within me crumbling in the moment. I saw myself in De-Nur and every victim, in Eichmann and every perpetrator. The split state sustained by hate and paranoia was healed by the horrible awareness of my identification with everyone. Auschwitz had become a place where my burden of shame and guilt was released on a selection platform . . . I am beyond amazed. Auschwitz, for me, under these circumstances, in 2014, had become a place of love.

You may think me mad, but I am looking forward to going back.

Peter doing Standing Meditation on the Selection Platform at Birkenau.
Photo credit: Shir Yaakov Feit

Maura

Interlude #3

Love and Auschwitz

Truth be told, it was a little harrowing sending my father off to Poland.

"I hope we get him back in one piece," my mother muttered when he hoisted his luggage into the taxi. *At least he's got the birds,* I thought, when we waved goodbye from the front door.

My sisters, my mother, and I had witnessed thirteen months of his dark-night-of-the-soul in preparation for this trip. Honestly, we didn't know if we were going to get him back in one piece. We really weren't sure what Poland was going to do to him. But he did return to us, intact *and transformed*.

Auschwitz had changed him.

He was still Peter, the competent psychotherapist, and our father, the enforcer of proper dishwasher-loading technique. But also, he was completely different. It was something that bordered on miraculous. Peter Sternberg (also known as Peter-the-Bombardier) went to Auschwitz and came back with peace in his eyes. Incredible! It shocked even me.

He began to write furiously, turning his journal entries into essays—pieces of writing he was hungry to have us read. I think he was looking for some confirmation that his experience really did happen.

"Yes, in Poland, the food was good, you were safe, and some of the music was lovely."

"Yes, there was peacemaking on those blood-soaked grounds, between you and the descendants of Nazis."

"Yes, it seems, even amongst the hauntings, you all had a wedding."

And also, I think he wanted us to be able to taste the immense transformation that was occurring, to show us the power of the great undoing and becoming he was in the middle of.

It's not every day that a daughter gets to watch her father transform.

Peter had been softly changing, somewhat under the radar, for many years since my early childhood. Long before he even met my mother, he had found a security of self in his study of martial arts, earning a third-degree Black Belt in Budo Aikido in his thirties. When I was young, he kept a tight hold on his fear, rage, and paranoia. He channeled that energy productively, building and teaching *Moves of Last Resort,* a humane self-defense course for providers working in the unpredictable environment of healthcare, and when he was called upon at the hospital he worked at, he created pediatric disaster-preparedness plans for mass-casualty events.

As a father, he was loving and invested. And, he was ever ready with his "Fuck off—don't trust anyone" attitude, kept at a low simmer at all times, for whenever he needed it. He was a man of explicit faithlessness, nowhere more at odds with that aspect of himself than in how he related to his children and in his unwavering faith in people's capacity to heal.

And he would have continued on that way, faithless and somewhat fearful, if not for the intervention of my youngest sister, Leah.

When Leah was in third grade, she expressed an interest in learning martial arts. Peter jumped at the opportunity. Up until then, his three daughters were far more interested in dance and music than in any fighting forms. The two of them went martial-art-school shopping. The local Tai Chi instructor permitted Leah to receive instruction only if a parent took the class with her. Both of them were intrigued. So, in the spring of that year, Dad and Leah studied Tai Chi on Wednesday nights, and occasionally practiced the flowing, dance-like movements together in the backyard on Sundays.

My father, however, was practicing every day.

By the conclusion of the semester, Leah's interest in the class waned. She never formally studied Tai Chi again after that. Which made sense, since her job was apparently complete; after one semester studying the peaceful practice, Peter was absolutely and unequivocally hooked.

He embarked on a decades-long study of Tai Chi and Qigong, known as "internal arts." These were a large departure from his previous martial and defense focus because the intention of these practices is very different. Peter changed from practicing martial arts to cultivate technical skill and force for defense, to a study of attunement, sensing, and calm.

Slowly, so slowly, the change was almost imperceptible, the grip of the hardness of his childhood and adolescence eased. He still stashed martial-arts sticks in the closets of our house. But he also became a man who spoke to trees and communed with the life force in the backyard.

As his years of study progressed, we began to associate him with those calming movements; in the park, in the airport, in the restaurant parking lot—we could find our father synchronizing his breath with the lyrical flowing motions of his arms and legs.

A few years into his study of Tai Chi, I caught him practicing under the incandescent lights of our kitchen. In what is now one of my most vivid memories of my father, I watched him raise his hands above his head and inhale deeply. At the top of the arc, his gaze tipped upward. And in the slow moments of pause, his body outstretched and extended, I watched those ceiling lights just above his fingers begin to flicker. They buzzed off and on in front of our refrigerator, as though in a lightning storm. And then, poof, normal again, as his arms lowered softly.

I whisper-yelled, "Dad—what—did—did you see that? You made the lights flicker—you with what you were doing, it made . . . your . . . Dad—your arms flickered the lights!!"

He caught my gaze, surprised that I saw him practicing. With a mischievous twinkle in his eye, he looked up at the now-normal lights and shrug-smiled nonchalantly, "They look just fine to me."

We were all a bit oblivious to the fullness of the change occurring within him, none more blind to it than Peter himself. In retrospect, it became clear that Tai Chi and Qigong opened him up to a spiritual experience. He didn't have to take the presence of *qi*, the connection to the universal energy, on blind faith. He wouldn't have been able to do that anyway, after leaving the Big Lie of the "Loving God" from his childhood behind. But he couldn't deny the feeling of energy that coursed through his body when he practiced, or the peace that remained in him after.

Thank God for daughters, because if not for Leah's interest in Tai Chi all those years ago, I don't think Dad would have returned from Auschwitz intact. Not only intact, he returned home and was even able to write the line, "Auschwitz had become a place of love."

After all the months and years of book-writing, I had learned to play it cool when I read his journal entries. I would read something I found so spectacular and awe-inspiring that I'd have to bite my tongue to match his nonchalance, so as not to scare him off. (A well-honed skill of mine, remember the birds.)

There were times, though, when I couldn't keep my cool.

"Auschwitz had become a place of love" was one of those times. When I read it, I wept.

I tucked my face quietly behind my computer screen, letting the tears roll silently down my face. For many moments, sitting at the kitchen table, I couldn't really speak.

"Dad, you—you went to Auschwitz, and you went to a wedding. *A wedding?*" I said quietly, after my first reading.

"A wedding. A wedding outside of the women's barracks. It's just. It's like," I always had trouble putting it into words he could receive. "It's inconceivable—how absolutely and transformationally beautiful that is. Each of you, playing your parts, to be standing on that desecrated dirt, so that love could live on that land again. It's . . . I don't know—it feels to me like God."

I saw the focus in his face. We didn't often talk about God.

"I—uh. I, well. Yeah, I . . . I think I get what you mean there, Maurz." He paused, reconsidering the writing on his laptop. His hand held his cheek. "I mean, we were all a part of some big unifying and kind of . . . *transcendent* thing. So, yeah," he shrugged—smiling nonchalantly, "Yeah, I can see it. . . . Kind of like God."

We were united in our incredulity at the power of his experiences. It was hard to fathom that something so beautiful could happen to someone who was so reluctant to see the beauty in the first place.

"How was Auschwitz? 'Oh, it was good! Amazing! Beautiful, even. Transformative,'" he'd say with a smile, when anyone asked about his trip. He was relaxed now, steady and content. "I'm looking forward to going back."

This, of course, always sounded a little bit insane. But it was good to hear. Good to have him back in one piece, good to see my father's burgeoning faith in love.

And good that he had been bolstered by his first plunge into reconciliation. Because shortly thereafter, he was Bearing Witness on a Lakota Sioux Reservation, and then in Alabama, Bearing Witness to the History of Enslavement in America. (More book-writing for us.)

And then, because he swore he never would, he was getting ready, finally, to go to Germany.

———

Conflict and Reckoning

Conflict and Reckoning:
Mr. New-Guy Goes to Germany

In *the 20th century*, Germany committed four crimes of mass murder. The first mass murder occurred between 1904 and 1908 in southwest Africa—in territory that is now Namibia—against the Herero and Nama people. This is territory that Germany colonized and, in doing so, murdered tens of thousands of African people who objected to having their land and labor taken from them. This was not a moral problem for Germans (or for any other White nation). Racial entitlement was commonplace and is why these crimes were morally (theologically) acceptable to Whites. The injection of race to determine worth, respect, and value is ego-aggrandizing for those with power doing the "judging."

Germany's second mass-murder crime had nothing to do with racism and nothing to do with antisemitism. It was based on eugenics to answer: "Whose life is worthy?" Eugenics is a discredited "scientific method" intended to improve the genetic stock of a people by weeding out of the gene pool those seen as defective, deformed, deviant, and unproductive. This was the effort of the *T4* program, with its incriminating story of German moral (theological) outrage because the victims of the crime were ***members of the family***.

Eugenics was *racialized* to justify the third mass-murder crime—the eradication of the *Untermenschen* (subhuman) Jews and to allow the theft of their property—a move that throughout the ages was intended to enrich neighbors, rulers, and the Church. It's hard to make the racial story work for Jews without antisemitism. The Jews had been outsiders for sure, but they were contributing to society since their appearance in Germany more than 1700 years ago. Jews were freed from the restrictions of ghetto-life when Napoleon imposed the French *Rights of Man* on Germany as he made his way to Russia in the 19th century. Newfound freedom opened space for rapid upward mobility of the Jewish population of Germany by giving them access to education, the crafts, and professions. This access antagonized the gentile German lower classes, who resented Jewish success, and it helped create a fear of Jewish influence (power and control) through all socioeconomic classes in Germany. This is the same experience of threatening and/or breaking the social order that Blacks encountered when they were "too successful"—experienced as an affront in America that could result in being lynched. In Germany and in the United States, this was experienced as a *racialized problem* of threatened hierarchy (something we in America are still experiencing as I write this in 2024).

The Jews obtained their standing as *The Other* through the time-worn method of antisemitism. In the hands of frenzied physician eugenicists and lawyers inhabiting the Nazi Party, it was an easy turn into **racializing** the Jews' *Other* status to justify their disposal. By designating them as *vermin* and *parasites*, the Jews lost their status as *Menschen* (humans) and became *Untermenschen* (subhuman). As with the Natives and Black people in America, the Herero and Nama people in Africa, the Roma and the Slavs, the hierarchy designation (subhuman) was made racial for ease of understanding, for the utility of persecution, and as a justification for immoral acts. It was a justification for an **orgy-for-the-ego** for those who were superior in the hierarchy.

You cannot smokescreen the third crime; it was and is too well known, with many remaining survivors, witnesses, artifacts, and locations. Crime number three was too big and too heinous to be concealed. It is fascinating to consider that only in the aftermath; shame and embarrassment (the moral judgment that Germany could not muster itself) flowed in from the rest of the world. Germany had gone too far, which is stunning when you consider getting *first-world* and *new-world* colonizers, thieves, and murderers disgusted with your actions!

Crime number four, the murder of the Slavic people of Eastern Europe and Western Russia, was begun in Poland with the murder of 1.9 million Poles. The Germans lost the war before they could get the program of larger-scale Slavic extermination up and running.

These facts created great cognitive dissonance in me as I prepared to visit a "normal" country, who was, at the time of its downfall, considered to be at the height of civilization. I kept thinking . . . *What could have happened to them? How could all of this have emerged from this place?*

In the midst of my confusion, I went to Germany.

———

When I returned from Auschwitz, Maggie greeted me—anxious to see what shape I was in. I saw the relief spread across her face as she saw me genuinely smiling and calm as I told her what an amazing time I had. She saw the letter I was sending out to friends and family giving a synopsis of the experience. She knew I had found some peace from the soul-reconstruction work I had been doing. She could see the lightness in me.

The storytelling went on and on with her, my daughters, and with Louie. He was beside himself with relief for what had been accomplished on this journey. Having seen all of my journal writings and, now, the outcome, he began saying, "You have to write a book." I could not give that serious consideration, as I had heard that the Zen Peacemakers were planning their first Native American Bearing Witness Retreat nine months later and had already signed up. After that, I was compelled to do my solo encounter with Black history by traveling to Alabama. And then, in 2017, I heard that two German women I came to know through the first retreat were going to be leading a healing-encounter at the Buchenwald Camp in 2018. This was the moment for Germany, and I jumped on it.

As emotionally challenging as all the preparation work was for each of these *Encounter Experiences*, I felt I knew how to walk the path. The path did not contain the same amount of charged traumatic material, since much of that had already been faced. I was kind of a *new guy*.

For the perversions and limitations of my "pre-catapult" worldview, I take some responsibility and leave some for others. Parents, extended family, the religion I was raised in, my teachers, and my country all had in common a narrow, self-interested "We are the good guys" perspective that severely limited my identity and knowledge of history. The guy I knew myself to be before Auschwitz, the guy who was paranoid about Germans, Poles, Ukrainians, Russians, *et al.*, ready to be hateful toward them, had morphed into someone else, someone new. Mr. New-Guy was willing to look beyond raw emotion, raw reflex. Mr. New-Guy was tired of thinking and regurgitating other people's thoughts to be in the "trust-no-one club" (part of the identity I was raised in). I had worked hard on my personal journey to arrive at this painful truth: thinking my own thoughts would distinguish me from my parents, separate me from them. But it was time to face that separation and pay the price.

Having learned from the Germans I had met that they carry the vibration of shame, I thought further about the shame and guilt I carry—my racism and the racism of my country came to mind. I think of how awful it would be if the story of my personal and collective shame and guilt were on display for all to see—if the shameful and/or guilty things I had done were memorialized so they could be visited and made a teaching point for how not to be a human. Public lessons about shame and guilt feel very difficult to bear. This process is beginning to occur in the United States as memorials and museums about genocide and the treachery of enslavement appear across the country.

Then I imagine myself as a German. I imagine that the deepest shame of my people, committers of heinous depravity which stands out among the pantheon of human perversion, is a stain I wear because I come from them. (Intergenerational "stain" is more than a moral imperative; I believe it is a true psychological phenomenon.) If I add that the places of heinousness became museums—I wonder how I would bear knowing these places exist—that, in the eyes of the visitors, I would see my people, my ancestors, and, by extension, me, judged and reviled. How do you get back into the family (of humanity) when *You* have done *This*? Can you ask to be let back in? Does your shame preclude your wanting and asking? Perhaps that is not how second and third postwar-generation Germans live. Or does this lurk inside?

I am driven to ponder this because it is hard for me to integrate: How might one live with the consciousness of it? That is not an accusation—it is a true question. Pity that the descendants of history's rogue's gallery of murderers, torturers, rapists, and thieves, whether a nationality or a religion, aren't in the same straits as the Germans. Couldn't we all do with a dose of feeling-our-shame? Acknowledging it would be a fine start. And then, right after that, how about we set up a *Truth and Reconciliation Commission* (see the operation of the same name started by Desmond Tutu that saved South Africa after Apartheid[25]) that every one of us in the rogue's gallery surely requires in order to come clean. . . .

I am acutely sensitive to those wounded by shame and guilt. I feel compassion for those bearing shame and those bearing guilt, even if the shame and guilt are correct responses to heinous wrongs. I hardly sound like "Peter-the-Bombardier" right here, now, do I?

To say, "I went to Germany" is so at odds with the person I knew myself to be for more than sixty years. Oh, man! The power of my former identity, and then the catapult, and then a shift.

Yes, I went to Germany in 2018.

———————

25 The Truth and Reconciliation Commission, April 16, 2024, *Welcome to the official Truth and Reconciliation Commission Website,* The Truth and Reconciliation Commission of South Africa {*https://www.justice.gov.za/trc/index.html*}

Conflict and Reckoning:
I Wanted to See My Work

My trip to Germany had two components: two weeks of intensive touring and then a five-day Bearing Witness-style retreat at the Buchenwald Memorial Camp (the former Buchenwald Concentration and Extermination Camp).

The first was two weeks of strenuous touring with an indefatigable octogenarian, a former United States government worker, musician, and tour guide, Daniel. My story of a five-year Reckoning and Responsibility Journey convinced Daniel to come out of retirement to facilitate my understanding of Germany and 20th-century Jewish history.

We began touring in Berlin, spending four days in the city and surrounding area. From there, to Dresden and the surrounding area for two days, swinging through Bautzen, down to Nuremberg, and then the Munich area for two days, and then to the Frankfurt area for a day, up to Celle, down to the Erfurt area for four days, and then concluding in Weimar for a day and a half. The organizing theme of the tour was my statement: "I can always come back here and go to a museum or get a tour of the Reichstag. Take me to the places that no one knows to take me to, and tell me your stories." And that, within the confines of two weeks' time on the road, we largely did. The trip was populated with people and encounters that were wondrous and unexpected.

Leaving Berlin, Daniel and I got on the road to Dresden to pay reverence to the terrible firebombing that city endured toward the end of the war. This visit was a straight-up confrontation for Peter-the-Bombardier. That bombing would have gladly been his work. I was a bit uptight about approaching the city and the history I had studied so closely—it felt a bit like going back to the scene of the (my) crime. I had watched documentary films and read vivid firsthand descriptions from survivors of those terrible hours and the aftermath of the two days of firebombing. There are movies shot from the air and the ground, and still pictures that I studied. I am in serious conflict when I study the firebombing of Germany and watch the films of those infernos. The part of me thirsty for revenge is not gone, even with all the fierce self-exploration I have undergone. I do not know that "gone" is a possibility for the impulse toward revenge. My effort was to, at the very least, try to connect to the source of pain and vulnerability that drives the press for vengeance within me.

Dresden is a beautiful city sitting astride the Elbe River, with a reputation for its cultural offerings in music, art museums, and Baroque architecture. Ninety percent of the City Center was destroyed as were some outlying areas and neighboring towns. However, large sections of the city were untouched by the bombs and fire. Historic buildings that were partially or totally destroyed were meticulously rebuilt, restoring the cityscape to its architectural splendor.

It was mind-bending to be in Dresden, to walk the areas where such devastation was inflicted and to feel horrified. I overlaid the pictures I had seen together with the first-person descriptions I read of the gruesome carnage—all the while imagining myself in the bomber, feeling quite satisfied. I visited the memorials to the bombing, and, as I stood there, I didn't know what to make of myself other than, at its simplest, there seemed to be two of me.

Sitting outside one of Germany's omnipresent bakeries, in a pedestrian moment with a pastry and coffee, drove home the surreal feeling. And then, as if to emphasize the bizarreness of that moment for me in Dresden, Daniel took me to a restaurant overlooking the river and a beautiful residential area, where I had some of the best lasagna I'd ever tasted. I requested that we return the next night.

The clearest, most integrated thing I can say is Dresden is beautiful and is the city of culture it purports to be. They have wonderful food. And I cannot get the two of me much closer (let alone integrated) than realizing they are both present.

Conflict and Reckoning:
The Bombardier Visits Dresden

Dresden was firebombed February 13–15, 1945.
Finally arriving in Germany in 2018,
the fantasy-bombardier inside me had to
see the place of his fantasy-work.

Two sides of me separated by a ragged line—
the man of compassion, respecting life
and a warlord thirsty for vengeance.

Studying archival films of the firebombed Dresden, Pforzheim,
and Hamburg,
I am horrified at his imagined work.
And delighted.
The warlord says, "Oh, do not stop."

And there I am sickened by how ugly the vengeance within me
can be,
how easily it is ignited by what their warlords did.
I walk around Dresden holding pictures of what my warlords did.
Smoke rising from the city takes me slant to chimneys elsewhere—
both belching flame and smoke of what, minutes before,
had been people.

Could a person be more split? I recall the American Indian lore
about how to be a good person . . .
It depends on which of the two wolves within you feed.
Warlord wolf—always on the prowl.

I'm ill.

And frightened.

In my mind's eye, I see me,
a smile on my face after writing *"Shalom"*
on my bombs, laughingly saying
as I trot to my plane,

"Look out below!"

———

Conflict and Reckoning:
Old Class Enemies

I *had just met Daniel and his wife*, Anna, in Berlin. They told me they were able to arrange dinner with their friend Salomea. Salomea is a Jewish woman who is Daniel's age, born in Germany. She emigrated with her family to Australia just before it was too late to leave Germany. In Australia as a young adolescent, she was drawn to the ideal of *fairness* and became an ardent communist—viewing that philosophy as a way to prevent persecution and promote fairness in a society. After the war, she returned to Germany and appealed to the German Democratic Republic (East Germany) for citizenship out of her idealism and commitment to communism. She eventually earned her citizenship and ultimately worked for the Stasi, the notorious Secret Police, committed to quashing any dissent from the party line.

The conversation between Salomea, Daniel, Anna, and me became a discussion about personal redemption as Salomea and Daniel spoke openly of unintentionally doing harm while "serving their masters." Here is the joke the two of them tell: "We are fast friends—two Jews who refer to each other as 'class enemies' (referencing how the communist party derisively referred to anyone who is not a part of the *working class*)."

The dinner conversation began at a restaurant and resumed at Salomea's apartment after brunch the next morning. To get to her apartment, we walked through a wide opening on the sidewalk between storefronts and emerged into a flower-filled courtyard. Salomea's place looked like the quintessential, fin-de-siècle, upper-middle class Berlin apartment I had seen depicted in films. It had a large sitting room filled with books, magazines, art, and photographs. I imagined I could have walked into this apartment one hundred years ago, and it would have looked the same.

We arranged ourselves around Salomea's spot at her desk, and Salomea began.

"I don't know how to calm my nervous system down . . . I know I overdid it for the first 80 years of my life. Salomea gestured with her hands in emphasis. "I can only hope that it is the reconnection with the enemy, with the enemy . . ." she paused, shook her head, "that *reconnecting energy* will bring me back to normal."

The slip struck me as poignant. "I love the way you said it: 'reconnection with the enemy.'" Salomea laughed heartily, "Okay. Right, Peter—that was a Freudian slip, wasn't it?" We all chuckled, recognizing the same reveal.

I went on and affirmed, "But it was exquisite. Can I use that as a segue—that reconciliation is making our way back, to *reconnecting with the enemy?*"

"Yes! Which drove me back to Germany. Which has been my dream all the time. To reconcile with the antisemites who made clear to me when I was four and five that 'you are a dirty Jew.'"

We listened with rapt attention as Salomea told her story, her eyes clear and her voice strong. ". . . the reconciliation that I have always longed for but didn't know, the men that I fell in love with had to look like those men who had abused me in the '30s. What I really wanted was for them to make clear to me, 'You are not a Jewish swine after all—you are a nice little girl.' *Little me* is what I need." She laughed and lifted her glass—"*L'Chaim.* That book there—*Shayndel and Salomea,* saved my life, because through writing that book, I reconciled with my mother. I was sixty-five but still a six-year-old girl.

"While we are on the question of reconciliation, I have to tell you this story about the second-oldest church in Berlin. In 1510, [the Christian community] had a trial of thirty-eight Jews for desecrating the Host and killing a Christian child to bake its blood into the matzos. They were tortured, and, of course, they confessed. They were offered that if they converted to Christianity, they would not be burned at the stake but killed by the sword. Thirty-five refused and were burned at the stake in 1510.

"I had been inside that church to attend a lecture. I sat there, and I had the feeling, *What a heavy atmosphere there is in here.* Six months later, I met a young man who had a British girlfriend. She was visiting when they went up the television tower, which is situated right next to the church. The girlfriend said to him, 'I'm a medium . . . there is a dark cloud around the spire of this church.' I could not get that out of my mind."

Salomea's voice was focused, her gaze direct. She was fully in the story, committed to conveying the power of this experience to us.

"In 1510, Jews got burned, and a dark cloud forms. 'Has anyone ever said Kaddish (the Jewish prayer for the dead) for them?' Hmm. I got the idea to go to the pastor of that church, which I did, and I said, 'Look. Excuse me. You will think I'm crazy, but I want to propose that such and such happened in 1510, and there's a dark cloud around your spire; I want to propose a Jewish-Christian service.' So, he didn't say 'You're crazy,' and show me to the door, as I expected. Instead, he said that was a very interesting proposal, but he needed the permission of the executive of the church. He rings me several months later and says they've refused. The reason is, 1510 was before the Reformation, so she should go to the Catholics. At which point I laughed my head off. As though the Protestants haven't been equally antisemitic. The pastor, though, is good friends with the boss of this church executive. The pastor says the boss will order them to do it, which he did. And so, I organized the presence of a rabbi and a cantor. The pastor made a speech apologizing to the Jews—it was a good speech—and then came the rabbi (the only one I could find who was willing to cooperate). At the end, the whole church sang, 'Eli Eli' (a Jewish song). And I had the feeling that the atmosphere in Berlin was a little lighter than it had been before." Salomea laughed heartily.

Salomea spoke her unconventional story without hesitation or concern about our receptivity to the paranormal. It was clear that she took the paranormal to be, in fact, normal. The three of us were in our private reactions when Anna guided us back to the friendship born between Salomea and Daniel when, in 2014, she realized she knew two Jews born in the same year, having worked in the same "industry" on different sides of the Iron Curtain. Anna realized the wounds of the Cold War that split Germany into capitalist and communist societies, were by 2014, less intense. Anna introduced Salomea and Daniel, and their friendship blossomed.

"What I'd like to know from each of you," Anna asked, "is what have these meetings between the two of you over these past four years meant to each of you—not knowing each other before, meeting your *former class enemy*, becoming friends—what has it meant to each of you?"

"Well, it's a number of years ago that I stopped having class enemies," Salomea replied. "I have simply enjoyed meeting Daniel, and I'm very amused at the fact that I would have been at his throat twenty years before that. Not literally, of course, but highly suspicious of him—would have tried to get his confidence to spy on him and report to the Stasi. So, when I actually met you, I was just amused at the fact that we used to be enemies, and I would have felt you to be one."

"Because you were indoctrinated as such," Daniel intoned.

Salomea agreed, "Yes, I was brainwashed. You can't call it anything else."

Daniel sat impassively. "You would not have been my enemy. No. Even though I was always told that those on the other side (of the Iron Curtain) were our enemies. But, for me, they were not enemies; they were human beings, just like me, living under a different political system. I respected these people. Maybe not all of them—there were politicians I met later that I respected as little as I respected some of my American politicians. For me, learning about your background, perhaps not as a Stasi, but you as an individual, there would have been a connection from Jew to Jew."

Salomea replied, "And to tell you the honest truth, I realized in 1972 that, in fact, all my life *I have been an antisemite*."

Quite abruptly, the feel of the conversation changed. Salomea confronted Daniel for working in the United States State Department, where he had to hide being Jewish from an organization that had been complicit in Germany's quest to murder the Jews of Europe. (Salomea was referring to this: before and during the war, the State Department stonewalled America as a safe haven for Jewish refugees. An example is the story of *The St. Louis*, a German passenger ship filled with Jewish refugees that arrived at the East Coast of the United States, only to be turned away and ultimately sent back to Germany.)

Salomea turned to Daniel, saying, "Knowing you were Jewish, how could Jews (you) work for these terrible people? That would have been another factor to make it even worse between us. How could you, a Jew, work for them?"

Daniel seemed taken by surprise. "Knowing about the strong antisemitism in the United States government—in the Department of State especially, as I did. . . . This is why I never outwardly showed that I was Jewish, because I knew there would be retaliation against me from my superiors."

Salomea seemed to acknowledge what Daniel said and what he kept unsaid. "Hmmm."

"If I may make the observation then," Anna added, "you had a work situation where you didn't want to come out as Jewish and you had a home situation (Daniel's first marriage) . . ."

". . . in which you did not feel accepted as a Jew," Salomea finished. At this point in the conversation, I watched Daniel carefully for the impact of their interpretation of his experiences.

Daniel explained, "It was a conflict situation and to keep all of this, these attacks (a reference to his marriage) toward me . . . this is why, in addition to the work I was doing, as I mentioned, I developed this 'Teflon coating.' It saved me."

"Yes, quite right," Salomea agreed. "But I would like to suggest that this Teflon coating you put on when you were a child in your family because there was no one there who really accepted you as you were. And therefore, *the Teflon coating had to cover you already as a child*. And then you thickened it as an adult."

"Yes."

"I know that as a small child, I did not feel my feelings. I repressed my feelings," Salomea offered.

"*I didn't have any feelings*," said Daniel.

Salomea threw Daniel a line, "Ahh, so we have that in common. And I didn't know this until I was past fifty, that I was full of fears. I found a psychiatrist in the GDR who helped me to realize that I had been a very traumatized child. It was only then that I realized, in my fifties, that I had made most of my decisions in my life from the basis of fear—unconscious fear, yes. It was only when I became suicidal that I started feeling my feelings. Yes."

"And my feelings," Daniel added. "I only realized that I had feelings after I met this woman right here." He pointed at Anna, his wife.

"So, how do you feel meeting now, in 2018?" Anna asked.

"I enjoy it!" Salomea exclaimed. "I find it a great pity that we are so far apart (referencing that Daniel and Anna moved from Germany to the States in 2016), and, consequently, we never see each other."

"I have to agree with you! I would love to spend more time."

Salomea added, "Yes. I should think of you as somebody who understands what's going on in me when I have certain experiences . . ."

"Very true!" Daniel interjected. "And even last night (the beginning of this conversation over dinner), the things that I said that I've been carrying around for decades, *last night is the first time I actually expressed these feelings, I've never been able to do that before. Suddenly it was there, and it started to flow.*"

Anna added with a smile, "I've never heard Daniel say that something hurts him (referencing his former marriage). This was the first time ever that he said: 'This hurts me.'"

"Wonderful!! Very good. Yes," said Salomea.

Daniel continued, "And I feel lighter. I'm getting this additional burden that I've been carrying around out of my body and off my shoulders. I always walk upright because, even at my age, I walk upright; I don't want to bend over. I've been carrying all of this, but upright."

"I realized that the most important thing is love," Salomea affirmed. "Without it, we can't live, and we need to embrace it. I'm sure that every individual has love within themselves—they only need to learn to feel it and to pass it on."

"And not to suppress it," Daniel added.

"And not suppress it because it can be so painful—which was how it was for my grandfather, my mother, and my sisters, and for me until I was fifty."

I gently interjected, "The interactions that I suspect you have from time to time with people who had been on the receiving end of your Stasi work—those are powerful moments, aren't they?"

"Very much so." Salomea nodded. "Look, as far as I'm concerned, I almost died in the year 2010 from a blood illness—it took me four months to recover. I asked myself, *Why did you recover from this?* I think the reason is that I talk about my life, and people, if they are able, learn from it and perhaps not make the same mistakes I did."

"Well, I would add that, from time to time," I reflected, "when you have interactions with people who were hurt by what the Stasi did, when you have those interactions, when you offer yourself that way, you offer them some healing."

Salomea nodded affirmatively and spoke of some of the ways she goes public with her need to reconcile the work she did "under the influence of a fierce ideology" with the citizens she hurt. With this, we closed our time together. I expressed gratitude for Salomea's and Daniel's candor. I was very touched by Salomea and her reconciliation journey, and she was touched to know that.

Conflict and Reckoning:
T4

Outside of Dresden, in a town called Pirna, Daniel searched for and finally hunted down a former T4 facility called *Sonnenstein*. The world well knows Germany's *third* mass murderous crime as the mass murder of Jews, Roma/Sinti, political prisoners, homosexuals, and prisoners of war. But few people know about or pay attention to Germany's first and second mass murderous crimes: the mass murder they committed in Africa and the extermination of "life not worthy of life" in Germany.

It is noteworthy how under-memorialized the second crime has been in Germany. Daniel pointed out that T4 sites did not appear in guidebooks, nor were they included in "must-see sites" in Germany, even for visitors specifically doing Holocaust touring. At least now there is an art installation at the site of the formerly Jewish-owned mansion which had been appropriated for the department implementing the mass-murder scheme—at the address Tiergartenstraße 4, or "T4."

Involuntary Mercy Killing was an idea conceived of by some of Germany's neurologists and psychiatrists. In 1939, these physicians offered to the Nazi leadership the idea and the method for the society to be "cleansed" of those who were intellectually, psychiatrically, and physically disabled. With Mercy Killing, they were ready to take the step beyond sterilization to prevent the spread of contaminated genes. They approached Hitler with the idea of eradicating "life not worthy of life," *a notion taken from the eugenics movement they had studied in the United States*. With Hitler, they saw a chance to go bravely forward and institute ideas for genetic purification. To the physicians, a bonus of these Mercy Killings was having the brains of more than one thousand people harvested and available to be studied. The dental gold taken from their teeth was to be repurposed for the Reich.

The Nazi leadership and the doctors envisioned this program outlasting the war and operating into the future—a remedy for the emergence of additional defectives and the burden of their unproductive mouths to feed. In addition to "the defectives" listed above were people living in German nursing homes, rehabilitation centers, and hospitals who had "lost their value" to society. As the war produced casualties, German soldiers with head wounds that were not expected to recover and elderly civilians living in old-age homes who became incapacitated by trauma after surviving bombing were added to the list for "special treatment."

With the medical community committed to the notion of genetic purification, Hitler and company could embark on three objectives: refine the gene pool by eliminating the defectives, unburden the State financially of feeding the non-contributors, and work out the most effective means of killing and disposing of large numbers of people.

It is a challenge for me to capture here the brutality of the medical-death experimentation and the banality of the "scientific conversations" the doctors had about *efficiency* and *cover*. It was hard on me to study this and fully realize the torture being done to babies, little children, and the helpless. There were many questions the doctors considered with a sense of ease and naturalness. I read the accounts. These were the problems they had to solve: Starvation? How long does it take? Injection? How much to inject for what size body? Asphyxiation? Which gas? How long does it take? And in each case, how do you get the patient to cooperate with their murder? These questions were all answered by hideous experimentation on adults and children. Once all that was worked out, how do you obtain the participation of physicians to administer the *medical therapy* required to "cleanse" and "heal" the society? How do you not arouse the suspicion of the victims' families? The nurses and the doctors, staff, drivers, and police were all required to keep the whole operation secret. The medical teams were not just active eugenics enthusiasts—some had to be co-opted to participate.

It is *our* capacity after all—not *their* capacity but *our* capacity—that staggers me, because, after all, what they did . . . *This Is Us*. Remember where they got this idea in the first place . . . it was America.

It was through experimentation in the T4 program, specifically at Sonnenstein, that doctors became extermination engineers who worked out—*on German citizens*—how to gas and starve people to death. Sonnenstein and a few other facilities for the disabled, once "cleansed" of their inhabitants, received shipments of inhabitants from other facilities in Germany.

After doctors made their "selections," the nurses would accompany their charges to the site of extermination in the basement and remain with them to maintain calm and order until their services were no longer needed. From its inception, physicians were necessary to "make the selections," administer the "special treatment," and write plausible death certificates. One can see in pictures on the internet children gathered around their nurses and adults with their aides. Those pictures make clear some patients knew very well they were going to their death.

Doctors wrote letters to family members explaining that their loved one had died from a disease, but the families began to suspect this was not true. There was a growing awareness among the general population that the government was killing their own. The Catholic and Lutheran churches took the step of publicly criticizing Hitler and the Nazi regime. Hitler was told he could not risk the backlash of going after church officials and, in 1941, closed the program down. Except, not really. T4 became Aktion 14f13, the less-visible, informal continuation of murder through the end of the war using injection and starvation. This went on at some former T4 centers like Sonnenstein, which also gave "special treatment" to overflow prisoners from the Sachsenhausen, Buchenwald, and Auschwitz concentration camps.

After the war, the Sonnenstein facility had its machinery of murder dismantled and repurposed. Not until the 1990s, with the interest and commitment of the public to honoring the memory of those slain, was there a memorial set up. A re-creation of the murder operation was set up as a museum. It was this museum that Daniel and I sought.

After some time driving around Pirna, we came upon a small campus of buildings that appeared to be a functioning healthcare facility. Daniel was not certain we were in the right place. There was no one in sight to ask and no signage to direct us. We finally found a pathway lined with small painted rocks, the only indication that this was a memorial site.

We walked around the facility, opened doors, and went up and down stairwells in search of a reception area. Daniel and I roamed around what seemed to be a functional, well-kept, innocuous, yet seemingly unoccupied building. After ten minutes, we came across a young man who asked us what we were doing. We explained our purpose, and the young man agreed to let us into the museum in the basement. He took us to a door, opened it, turned the lights on in the stairwell to the basement, and as he left, mentioned when closing time was, and asked us to turn out the lights on our way out.

At the bottom of that eerie stairwell, we opened the door to the basement and stepped into a replica of the killing center that had once been there. The eeriness of the stairwell presaged what came next: in the exhibit's undressing room and the body-collection room, were pictures of the murdered residents while in-life, descriptions of who they were, and descriptions of their families. It was an active memorial site with fresh flowers left by families and lit memorial candles burning beside the pictures! The residents were almost exclusively Aryan Germans. It took my breath away. The shock of seeing the apparatus of death in the basement of a healthcare facility, in an immaculately clean basement, was hard to take in. I took deep breaths and stood still to mentally arrive where my body was standing. Before me, complete with an undressing area, were gas chambers, and an oven.

We took our time in that sanitized, compact, surreal, and yet very real, place of horror. Once we completed our exploration of the basement memorial, Daniel and I walked upstairs, turned out the lights, and went around to the back of the building. We were standing at the top of a ravine. It was into this ravine that the ashes of the murdered had been dumped. We stood in silence for a bit. Words felt out of place. I was looking at a lush ravine with the streets of the village just beyond. Standing on the grounds of a quiet, unassuming facility tucked into a residential area of a very regular town, I was doing the work of realizing I was at a crime scene. I did standing meditation for a few minutes, as I had four years earlier, while facing the red boxcar on the siding at Auschwitz.

Sonnenstein's T4 museum was one of the most eerie places I visited. Walking into a death or labor camp, I pretty much knew what I was going to be confronted with, whereas, at Sonnenstein, there was nothing to suggest horror, or being shocked with pictures and gravesite memorials, or plunging into deep sadness for the crimes and how and where they were committed. The fact that it was largely hidden and part of an active healthcare facility I found mind-bending. What was it that was affecting me so powerfully? Beyond the juxtaposition of the healthcare and death center, there was something else. But it was unclear, unclear . . . and it left me unsettled. The nagging deviancy about this place stayed with me and did not resolve until long after I had returned home.

Later, when I had time to parse through the experience, I realized what was so eerie and unsettling about that place. I had been to the ghettos, camps, and forests. At the camps, I was accustomed to train tracks, barracks, buildings for torture, buildings for the storage of valuables, buildings for eradication. The camps were factories. They looked like factories. They were mechanized for efficiency through terror. But in Sonnenstein, none of that existed—unless you looked in the basement. Sonnenstein looked (and had been) regular and normal—a safe place for people who needed tending. At Sonnenstein, what was disorienting was the *treacherous intimacy* of it all. This place had been *home*. The residents of Sonnenstein were murdered in the basement of their home! One day their doctors and nurses were benevolently looking out for them, and the next, they were murdering them. And there it was, the first part of the answer that had eluded me: the depth of the betrayal of the relationship and the possibility that the betrayal could be accomplished so completely and easily just unmoored me. The pictures and flowers maintained in the basement by the families and the pictures taken by the SS that one can view on the web made that unmoored feeling all the more powerful, real, and so very heartbreaking.[26] To me, T4 was treachery in its most insensate form.

---

26 The United States Holocaust Museum, Museum established in 1993, *Euthanasia Program— Photograph* {*https://encyclopedia.ushmm.org/content/en/gallery/euthanasia-program-photographs*}

Conflict and Reckoning:
Orgy-for-the-Ego

traveled to Alabama in 2018 to plunge into an encounter with racism and enslavement in America. At that time, there weren't organized retreat offerings as there are now (Zen Peacemakers and Compassionate Listening, to name two) so I went on my own. I traveled to Birmingham, Selma, and Montgomery. In Montgomery, I attended the newly opened *Legacy Museum* and the *Lynching Memorial*—two exceptionally powerful and instructive places for encountering racial atrocity in America. It was during this solo Bearing Witness Retreat that I had an insight into racism and our predilection for inhuman behavior.

There are many compelling aspects to the Memorial Museum, not the least of which is that it's housed in a former slave warehouse. One exhibit brought me to the insight that travels through this book. . . .

There is a section of the museum that has displays, posters, and newspaper articles that advertised, announced, and covered lynchings. In one instance, a Black man had been falsely arrested for the travesty of having in some way challenged the social order (this occurred routinely to Black people by simply being too successful in business, failing to be adequately deferential to Whites, or daring to make eye contact with a White person—especially true if it was a Black man accused of looking at a White woman). The offended citizens demanded justice. They demanded a lynching. The lawmen holding the Black man in jail said they had no choice but to acquiesce to the demands of the people. But lest you think the people were acting impulsively or spontaneously in the heat of the moment, the righteous outrage about the continued existence of the jailed Black man was advertised in newspaper articles, along with "the call-to-action." The lynch mob was a crowd of five thousand people, some traveling a significant distance to be in attendance.

Five thousand White men, White women, their children, their preachers, reporters, and photographers all came to be a part of a blood spectacle. The newspaper description was of "a carnival atmosphere." The black man was slowly hanged, meaning his body writhed, twisted and jerked while struggling to stay alive and to die at the same time. From his dead, hanging body, the White seekers of justice cut off his fingers and sold them on the spot as souvenirs. Once out of digits, they proceeded to shoot his body two thousand times. They shot the rope holding his body, bringing his body crashing to the ground. Then they set his body on fire. Pictures of the carnage became postcards that were sent through the mail.

Standing in the museum, seeing those photos, and reading the newspaper account, I was staggered, sickened, and ashamed. I moved very slowly around the exhibit, pushing myself to take in the horror of it. It was my duty to bear witness—not to look away from what my race did, and to acknowledge the depth and breadth of the horror inflicted upon another's life, a family's life, and the lives of an entire race. I looked closely at the photos of the White people gathered around their dying or dead victims: the hanged, the burned, the mutilated. One photo shows the male victim from mid-shin down. I studied the faces of the adults and children who were gathered around, looking straight at the camera. I tried to fathom how they were impacted by their participation. The child abuser or the spouse beater sometimes has a passing moment of remorse, or of regret, or even fear of being caught once their frenzy has passed. Was that possible here? And for all my studying of those photos, only once in a while did I see on a White face anything that approached apprehension or consternation—that a deed had just been done that was a desecration, a crime, and that they had participated in a sadistic frenzy.

Now the insight: that five-thousand-person carnival of sadistic frenzy, complete with souvenirs, was an orgy. Not an orgy in the usual sense of the word; it wasn't sexual—it was an **orgy-for-the-ego**.

In his books *The Denial of Death* and *Escape from Evil*, Dr. Ernest Becker developed the idea that humans organize themselves to obscure their awareness of their death and the deaths of their loved ones. Becker references and synthesizes the foundational works of early psychoanalytic thinkers, cultural anthropologists, and philosophers, and offers insights into how human beings reconcile with the sense of insignificance that death conveys and the existential challenge of no-longer-existing. Becker believes that awareness of the fragility of our existence is so powerful, can be so intense, as to render us non-functional if we were to remain conscious of our precariousness. Ergo, our need to, from minute to minute, be in denial of our death. Becker's notion is

that we can block, transform, or transcend the nagging awareness of death, by either committing ourselves to something we
can regard as a *heroic cause* or *project*, which, by its importance,
moves us beyond our insignificance, by *numbing our consciousness*
with self-medicating addictions, or by the boredom of a narrow
and constricted life.[27]

Humans are symbol-making animals, and, through symbols
(a building, an idea, games, play, a practice or ritual, offspring,
a piece of art, a belief, the conquest, etc.) are able to leave a bit
of ourselves behind. Through our productions, we get to cheat
the *smallness* and *obscurity* that death brings. In Becker's view, the
heroic project can be virtually anything: becoming a healer, a parent,
being a protector, performing service to others, or (*ahem*) writing
a book.[28] We can also have hero projects that place ourselves *in
opposition* to culturally accepted mores and values; as examples,
we can be a rebel, an outlier, a criminal, a revolutionary. Doing
so places us in opposition or resistance to the dominant culture's
endorsed hero-projects.

It is my contention that the ego's discomfort with death (the
ultimate vulnerability) forces us to desperately associate ourselves
with *the power larger than ourselves*—with the *Creator/Destroyer*.
To further our association with the *Creator/Destroyer,* we imbue
ourselves with magical powers that provide us with an imitative
sense of power and control over our lives and existence. But our
imitation of the *Creator/Destroyer* does not stop there. The natural
extension of feeling this power over life and death is to expand
it, to express it over other sentient beings, over our immediate
environment, and, ultimately, over the very planet itself. And
right there, in this association, in this *transference*, in this quest for

---

27 Becker, Ernest, PhD., *The Denial of Death* (New York: The Free Press, 1973) 123, 127–139
28 Becker, *The Denial of Death*, 284, 285

expanded influence, in the hands of humans, is the birth of our capacity for evil.

The descent into madness on display in those pictures I saw in the Memorial Museum in Montgomery was, for the mob (as it is for us all), a desperate effort to identify with the force that orders the universe, the force that puts us here, and the force that takes us away. In our identification with the *Creator/Destroyer*, in our imitation of the *Creator/Destroyer*, **we** get to say who or what matters, and **we** get to say what value anything or anyone has. In our eyes, we have turned ourselves into junior gods. *This* is the triumph of the ego—elevating itself from the status of mere dust to the status of a demigod. Status, hierarchy, rank—all ways of measuring our value and powers as demigods. This maneuver can be relatively *benign* and even necessary, e.g., someone must take charge of the group or an undertaking so it can function. Or the maneuver can be *malignant*, e.g., "We are better than them because they are different, inferior, or a threat to us—they are the *Other*." This negates the meaning, value, and worth of *the Other*, and it solidifies the belief that *the Other* is "not connected to me—not 'part of the family,'" if you will. Now we believe we are justified and free to dominate, hate, exploit, or exterminate them—we can have an orgy for the *Creator/Destroyer* ego.

Not that long ago, if you were a White person in America who felt your special status had been maligned or trodden upon by "a racial inferior," you were able to remedy that insult to your *natural-born entitlement* by inflicting terror, torture, and murder with impunity. Humans have been using *orgies-for-the-ego* to prop up their individual and communal egos forever. The stories are ubiquitous. *Orgies-for-the-ego* (the evil *hero story*) are a time-tested way to imagine, if only for a while, two things: that someone wasn't standing on *our* back in order to elevate themselves and/ or that our fate as failing sentient beings wasn't waiting for us.

Greed, devastated pride, jealousy, subjugation, and religious rivalry (all manifestations of the injured, fragile ego) seek the balm of grandiosity and entitlement. This happens as part of our daily lives. In Germany in the first half of the 20th century, the confluence of those forces became a frenzied, communal *orgy-for-the-ego*. And as we see throughout world history, the price for any sordid carnival (Nazism, the enslavement of Africans, eradication colonialism, and ethnic cleansing, among others) is the dignity of humanity for *all*, whether directly or indirectly involved.

Conflict and Reckoning:
Luckier than Hitler

And *now for a romance.*

Hitler is the icon of evil, and as the icon of evil, he is seen as not human. What is handy about that for the rest of us is that we don't have to recognize his humanity, nor are we confronted with the leap from what *he* did and who *he* was to who *we* are.

I read his autobiography, *Mein Kampf.* His writing reveals his disorganization, his capacity for distortion, his grandiosity, and his paranoia. Adolf Hitler was a mess. Adolf most certainly had PTSD—something people tend not to mention. His experiences in World War I would account for that. His experiences as a child would account for that. He experienced violent subjugation as a child, as a soldier, and as part of the collective in post-World War I German society. His sense of pride was as shattered and twisted as it could be from those experiences, with the additional influence of a psychopathic narcissism we can imagine stemming from his disturbed, alcoholic, violent family. Adolf was haunted by the loathsome fear that he was infected with the *disease of Jewishness*, as his father's father could have been Jewish. He was infected with the brutality and the distorting false-love he experienced in his childhood home. In his eyes, his drunken, abusive, persecutor/father was "infected with Jewishness," but Adolf could never approach that reality. Instead, his father was "the old gentleman" whom he "honored" yet whose authority he steadfastly resisted.[29] To his body-gnarling mental and personality disorders, add a delusional disorder of messianic grandeur. Throw in some factor of clinical hysteria and god-knows-what sexual perversion he was reported to have had, on top of PTSD x 2 or 3, and you have a flaming mess of a human who acquired a gift for oratory at the hands of those who wanted to exploit him. As I studied the old films of him, what is stunning is to watch the otherwise stolid German people getting whipped into frenzy by his affected ravings. In their own words, they literally "fell under his spell."

In studying *The Psychological Analysis of Hitler for the OSS*, by Walter Langer, I was confronted with Hitler's humanity. In the early 1920s, he was a guy who was so out of it that he looked absurd walking down the streets of Munich. His dress and the manner of his walk were similar to other PTSD-stricken vets from World War I, who, like Adolf, were ostracized by German society. This description drives the point:

> *He frequently wore the Bavarian mountain costume of leather shorts with white shirt and suspenders. These were not always too clean and with his mouth full of brown, rotten teeth and his long, dirty fingernails he presented rather a grotesque picture. (F. Wagner) At this time, he also had a pointed beard, and his*

---

29 Hitler, Adolf, *Mein Kampf* (Cambridge; Houghton Mifflin/Reynal and Hitchcock, 1939) Chapter 1.

dark-brown hair was parted in the middle and pasted down flat against his head with oil. Nor was his gait that of a soldier. "It was a very ladylike walk. Dainty little steps. Every few steps, he cocked his right shoulder nervously, his left leg snapping up as he did so. He also had a tic in his face which caused the corner of his lips to curl upward.[30]

Langer continues with a picture of a stricken individual:

Sleep is no longer a refuge from his fears. He wakes up in the night shaking and screaming. Rauschning claims that one of Hitler's close associates told him that: "Hitler wakes at night with convulsive shrieks; shouts for help. He sits on the edge of his bed, as if unable to stir. He shakes with fear, making the whole bed vibrate. He shouts confused, unintelligible phrases. He gasps, as if imagining himself to be suffocating. On one occasion Hitler, stood swaying in his room, looking wildly about him. 'He! He! He's been here!' he gasped. His lips were blue. Sweat streamed down his face. Suddenly he began to reel off figures, and odd words and broken phrases, entirely devoid of sense. It sounded horrible. He used strangely composed and entirely un-German word-formations. Then he stood still, only his lips moving . . . Then he suddenly broke out 'There, there!' In the corner! Who's that?' He stamped and shrieked in the familiar way."[31]

After Hitler was cleaned up by the elites of Munich and taught how to navigate within political and business circles, the courtship

---

30 Walter Langer, Ph.D., Henry Murray, Ph.D., Ernst Kris, Ph.D., Betram Lewin, M.D. "The Psychological Analysis of Adolf Hitler: His Life and Legend," https://archive.org/details/A Psychological Analysis of Adolf Hitler Office of the OSS (later the CIA), 1943, republished July 29, 2020, 99
31 Langer, et al., *The Psychological Analysis of Adolf Hitler*, 145

with Germany was on. And again, from Langer, a picture of that courtship:

> *A policeman who is noted for his antipathy to the Nazi movement is sent to a Hitler meeting to maintain order. While [the policeman was] standing at his post. Hitler enters: "He gazed into the police officer's eye with that fatal hypnotizing and irresistible glare, which swept the poor officer right off his feet. Clicking to attention, he confessed to me this morning: 'Since last night I am a National Socialist. Heil Hitler.'"*[32]

Notice the romance language of the police officer, "swept right off his feet." The mutual courtship swells. Langer quotes Gregor Strasser's first-person experiences:

> *Many writers have commented upon his ability to hypnotize his audiences. . . . His meetings were always crowded, and, by the time he got through speaking, he had completely numbed the critical faculties of his listeners to the point where they were willing to believe almost anything he said. He flattered them and cajoled them. He hurled accusations at them one moment and amused them the next by building up straw men which he promptly knocked down. His tongue was like a lash which whipped up the emotions of his audience. And somehow he always managed to say what the majority of the audience were already secretly thinking but could not verbalize. When the audience began to respond, it affected him in return. Before long, due to this reciprocal relationship, he and his audience became intoxicated with the emotional appeal of his oratory.*[33]

---

32 Langer, et al., *The Psychological Analysis of Adolf Hitler*, 22
33 Langer, et al., *The Psychological Analysis of Adolf Hitler*, 22

It was this Hitler that the German people knew at first hand. Hitler, the fiery orator, who tirelessly rushed from one meeting to another, working himself to the point of exhaustion on their behalf. Hitler, whose heart and soul were in the Cause and who struggled endlessly against overwhelming odds and obstacles to open their eyes to the true state of affairs. Hitler, who could arouse their emotions and channelize them toward goals of national aggrandizement. Hitler the courageous, who dared to speak the truth and defy the national authorities as well as the international oppressors. It was a sincere Hitler that they knew, whose words burned into the most secret recesses of their minds and rebuked them for their own shortcomings. It was Hitler who would lead them back to self-respect because he had faith in them.[34]

PTSD makes everybody vulnerable to social hypnosis. How powerful is a demagogue who is tapping societal Post Traumatic Stress Disorder, his own PTSD, and the magic and promise of romance? Here it is:

Once Brueckner, seated on the platform, showed me his watch at the moment Hitler began speaking and asked me to note the time. About three and one-half minutes later Brueckner nudged me. Hitler had pushed both hands, fingers extended, upwards along the side of his head and started bellowing for reasons wholly unrelated to the context of his speech. "See," whispered Brueckner, "the holy ghost has taken hold of him." That was also the moment when men and women began to faint and were carried off by Stormtroop stretcher bearers.[35]

---

34 Langer, et al., *The Psychological Analysis of Adolf Hitler*, 24
35 Shirer, William, *Berlin Diary: The Journal of a Foreign Correspondent 1934–1941* (New York: Alfred Knopf, 1941), 10.

How could a PTSD wreck like Adolf Hitler become an irresistible demonic force? *He was welcomed, needed, and received by a PTSD'd society literally in a state of dis-integration.* The evidence of this dis-integration can be seen in the rampant drug abuse and addiction following World War I, right into the abuse of substances in the Army and Nazi leadership in World War II.

From Ohler's *Blitzed: Drugs in the Third Reich*:

"In fact, Germany was in dire need of artificial assistance: the war had inflicted deep wounds and caused the nation both physical and psychic pain. In the 1920s, drugs became more and more important for the despondent population between the Baltic Sea and the Alps.[36]

"Coke spread like wildfire and symbolized the extravagance of the age. On the other hand, it was viewed as a 'degenerate poison,' and disapproved of by both Communists and Nazis, who were fighting for power in the streets . . . Nazis had their own recipe for healing the people: they promised ideological salvation."[37]

Ohler describes Hitler as requiring injections of a drug containing oxycodone in order to function. By the time Hitler was fighting his war, he was being ***propped up by as many as 90 different substances*** administered in different combinations to prevent him from thinking he was addicted to any of them.[38]

If Ohler is even half correct, the pursuit of the Third Reich extracted a toll on its leaders and foot soldiers. The demands of the Reich created psychological disturbance, sleeplessness, and physical pain. An example of this would be the steady use of cocaine

---

36 Ohler, Norman, *Blitzed: Drugs in the Third Reich* (New York: Mariner Books, 2018), 8
37 Ohler, *Blitzed*, 8
38 Ohler, *Blitzed*, 104

to remain alert for three or four days and nights running by the general staff and the enlisted men to maintain the advantage of rapid and sustained troop movements and patrols; we know this as *Blitzkrieg* (lightning war).

After World War I, Germany was a society that was rootless, in political chaos and civil war, pushing avant-garde to the extreme, running on drugs—out of control. It turned on itself, pulling everyone into the black hole of depravity.

As a man whose wretched destiny was to dwell in the torment of PTSD-induced madness, Hitler is, like the country he seduced into madness, a poster boy for how bad we can get. I mean any of us, at any time. This is why I needed to look at him so closely.

Here is another approach: Am I better than Adolf Hitler? He lived the perfect storm of horror and injury, at the perfect time in the world's history to find himself offered up for a singular infamy.

I contemplate his nightmare lived day after day, with no way out, and think, *Huh. What if that were me?* If I found myself in similar foundational circumstances and then later found myself having been remade with popularity and fame, with power and glory nipping at my heels—might I have done what he did—let the madness envelop me further, all the while thinking I was on the verge of being free of it?

Am I better than Hitler?

Not relevant. I am simply luckier than Hitler.

Conflict and Reckoning:
The Confederacy and Germany

Daniel and I were driving to Seelow Heights, the place where the Soviet Army launched their drive for Berlin toward the end of the war.

Daniel said, "We are in Brandenburg, one of twelve federal states."

Me: "Hey! I just saw a Confederate flag back there!"

"Yes. What does a Confederate flag have to do with East Germany?"

"Or Germany?!"

"It is political expression for some people in Eastern Germany who still believe in the past, especially in Germany's past. They identify with the Confederate aspect of American history, with cowboys, and with the concept of the Wild West. In the past, there were annual 'Wild West Festivals' in Germany, in both East and West Germany. And the men who participated dressed up as cowboys and the women as frontierswomen." Whether in alignment with glorious and rightful theft of land or the enslavement of "lesser beings" for the aggrandizement and enrichment of the entitled, the Germans identified with the two overarching racial crimes committed in and by the United States.

"Wow! I understand the explanation and understand there were those ideological links between American and German history, but I never expected to see a Confederate flag here! That is crazy! There are some folks back in the States who would be proud of that!"

Once again, this time in a flag, the strong ties between Germany and America are clear. In pursuit of "doing business," American banking, industry, and government took an amoral view that business was booming in 1930s Germany because of Hitler, fascism, and the grand theft. And beyond that, America was a modern model for how to do colonialism. That model, which worked so well was *Eradication Colonialism*, which builds on the principle that getting rid of the indigenous people gets you rid of the problems of being a colonizer. We see this amply demonstrated in the treatment of the Native Americans in the Western Hemisphere. Or, if you need cheap labor, you can be "rid of the people" (as people) by disenfranchising them to subhuman status in the hierarchy and use terror to subjugate them—again, amply demonstrated by the enslavement of Natives and Africans.

Hitler and the Germans followed the model of Eradication Colonialism and its amorality as a blueprint. That blueprint was very, very good for business—and by that, I mean American businesses which had subsidiaries in Germany before the war. Many of those companies continued to operate *during* the war and then continued or resumed business after the war. The opportunities for American profits were huge. Looking at the list of those American companies provided by Daniel, I felt my stomach turn when I realized that members of my family and I had been and, in some cases, still were stockholders in those companies. Which leads me to wonder: Can I imagine myself insulated from the long and sometimes subtle reach of greed? Imagining a way to accomplish that through some radical change in lifestyle, would I do it? I sense my hypocrisy would win that contest . . . and does.

I no longer view fascism as an extreme position on the right of the political spectrum. I understand fascism as a *state of tyranny* emanating from authoritarian leaders and rigid social, political, or religious movements, regardless of the particular ideology espoused by the leader and the movements. Fascism is available to be applied within *any* system. I can see this on the right and the left of the political spectrum in the United States as I write this in 2025. As someone who inhabits the "liberal/center" end of the political spectrum, it was eye-opening for me to see tyranny becoming commonplace and acceptable on *the left* in the ferocious way "cancel-culture justice" is meted out in the court of social media. That is a demonstration of how fascism is not a point on the political spectrum, but rather, the condition of tyranny.

Contemplating the Confederate flag in Brandenburg, it occurs to me how the Confederacy embodied fascism. The fact that there was a form of representative government in the southern states does not obviate the rigidity of hierarchy, the disenfranchisement of all but the highest tiers of society, the disenfranchisement of females, and the use of subjugation, terror, and abuse to maintain the elite in the hierarchy. You know . . . fascism. And the north? Rigidity of hierarchy, power and control closely held by the elite, the disenfranchisement of females, and the use of subjugation, overt and subtle, to maintain the power differentials with those held as lesser (the immigrants that became the labor force) . . . Hmmm.

Conflict and Reckoning:
Klezmer Music

Daniel *and I were joined by three* of my soon-to-be fellow
Retreat participants in Erfurt, a charming town with many
structures dating to medieval times. Notable among them was
the bakery we stopped in for a rest. Two bakers were baking
bread and pastries in an oven built in the 1500s. Standing in the
square, I could imagine the place 500 years ago. In Erfurt, there
is an undamaged synagogue built in the late Middle Ages and
a *mikveh* (a Jewish ritual bath) which dates to the 13th century.

Daniel had a less-charming stop lined up for us there: the
Topf und Sohn factory (now a museum). This engineering and
manufacturing concern has been around for approximately 150
years. At the outbreak of the war, the third generation of Topf
sons had to join the Nazi Party in order to sustain the business
and their presence in it. They obtained the contract for the design
and production of the crematoria needed by the Third Reich that
could handle the endless number of bodies of the murdered. The

museum details the banal descent of a common business into an industrial accomplice of mass murder. The story of co-option can serve as an object lesson for us all.

While touring the museum, we discovered there was going to be an event that evening. A couple of authors were going to read from their new book about Germans and Jews. Refreshments and entertainment were to follow. The five of us decided to attend.

The reading was in German, leaving Daniel having to whisper bits and pieces of translation to me, which I then passed on to Janice (the one other American) sitting next to me. With the reading concluded, the entertainment began, which turned out to be four non-Jewish musicians performing *klezmer* music (the Jewish folk music of Europe).

At the first cry of the clarinet, I reacted. This is the one time in all my travels throughout Germany that I was destabilized. The musicians played at being *klezmer* musicians, right down to the exaggerated effort at affected singing with quavering emotion in their voices, and corresponding facial and body expressions. I looked to my left at Daniel. We held each other's gaze for a moment, wordlessly incredulous. It dawned on me that it was quite likely that he and I, along with Janice, were the only Jews in the building.

As I sat there, I felt pulled into an ever-darkening place. It would have been disruptive for me to bolt out of there during the performance, and I did not want to make a scene. Instead, I became a human pressure cooker—containing mounting anger and grief within. One song led into the next to the great joy of the crowd and revelry from the musicians. The merrier the room became, the more it seemed the murdered, missing, and disappeared had become caricatures to be enjoyed as relics from a bygone era. From the emotion burning inside I wanted to yell: **"No! Oh,**

Hell No! We are gone! You got what you wanted! We're gone! Fuck you, having a quaint touch of Jewish culture made palatable and interesting to you by our absence!" But I held my tongue, and I kept my charged-up limbs still.

When they finished, amid everyone's smiles and bonhomie, and surely looking a bit crazed, I clambered over Daniel, scrambled for the door, and made my escape. I flew down three flights of stairs and was finally outside. I was in a very agitated state. It took what seemed like a long time for my companions to come out of the building. They were oblivious to my situation. I handled it poorly and did not convey to them what had happened to me in there. Sadly, an autopilot defense took over—I withdrew. An opportunity to be vulnerable in grief and in anger, to release it openly, was lost. It took me until long into the evening to calm down.

It was more than a year later, in a conversation with Janice, that I felt I had an opening to bring up what happened that evening. I explained to her what it was like for me. I owned my failure to speak of it at the time, saying how undone I was by the experience—the wrenching emotions and vulnerability set loose within me. I so wish that, in that hall at Topf and Sons, listening to pretend *klezmer* music, I had been stronger and simply, openly wept.

Conflict and Reckoning: Track 17

I left my red carry-on case on the empty platform of the Track 17 Memorial, the point of deportation of Berlin's Jews to concentration camps between 1941 and 1943. Track 17 is the last train platform at the Berlin-Grunewald railway station. Because our car broke down and we could not get a replacement until the next day; because then I had to schlep all of the recording equipment I had with me in the red carry-on; because, for a few minutes, Daniel and I were the only people walking around Track 17, I set my red case on the platform and walked on to read the inscriptions in the inlaid iron plates along the edge of the platform.

The tracks now, literally, lead nowhere. At both ends of the platform, the tracks are swallowed by brush—it is visual poetry. I happened to look up from my study of the plates with the names of the camps and the dates of deportation on them and caught sight of my red case, sitting on the platform, as though someone departing had left it behind. I had to photograph it just that way. Upon the snap of the photo, a young man riding his bike on the gravel path alongside the track saw me photographing the bag and stopped. He approached me and began speaking excitedly and pressured, in German. I made it clear I didn't speak German. He pressed on in broken English: "Did your father fight in the war? Your grandfather? Were your people killed? I'm so sorry for . . . I'm sorry to . . ." He couldn't find the English words to adequately express his distress. At this point, I made a grave mistake. I mistook him to be apologizing for interrupting me on the platform. Through our troubled communication, I kept saying, "No, it's alright, I'm just touring, visiting, you are not interrupting." On he went with still more emotion; "If I had been alive then, I would have done something! I would have unlocked the doors of the train; I would have shot myself!"

By this time, Daniel was standing with us, and even his fluency in German could not penetrate the misunderstanding I had begun. Although I *knew* that he was talking about the war and the Holocaust, for some reason, I could not grasp that he was apologizing to me in such a desperate way. Picking up on my misunderstanding, Daniel, too, thought he was being apologetic for interrupting what we were doing on the platform of Track 17. The German man gave up on his anguished monologue, got back on his bike, and rode off. I felt deeply unsettled. I knew something wasn't right, but couldn't grasp it. Half an hour later, I told Daniel that I had gotten him all wrong. I couldn't believe how I had just missed my first (and what would have been the most random and therefore the most meaningful) opportunity to break through the barrier, to connect into reconciliation. And, maybe, to heal a bit.

This was and is such a deep regret for me. What a moment— and I could not grasp it! Everything I had been contemplating in preparation for this trip was happening in front of me, and I did not grasp it to enter it. There is so much I would have asked this man and so much I would have attempted to say in response to his desperate pleas for forgiveness. I wish I could have assured him that, in my eyes, he had no guilt for what had been done to my people. And I would have reassured him that we share the perspective of being a citizen of a current and past bad-actor country. I understood the sense of inherited, transgenerational guilt he could not shed. I would have tried to join him in the painful acknowledgment of that-from-which-we-cannot-get-away. I could have referenced the commonality we share of genocide and enslavement committed in our countries and how dominating people on their own land, held and ruled by America, is still going on all over the world: see *How to Hide an Empire*, by Daniel Immerwahr.[39]

In my imaginary redo of those moments, I would have received his pleading. I would have asked about him and told him a bit about me and what I was doing there. That German man and I would have realized the ways in which we are brothers in our respective—yet very similar—soul-struggles. I would have asked for his name and contact information. Perhaps we'd have become friends.

Years later, in a conversation with my daughter amidst my struggles to write of this heartbreaking mess, she said, "Sometimes the point is to let things go; sometimes the reason something arrives is for you not to get to have it. It's so profoundly clear that this was not meant to be."

I heard her, but her words could not quell my angst. With agitation in my voice, walking around the room and gesturing

---

39 Immerwahr, Daniel, *How to Hide an Empire: A History of the Greater United States* (New York: Random House, 2019), 3–19

wildly, I said, "We, the three of us, the German man, Daniel, and I, together are banging our heads against the wall, . . . the wall, . . . the wall, and we give up, and *fuck!*—we walk away, and I'm going *fuck!* We were *so close*; it was a wall that was only microns thick **that I could not penetrate!**"

The air seemed to freeze between us. And then my wise daughter spoke.

"Because," she whispered, "this wall wasn't supposed to be penetrated . . ."

And the truth of that collapsed me into my chair and brought tears to my eyes.

Red Carry-on on the train platform.
Photo Credit: Peter Sternberg

Conflict and Reckoning:
Peter's Heart and Daniel's Knees

After two weeks of emotionally intense and academically enriching touring, it was time for Daniel and me to part in Weimar.
Having formed a friendship, we were both sad to say goodbye.
We ignored what was most assuredly true: that he had come out
of retirement when he heard my purpose in touring Germany
and that, due to his age and circumstance, we would not be
touring together like this again. Linking up with me on this tour
offered Daniel an opportunity to memorialize his fifty years of
unusual, personal, and in some cases, hidden experiences through
my recording him. We had become trusted friends. I wished we
could have spent more time together. I saw Daniel as an excellent
historian and someone whose input could help me explore and
synthesize the connections I was making about history and my
own life. He saw me as someone who could absorb the experiences we were in and the meaning of the stories he shared. At
times, our musing together seemed to deepen his understanding

of Germany, the history, and himself. And Daniel also found me, well, interesting. . . .

At one point, Daniel and I were making our way to the Dachau Concentration Camp. We stopped at various sites in Munich along the way. While I was walking about one of those sites, Daniel struck up a conversation with an employee there. When I finished what I was reading, I came over to the two of them. I was introduced to Lily, who turned out to be Jewish. When Lily heard about the nature of our tour, she eagerly began telling us her family story: one grandmother was the sole surviving resistance fighter of her group, and the other grandmother had been herded onto a train with her children for deportation, but the train mysteriously never left the station.

I found Lily to be a very determined, angry, and obsessed person: she wanted to repopulate Munich with Jews.

Lily is a problem for me, as are the Jews who donated big money to build the museum of Jewish history in Warsaw, just as the Jews who are repopulating Poland are a problem for me. The problem is my imagined *klezmer*-music rant: "We're gone! Don't you get it? Gone!"

Munich will not escape having to contend with Jews in their midst if Lily has anything to say about it—unlike me, who ponders: *Why the hell are we trying to go back to places where we were burned?*

Can it be that the Jewish people do not realize they will burn again? You can see my problem—and so does my wife, who, when she heard my exasperated question about Jews returning to get burned again, deftly and brilliantly pointed out: "It is easier to leave hope before hope leaves you."

It is a complex problem. One part of it is logistical: exactly where would we go that isn't Israel and not face burning? Off the top of my head, I can think of four places from the recent past: Bulgaria, Denmark, Singapore, and India. Yes, Singapore and India have welcomed Jews to their countries. Bulgaria and Denmark resisted intense pressure from the Nazis to turn their Jewish population over for destruction—they did not cave.

The second problem is intensely personal; it is the young and defiant voice within me that says with a full-on smirk, "I'll show you." That was my unspoken message at age fifteen—silently staring down the tormentors who hung me on the wall to crucify me. Throughout his young life, other than complete collapse, that defiant boy had one move only—"I'll show you." Which brings me sliding into the punchline—how very hard it is to discover and hold the truth buried beneath that rubble: "I really cannot do anything to stop it . . ."—I, and the Jews, **will** once again burn. My powerlessness burns now. . . .

We arrived at Dachau and were about to go into the camp when I looked at Daniel and saw how drained he was. I said, "Daniel, I don't need you to take me on a tour of this place. Wait for me out here." He protested that he could do the tour. I said that may be so, but it wasn't necessary. He agreed it took a lot out of him whenever he went into a camp. He asked me if I was sure; I said I was, and he thanked me. I left him at the entrance.

When I emerged, I asked him if we could find a quiet spot on the outskirts of the grounds of Dachau where I could do some Tai Chi. We found a spot and I did a short set. He asked me what I was doing. I explained a bit about Tai Chi and the form I'd just done. I explained that it harmonized the energy in the body, moved energy, and that, when viewed, its aesthetic had been known to have healing properties for people who were ill. He said, "When I go to these places, it hurts my body, especially my knees. Watching you do that made my knees feel better." We were both astonished.

———

In Weimar, Daniel and I were having our last breakfast together. I walked him to the car for his drive back to Berlin. I joked with him, wondering if he'd be able to navigate the way back without me there saying the three phrases of German I had mastered while in the car with him: *geradeaus* (straight ahead), *links abbiegen* (left turn) and *rechts abbiegen* (right turn). Every time I blurted one of them out in concert with the GPS, it would incite laughter.

We had made plans to continue our conversations and even do some virtual touring together from home. We said our good-byes, and I watched him drive off, feeling the loss of his company. "Wait!" I wanted to say. "We still have the rest of Germany to do!"

Instead, I met up with my cohort in front of the Weimar train depot for the short bus ride to the Buchenwald Concentration Camp and another time and world.

———

Beauty at Buchenwald

Beauty at Buchenwald: Retreat

checked into the *Days of Peace and Reconciliation Retreat* at Buchenwald, staying in accommodations on the grounds that once housed the SS guards. Today, these are pleasant-enough accommodations; some rooms are dormitory style, some shared, and some private. There are meeting rooms and a dining facility. I found it worth imagining being there as an SS man (note: many of these "men" were mid- and older-adolescent *boys*) or one of the SS doctors (the fellows who did the "selections"), having breakfast and getting ready for the day's duty—where yards away, people were being starved, experimented upon, tortured, and worked to death. I try to imagine conversation over morning cereal: "I might have to beat some prisoners to death in the quarry today, but at least I'm not on the Eastern Front! Phew! Lucky me . . ."

It was effortful for me to remain in that consciousness, to be present in every role, to approach the fullness of the place and the time—to not simply settle into the familiar identity as a victim. It was a lot of work—it was good and instructive work. Here is how I know it was good and productive: things became more complex, the suffering more entangled. An example of that complexity might be the effects on some of the SS and soldiers when they found their enthusiasm and exaltation giving way to the realization that they and their families had been fed a lie.

This was the invitation to the retreat:

DAYS OF PEACE AT BUCHENWALD
"Our Vision:

We feel the need to turn to our personal and
collective wounds. We see this turning as loving
action on the way to inner and outer peace.

We feel called to acknowledge the wounds of our time,
to learn from them and to heal them where possible. This
strengthens our determination not to cause new wounds.

We recognize our fears, defense strategies, and indifference
and let arise from this the strength for acting courageously.

We commit ourselves to embodying the insight
that the recognition of differences and diversity
makes interconnectedness possible.

We want to understand what causes war and what
causes peace, so that we can act peacefully.

We see ourselves as part of a learning community and
are ready to contribute to peaceful vividness.

If this vision inspires you, you are welcome to share
the Peace Days in Buchenwald with us."[40]

The tenets of the retreat were similar to the Zen Peacemakers: Allowing oneself to be in a state of "Not Knowing" (letting the place teach you), "Bearing Witness" to the uncensored and spontaneous fullness of feeling and awareness that can flow from an encounter, and allowing "Right and Loving Actions" to arise as they will.

In addition to familiarity with the Zen Peacemakers approach, the four leaders also guided us in the practice of *Inquiry* from the *Ridhwan School* of personal development.[41] Done in pairs, *Inquiry* allows a chunk of time, say, ten minutes, for a monologue of introspection of self-questioning, thoughts, feelings, associations, and quiet, all in the service of deepening one's attention to find and express the hidden aspects of one's internal world. The listener receives the speaking. Only after the speaker has finished is there some dialogue for clarification. Then the roles reverse. It is an interesting way of giving interpersonal and personal space for focused self-reflection and sharing.

And like the Zen Peacemakers approach, there was intensive and extensive touring of the grounds with a guide from the Buchenwald Memorial. He was very knowledgeable, responsive, and dedicated to helping people get to know the place. We had

40 *Credo of The Days of Peace* for the 2022 Buchenwald Retreat, Kathleen Battke, Reiner Hühner, Dorle Lommatzsch, and Judith Beermann Zeligson (2022), used with permission.
41 The Diamond Approach, Almaas, A.H., *Diamond Approach: Glossary of Spiritual Wisdom from the Teachings of A.H. Almaas* {*https://www.diamondapproach.org/glossary/refinery_phrases/inquiry*}

an opportunity on three occasions to do restorative work for the camp, which I found quite meaningful.

There were twenty-three of us, counting the four leaders. Three of us were Jewish, one of whom was a retreat leader from Denmark. The other was a new friend to me from the United States—we were previously introduced because of our intention to participate in the retreat. Most of us were in our fifties, sixties; a few were in their twenties and thirties.

Each day opened with meditation at The Quarry—a place of horror now made beautiful by the restorative action of the passage of time and nature. Back in the day, it was the site of person-crushing work, administered the Nazi Way. The quarry work required weak and sick prisoners to do heavy labor, breaking limestone into rock, loading it into carts, and pushing/pulling those carts up an incline out of the quarry to the new railroad bed on the other side of the camp that was to terminate in the town of Weimar. The quarry was famous for random and often sadistically delivered death. Two of the Retreat organizers who had met me through the Auschwitz Retreat knew I practiced Qigong and Tai Chi. They asked me if I would lead the group in ten minutes of Qigong exercises as part of the daily meditation in The Quarry, which I did. With the images of brutality I had seen in SS photos held firmly in my mind, I sought to hold contemplative space for the heavy energy in that place and the heavy energy within us. The group moved in unison—the movements settled us into our bodies, while we did our work of appreciating where we were and what madness can do.

Buchenwald is a large camp, and it was a training facility for the SS. It was a site for medical experimentation. It was a central warehouse for sub-camps where slave laborers were distributed across the region to industrial and farm concerns needing labor.

It was a torture center, and it was a killing center. It held political prisoners, Sinti/Roma, Jews, POWs, and homosexuals. Children were held in the children's camp before they were sent to other camps to be murdered. Our guide spent several hours each of the five days taking us around the camp in detail and getting us connected with different restoration work projects. I worked just outside the camp, spreading gravel to make a parking lot alongside the train embankment that the prisoners created with the rock from The Quarry to extend the train line from Weimar to Buchenwald. I was very aware that my work abutted their work. I got to rest; they did not. I got water; they did not. I was well nourished from breakfast and could look forward to lunch. They were starving. I could work at my own pace; they would be beaten if their pace faltered. My work and its proximity to the embankment the slaves built was a powerful meditation on atrocity and their suffering. I worked hard and was very aware that people my age were not chosen to work but were sent instead to be immediately gassed.

When we weren't meditating, working, or touring, the group met as a whole. During the five days, wondrous moments occurred.

———

Beauty at Buchenwald:
Our Yellow Star of David

Before my trip to Poland in 2014, I went to a fabric store, bought some yellow cloth, cut and then sewed a Yellow Star of David—a symbol forced upon the Jews of their disenfranchisement, ostracism, and relegation to subhuman status during the Third Reich. That Star traveled with me through Poland and the Auschwitz Retreat in 2014. I kept it in a baggie along with the small stones I'd brought to distribute at the places of atrocity I was going to visit. Only my wife had seen the Star. When I attended the Zen Peacemakers Native-American Bearing Witness Retreat in 2015, I added a companion object to the baggie: an American Flag arm patch, which signified to me my identification and classification as *the perpetrator* in the Native eradication story.

I had no intention of displaying the contents of the baggie. And yet, nervously, with a racing heart, on that first day of the Buchenwald retreat, at our first gathering as a group, when we were going around the circle, each doing a two-minute introduction to say why we were there, I spontaneously pulled the Star and the patch out, saying to the group, "A picture is worth a thousand words. I wish to be aware of it all—the full catastrophe, if you will, the story of the victim and the perpetrator, in all manifestations."

Sixty seconds. I have never explained *anything* in sixty seconds. Thinking I was finished and pleased with my economy and precision, I had replaced the baggie and was zipping up my backpack when Dorle, one of the retreat leaders, asked me if I would consider adding the Star and the patch to the objects sitting on a fabric mat in the center of the circle. The mat was an altar of sorts, and the various objects on it were talking pieces. Any talking piece could be chosen by a speaker. Once finished, the speaker could replace the object or pass it to the next speaker, who could use it or choose another.

I paused for a moment, still quite taken aback that I had even pulled these objects out of my backpack and now had just been asked if I would allow them to sit out in the open. Despite feeling caught off-guard, I gave in to an impulse and said, "Sure." The room was silent, and I felt all eyes upon me as I took the Star and patch back out, walked over, and placed them on the mat. A sense of shock had come over me, and my head felt fuzzy. With the introductions concluded, the group had finished its business for the day. As I left the room, I looked back, surprised that my Star and patch were where I had left them, artifacts of my life, sitting out in the open. Bewildered by this sight and thought, I paused a bit longer, shook my head in lingering disbelief, turned and left the room.

The next day, we were going around the circle, speaking about ourselves in greater detail and depth than in our introductions. Partway around the circle from me sat Dorle, and when it was her turn to speak, she asked me if she could use the Star as a talking piece. Caught off-guard again and momentarily dumbfounded, I nodded my assent. As she walked over to pick it up, my apprehension grew. Something large was happening, and I knew to take note: my breathing was shallow, my eyes were wide, my body was tense; I was and wasn't tracking what was unfolding in front of me. Dorle sat down, holding the Star gently, and began to speak. I was looking at her when I was not glancing around the room. I cannot recall what she said, since I was in a daze. I can recall *how* she spoke—with solemnity. She finished and paused.

I briefly closed my eyes, opened them, and said to myself, "Phew, that's over!" But then she calmly passed the Star to the person on her right. Rather than take up a new "talking piece," that person held onto the Star, my Star, that Yellow Star of David, and then solemnly spoke. My shock continued and deepened. Again, I vaguely heard speaking; tone, cadence, and posture were coming through, but my poor brain could not take in the words, as I required more concentration than usual simply to breathe. Mercifully, that person concluded their speaking, giving me a chance to draw a deep breath. I thought I might be coming into clear-headedness, but then, in a jolt, my shock was renewed as *that* person passed the Star to their right.

Apparently, I was oxygenated enough to form this thought: "What is going on here?" I was incredulous to myself. "I am being passed around a circle of Germans. My people are being passed around a circle of Germans! **What was happening?? What have I done?!**"

I tried to stay with what was occurring in the room right in front of me. One person and then another took and used the Star to speak. Finally, I could begin to take in words and what they were saying about the Star.

Each person reflected on having the Star in their hands. They received it silently—they held it reverently. They caressed it. They turned it over and studied it. They rocked with it. They held it tenderly. One woman pressed it to her chest and burst out in deep sobbing. They said they had never touched a Star of David before. Holding my Star of David in their hands connected them to the reason they'd come to Buchenwald in the first place. They remarked that I had made it by hand. They said they had heard my description of the pain the Star represented and held.

The power of their words, feelings, and actions penetrated my shock, and my tears could no longer be restrained. By a stroke of synchronicity, my new friend from the States and fellow Jew, Janice, happened to be sitting next to me and saw I was struggling. She gently put her hand on my leg, which helped me to stay with the feelings of the moment, because I was completely overwhelmed with this: I had offered myself, in my Jewishness, to the Germans.

On it went.

"Stay in the room," a small voice inside me repeated over and over. "Stay open to what is taking place around you—with a part of you." I watched the Star, a symbol of the people I come from, a symbol of their relentless persecution and endurance through the ages, right into and through my life, passed among strangers, among Christians, among Germans. Whatever lies beyond surreal is where I was at.

I had lost control, literally, lost control of my Self—the Self that was in that passed-along Star. I watched my Self being passed from one stranger, one German stranger to another, held in reverence and tenderness because I had said "Yes." It was bizarre, and the bizarreness reached a stupefying crescendo. In what felt like a startling crack of thunder, what had been preposterous and surreal instantly became awesome and beautiful. Tears rolled steadily down my face. I looked about—*we* were crying.

The Yellow Star of David had cracked us open. My co-retreatants were blown away; I was blown away. They cried. I cried. It did not stop until each person in the circle had spoken. When the last person returned the Star to the altar, there was silence. I stared at the Star, rocking in my chair, taking deep breaths, overwhelmed by it all. We sat in silence and awe.

After some minutes had passed, one of the leaders closed the circle for the day, and the group slowly and silently dispersed. I watched my fellow retreatants leave the room. Still overwhelmed, I remained seated. Janice had started to leave and then came back to check on me. I told her I was okay and thanked her for checking in and for her support. It was clear from her look and tone—and mine—how touched, how blown away we both were by what had happened. I told her how important her presence had been to me during the circle.

I sat there as though coming out of a dream—trying to comprehend that I had let my Self be so exposed. My Star/Self had been shown such care, tenderness, respect, and depth of feeling. I realized in retrospect that I had let myself be an offering and that I had been deeply received.

I could not have anticipated the exhaustion I was in. I finally got out of the chair and very slowly walked out of the room. Dinner followed, but I recall nothing about it or the rest of the evening. Lying on a thin, hard mattress in a heat wave and no air conditioning equals poor sleep for me. But that night was the one night I slept well.

The next day, someone commented to me that they had been afraid to touch the Star for fear of being burned by it. One of the leaders, whose name was Reiner, later said to me: "The Star was a great gift to me as a German—it was an honor to be seen by you as worthy (to be entrusted with it)." In his statement, I understood that dignity had been restored to us all by the Star being passed as it had.

The Altar

A couple of days later, one of the participants brought out an instrument to play some music. She approached me and asked if she might play a Jewish lullaby. I thanked her for her sensitivity and said yes to her request. She played a melody I recognized and had always found mournful. The differences between this moment and the severe reaction I had to the *klezmer* music played at the Topf factory were clear. Here I was, in a heavy but respectful setting, and I had been asked. And I noticed that through the five-day retreat, at a place that held obscenity, Peter-the-Bombardier, the guy whose fantasy was the annihilation of every living thing in Germany, was quiet—oddly at peace.

———

Beauty at Buchenwald: SS University

Throughout *the retreat*, I spoke of my intention to get to the full catastrophe. This intention was symbolized by adding the American Flag patch to the pouch containing the Star of David, in working to imagine the crushing disillusionment for some Germans when Hitler's spell was broken, and in owning the awfulness of having an *Inner Hitler.*

Our guide explained that Buchenwald had been used as an "SS University" for training the guards they would need for the other camps. He explained that the average age of these *men* was eighteen. They were as young as sixteen. It was clear to me, in full remembrance of my impressionable, eager-for-elder-acceptance-Self at that age, that these boys (for that is what most of them were) did not have a chance. In most cases, there was no real option for taking a moral inventory of what was being required of them and, hence, no choice about participation. Overcoming the pressures of herd insanity that brooked no deviation, and the resulting terror that had overtaken Germany would have required a psychological, familial, and moral structure that was a stretch for *anyone*,—let alone an adolescent!

On the second-to-last day of the retreat, the group went on a day tour of the nearby city of Weimar, one of the early bastions of National Socialism. Janice had been with me and Daniel when we toured Weimar just before the retreat, so neither of us felt the need to go back. Instead, we both felt there was more to see and experience on the grounds of the Memorial. We stayed back. Janice suggested going to the art installation.

Straining belief, amid the degradation and deprivation of that place, with virtually no access to supplies, some prisoners felt compelled to, and somehow did, make art. The art in the collection had been produced by them during and after the war. The installation did what art does well: bypasses the verbal mind and gets the distilled experience across in a way from which we cannot readily distance ourselves. Rough, raw, and extreme experience was portrayed in the work all around us: people at their worst, people in hope, people in torture, people acting their monstrosity, people in strength, people in states of demise, people in faith . . . people reduced to their component parts. It became clear to me that the brilliance of the architects of the obscenity of Buchenwald was to reduce people to their component parts, whether victim, observer, or perpetrator. In Buchenwald, every creature was turned into a piece of machinery. Every person was reduced to person-as-collection-of-component-parts. Bucolic scenes reminded the imprisoned of life-before-reduction, or gave them a sense of hope, or gave them a sense of separation from their current reality. Acts of kindness, retained faith, the random stroke of luck—all were humanity being pumped into the humanity-consuming process of reduction-to-component-parts.

And in the end? The perpetrators failed. In the end, shreds of humanity, of soul, if you will, and even dignity, prevailed. They failed. The art showed that the perpetrators' efforts at reducing humans to their component parts and "boiling off" their humanity—failed.

When we look at their art, when we talk about them, when we look at the photos the Germans took, we make them—the victims *and* their perpetrators—real people, right now.

Another way of saying it is that I was taken with profound wonder (perhaps *awe* is the better word) about the participants who survived; that starvation yielded to nutrition, that the broken hearts yielded to care and respect—never to become undamaged, but in so many cases, brought back into some altered form of humanity. I wondered if there was anything that restored the brokenness of the perpetrator who, like his/her victim, was also reduced to component parts—except that the perpetrators had to carry on *in hiding.* They were left with hidden distortion, the hidden damage of having been taken apart—forced to discard parts of Self as "sentimental, burdensome, and weak." Once the madness was over, the mangled perpetrators were left with the joy of remaining alive—all the while having to hide any sense of brokenness. How does one live in the "as-if" state, "as-if everything I have done, I have not done"? (So many perpetrators handled that problem with the same method described by Adolf Eichmann at his trial: by splitting. I observe this method silently woven into everyday life.) These were the questions swirling (again) in my mind as I left the art installation.

The art installation was the most visceral experience I had while touring the camp. Janice and I staggered out of there. She said, "I need to sit in the forest and get calm; maybe you can do some Tai Chi." I agreed. We started walking. We walked outside the fence on the path the guards had walked. The camp is surrounded by an exquisite forest, and we happened upon a section of it. We noticed a sign. It said: "Soviet Special Camp No. 2—more than 7,000 men are anonymously buried in this mass grave." The story is this: after the war, in the section of Germany they occupied, the Soviets had rounded up as many SS men as they could find and sent them to Siberia. Their need for vengeance not mollified, they continued to round up anyone they could (rightly or wrongly) identify as a Nazi functionary or as having belonged to the Nazi Party. Into the Soviet net went landowners, mayors, architects, librarians, etc.—all men in their forties. Was it to make way for the communist government they were installing? Was it for retribution? Maybe both. Over several years of being "disappeared" and held out of contact, those German men were starved to death and buried in the mass grave. Only after the reunification of Germany were family members of these disappeared able to find out what had become of their loved ones. Many families consecrated the mass grave by erecting memorials. Those memorial crosses and gravestones are in a small clearing in that forest. Those stones and crosses have names and dates on them. Many have expressions of anguish engraved on them.

The previous day, the group had reflected on Simon Wiesenthal's book *The Sunflower*. As you will recall, the nub of the story is this: close to the end of the war, while walking through a village as part of a work detail, Wiesenthal was randomly chosen to appear beside the bed of a young, badly burned, dying SS man. The SS man had insisted that his nurse break the rules and bring a Jew to his bedside. Once Wiesenthal was there, the SS man confessed his participation in atrocities against Jews—including, ironically, in one instance, setting a building filled with Jews on fire. He was in anguish. He begged Wiesenthal for forgiveness. Wiesenthal said nothing. This went on for some minutes as the SS man reconnected with the Self he had before the insanity got him. Wiesenthal described the man as being in profound moral torment (my words). At a point in his desperation, the man took Wiesenthal's arm and continued to beg for forgiveness before death. Wiesenthal remained at the bedside but said nothing. This is how the interaction ends. In the book, Wiesenthal then turns to the reader and asks what the reader would have done in his place. The last section of the book contains brief essays by various philosophers, ethicists, and religious figures commenting on Wiesenthal's decision to say nothing.[42]

Without suggesting that Wiesenthal (or anyone else) should have done anything different, I contributed to our discussion saying that the German people, who were swallowed by madness, received a profound moral wound—whether they realized it or not.

While Janice and I walked on to discover what the clearing held, all the reflections about *The Sunflower*, the teenage SS "men," and perpetrators living their lives stuck-in-hiding, were in my troubled head. As we walked, a clear impulse formed: I would do Tai Chi here, the same Tai Chi with the same intent I had previously brought to all the other places of atrocity where I used the form as a ritual of presence and of healing. I turned to Janice and said, "A former version of me would now be putting my backpack down and gleefully dancing on, literally stomping around this mass grave. I can picture it." I continued, "Now, it appears I've lost my mind—the mind I once had for sure, for I am about to do this . . ."

---

42 Wiesenthal, *The Sunflower*, Books One and Two

Janice sat down at the memorial site. Holding the idea "That could have been me," I put my backpack down and, without thinking further, I allowed myself to be led by the impulse that had spontaneously arisen within me. I commenced. In a clearing at one end of the memorial site, I did Tai Chi.

Photo credit: Janice Jacobson

To be clear, I was doing Tai Chi to memorialize German victims of a Soviet atrocity—likely perpetrated in response to the heinous atrocities perpetrated by the Germans upon the Russians. And the ritual also memorialized the Soviets-turned-into-perpetrators who had been inexorably caught in the trap. When I finished the Tai Chi set, Janice and I talked. I asked, "Why is this not part of the tour of the camp? Why is this overlooked?" We realized that overlooking this place is what our German co-retreatants had been alluding to when they said they were in deep conflict about having feelings of grief, of loss, of victimhood for being deprived of fathers, uncles, grandfathers, of a moral universe to grow up in, of pride in one's country and of desperately wanting to be able to grow and live outside of the stain of depravity and madness.

To me, the avoidance of this place was exactly that problem. In that moment, I understood the Germans were frozen, left in guilt and shame, incomplete, unworthy to feel, to own the rest of their experience, to own or re-own their humanity and the rest of the feelings of profound loss therein.

I said I knew what we had to do. *We* had to bring the Germans here. We, the two Jews, had to acknowledge and endorse the full German catastrophe. To do otherwise would contribute to their continuing distortion and stain of unworthiness. I said we had to offer them a way back, to be a conduit to the rest of their humanity.

After reckoning, after responsibility-taking, and after reconciliation with the other comes the possibility of redemption when one finds a path (not back, but forward) to the fullness, the worthiness, of humanity. I knew this from having to face this process of reckoning and responsibility-taking about my work on lab animals. I also faced myself as a civilian who was comfortable and content to distance myself from the people in the military that I, as a citizen, insisted take up arms for me. And I knew this process of reckoning, responsibility, and reconciliation from the ever-widening crack in my denial that allowed me to see all those (even inadvertently) left in my wake while I was going through life as a white male.

When the group was together at dinner, Janice and I spoke with animation of our experience at Soviet Special Camp No. 2. I offered to accompany anyone who wanted to go to the forest and to the memorial. I was excited to make this offer—it felt like the most important thing I could do on this retreat. The immediate reception was lukewarm. I was momentarily surprised, but then realized my German co-retreatants were unprepared for this moment and my offer.

The next day after lunch, seven people took me up on my offer. (Others approached me later and I made multiple trips to the mass grave.) We had a solemn walk there and a solemn exploration of the area. My German co-retreatants translated the gravestones for me. Hearing the lament and the wail arising from those stones and crosses deepened the place for us all. One of the men suddenly reacted with anger, anger at the dead Germans and their grieving families, saying, "You fools, you brought this on yourselves!" I touched his arm and quietly said, "It is time for a different encounter just now." He let my words come in, and then his grief bubbled up.

The group asked me to do Tai Chi. I felt it was important for us to do a practice of harmonizing energy as a group instead of them watching me. I suggested that we do Qigong as a group because Qigong, unlike Tai Chi, is a practice done standing or sitting in one place and therefore is less complicated to demonstrate and replicate. They agreed. I taught them a Qigong move. In the shaded clearing of the memorial area of a stunningly beautiful forest that grew out of a mass grave for seven thousand people, we faced each other in a circle. As we inhaled, we bent our knees, and our hands came up to chest height. We slowly exhaled as we gently pushed out and straightened our knees. As we inhaled, our hands retracted back to our chests. Exhale—extend out, inhale—retract. We did that in silence for thirty-six repetitions. Then, still in our circle, we turned around. Facing out into the forest, we silently did another set of thirty-six. It was stunning in its silent power.

Flowing from our extended hands was the energy of acceptance. It was the humanity and humility of the *bridge experience*: "I could easily have been you; I'm sorry it was you; I'm sorry for the agonizing loss your families had chiseled into the headstones they placed here." Our Qigong was acknowledgment that an atrocity had been committed in this place, to these people, without regard for who was deserving of what. The living, the dead, and the perpetrators of the atrocity; all three groups were there; all were accounted for.

It is difficult to convey how profoundly my co-retreatants were affected doing this practice in a place of atrocity toward Germans. I saw it on their faces as they registered sadness. They also looked surprised to be in a place that had been off-limits to them. They knew a barrier had been broken, that they had gained access to something they had not had before—***an entitlement to their pain***. They said that to me. They felt the power of us as a small group, gathering, moving, and sending energy cultivated in that moment, to each other and to the place. They told me they would never forget what had just occurred. There were tears, hugs, and deep breaths of release.

The experience was clearing and cleansing in ways we could and could not articulate. We were all deeply touched. I was profoundly thanked. I felt I had done the exact right thing. I smiled into the mind-bending, head-shaking irony of being the mildly-to-moderately paranoid, quietly smoldering-with-rage Jewish guy who had fantasies of annihilating them all, as I detailed earlier, now bringing Germans to this place, acknowledging them, acknowledging the truth of their experience, and simply Bearing Witness to the place. I had become a conduit for them to reclaim the parts of themselves left un-entitled by the shame of simply being born German. Buchenwald would have been heartbreakingly incomplete had Janice and I not stumbled upon Soviet Special Camp No. 2. The experience with the Star of David would have been incomplete without this discovery and the immersion into the denied story of Buchenwald.

The play on words I landed in is so poignant to me: "I'll **show you**!"—the silent war cry of the defiant young boy who must answer his powerlessness. With my German friends, it became, "I'll show you . . ."—the place and thereby a path to acceptance and dignity restored.

And this is why my time at that spot with Janice and my German friends was the denouement of my journey, up to that point.

———

Maura

Interlude #4

Catapults

I*'ve gotten to learn a thing or two* about bravery, watching Peter on his reconciliation adventures and helping him put his experiences to paper.

I'm a writer, but I've never written a book before. I'm a daughter, but until this experience, I didn't really *know* my father, not like this. There have even been times here and there where I've had flashes of regret at the vow I pledged under the pergola all those summers ago: *We're gonna write you a book, Dad.* Honestly, I don't know who I thought I was, making that wild promise. Damn my reckless tongue.

And, I don't think I would have gotten through what life had in store for me, if under the pergola all those summers ago, I hadn't said, *Yes.*

This process has been a study in what it truly takes to transform, a demonstration in the willingness to let everything once held as fact, fade away. The facts were that my father hated Germans, that my grandfather was an asshole, and that Auschwitz was a stain on humanity's collective soul. But now, the facts are that my father is friends with Germans, that my grandfather visits us as a hummingbird, that Auschwitz can become a place of love.

It was necessary for me to watch my father (by the grace of Tai Chi) loosen his grip on what he thought he knew to be true, to make way for someone and something new. Because, over the course of the years it took for my father to journey through reconciliation and for us to write the book, all of the facts of my life that I had previously gripped so tightly, shattered.

See, we don't hear the creaking and the groaning of the catapult, or the ominous *click* of the ratchet gear loading, preparing for grand release.

Before my life fell apart, I had put myself smartly on the right path, doing the good-girl thing, and pretending to be normal. [Click] I married responsibly, in a fucking white dress, and dreamt, of course, that babies were well on their way. [Click] I dazzled the administration and the students in my classroom at a top-tier high school. [Click] I bought a house, planned a garden, and sat myself with prim ignorance on my catapult's rough seat.

[Click]

In the time it takes to shut a door, that catapult released. The man I thought I would love for all my life left, and I went from imagining the baby furniture to burning in the forging fire of heartbreak.

Stripped of myself and crumbling, I sat dumbly in my parents' front room, where years ago we watched the sparrow cyclone. I called lawyers for the papers and real-estate agents for the garden-less house. I planned the burning of my wedding dress, in between teaching Shakespeare during Covid to students on deadening Zoom screens, as the world seemed to fall apart.

Dumb, blind, and somewhat faithless, I tried to learn to be brave in the face of heartbreak. During those months and years, I was barely keeping my head above water, furiously treading to avoid full dissolution. And a few Sundays a month, squeezed here and there in between our work schedules, my father and I would sit down with his writing, trying to take his journal entries and turn them into a book.

Each time my father would share another piece of his journey with me, in order to cover my tears and my choking throat, I'd shriek something like, "Why didn't you tell me this one first? How have I not heard this one before?"

We often wrote at the kitchen table, over leftover Thai food. Me with a heart already in pieces, and him constantly being re-stripped by his memories and our conversations.

One time, we were writing about his experience being identified with the Yellow Star of David, passed around the room of Germans with love. In the midst of my stricken silence at the power of his story, I looked up to see the emotion welling in his eyes.

"This whole thing, Dad—it really requires heartbreak, doesn't it?" I managed to warble after gulping some tea.

"Yes, yes it—"

"And," I interrupted loudly, "we can't know what we're getting into before we're in it."

In these moments, I danced around the ruining I had recently experienced. My dad was gracious enough not to press me about my own heartbreak. And in retrospect, I don't think I would have known what questions to ask him without that heartbreak.

"Could you have conceived," I continued, "would you have even *considered*, when you made the Star of David during your dark-night-of-the-soul before going to Poland in 2014, that you would reveal it and then allow it to be passed among a circle of Germans?"

"No. Not even a little bit." He shook his head, a sort of awe lighting up his eyes. "No, it would have been inconceivable to me back then."

He's brave, my father. Sometimes dumb, and blind, and faithless. But brave.

Of course, he couldn't have known what was up ahead, what the journey was going to actually require of him, before he made that Star of David. None of us can.

I relate.

Apparently, transformation requires blindness.

Had I known ahead of time the price I'd be paying for my transformation out of my identity as a normie wife-good-daughter-teacher, I don't think I'd have been brave enough to go through with it. And had I been without a model, an example of what it takes to truly transform, I'm not sure I would have survived it.

The blindness made it hard for my father to wrap his mind around his experience, because he couldn't quite explain the *why* of it all. He wrote it in one of his early drafts as he digested his experience at Auschwitz:

I am trying to work out the correct language for my survivor's-guilt problem. How about protected-from-the-fires guilt? Or, has-good-dental-care guilt? Or maybe not-currently-fleeing-atrocity guilt? How did being on Earth go so wrong? And still goes so wrong? And I am enjoying my beautiful backyard. What the fuck?

He's wracked with guilt and left immobile at the vast inequity, at his unearned ease. He continues:

A spiritual teacher once said to me, "You are not forgotten." Me? Not forgotten? All those souls in the camps, also not forgotten? Worse—they were used.

Elie Wiesel, while a captive in Auschwitz, was asked by a comrade, "Where is God?" He pointed to a child hanging on a gallows and said, "There is God."[43] *And I say: Don't stop there Elie, don't stop too soon. The child who died slowly on the gallows: God. The poor wretches witnessing it: God. The child's mother and father: God. The SS man or woman who did the hanging: also God. There, now we have a comprehensive view of God.*

The spiritual teacher is on shaky ground with me. She is smoking way too much weed—and I am not. If I buy her line— "You are not forgotten"—it intensifies my guilt. Why does Peter get to live in his "nice backyard" world? And other people, no less worthy, do not?

It's easy to see why I'm so reluctant to speak in ways that remind him of the spiritual teacher smoking way too much weed. When we speak of this conundrum, his gaze is shuttered, and his hands will wave in an effort to fend off the horror.

"I'm wrecked by this, Maurz," he said to me. "If the birds have meaning, if they're some sign from something greater, if there is something greater, then why, *why* do I have the nice backyard and some other poor soul is running for their life?"

I know about the pain of wondering why. I have touched some of the wracking guilt, the crushing uncertainty, the fathomless

---

43 Elie Wiesel, *Night* (New York: Bantam Books, 1982), 61–62

grief. I have some small comprehension of the bravery it takes to look at the whole mess dead on.

When he asks these questions, I tread gently. After all, I'm just his daughter, and it's not like I'm some great authority on God or purpose or how catapults work. But finally, I couldn't stop the words from tripping off my tongue:

"Because, Dad, there's a bigger reason you can't see."

I have to point to it as lightly as possible, like greeting a deer in the woods.

"You have a nice-backyard life, yes. And also, you went to Auschwitz and named your monkeys. You offered the Jewish Star that cracked open everyone's hearts. You brought the Germans to name and grieve their dead. You went to a Women's Barracks Wedding, for fuck's sake. You have no possible idea what greater purpose that served, what knots that unwound, whose lives are different now because of those moves you made."

I pause and hide my eyes. I'm going in for the kill now, moved by some Sense-Making Force that even I don't fully understand.

"It's just like 'Parallel Tracks,' Dad. In the moment, you can't see it; you don't have a far-enough-away perspective to know the *why*. Why couldn't you and that German man have penetrated the wall between you, only microns thick? It's because, in the heartbreak of that moment, in the experience of the missing, you awaken the desire to become a friend to the Germans. You miss reconciliation on Track 17 to awaken the part of you that is ready to be passed around German to German, as a Yellow Star of David. Don't you see? It's all woven together, each experience getting you ready for the next. And we have to be blind to the *why* in order for it to line up as it's supposed to. We just aren't allowed to know."

He looked up at me with a stark openness. I can feel my words bouncing between us. On the one hand, these words are for him, and his survivor's guilt, his spiritual questioning, are for his faithless and wounded-child self. On the other hand, these words are for me, and my enraged sense of betrayal, my crisis of faith, my bone-aching uncertainty at whether my life would ever feel like mine again.

It's clear, in moments like these, just how much I am writing this book with him to ease the intensity of his transformation, and how much he is writing this book with me to ease the intensity of mine.

He often has a foot in both worlds, unable to deny either. It's true—his good fortune is undeserved and unfair, and his actions were real, some of the experiences mystical and wondrous. He was Arjuna being told by Krishna it was not for him to understand, only to do his duty (to live his life as he was).

"And I think, Dad, I think the guilt only covers up the truth of the bigger purpose. You're just someone who happens to be luckier than Hitler. You're someone who can even *say,* 'I'm just luckier than Hitler,' which is remarkable in its own right. Luckier or not, the world needs you to just be you. Not guilty. Mindful, in your nice backyard—which you god-damn well better enjoy!"

For once, I had him. I very rarely could land any of my God/Universe/Everything Has a Purpose arguments, but this time, he smiled at me full and deep.

Then he wiped the tears from his face and cleared his throat. I swallowed hard against the thickness in my throat.

And then, we turned back to our laptops—back to making good on the promise we made to—come hell or high water—write the book.

———

Peter

Not Psychotherapy

Not Psychotherapy:
Reflexes

first met Reiner at The Days of Peace Retreat at the former Buchenwald Concentration Camp in 2018. He was one of the four leaders. We shared the impact of the Star of David being passed around the Council circle and the intensity of being at Buchenwald. Reiner was not able to go with me to Soviet Special Camp No. 2, where a number of us created a ceremony at a mass grave of Germans. He explained that, in the moment of decision, he found it overwhelming and then regretted not pushing through that to go with me. He made it clear that the baggage that overwhelmed him had to do with his father. I shared that I, too, carried baggage from my relationship with my father. I said we would go there when we are back here again for the next retreat. And that launched our ongoing communication with each other and our friendship.

Due to two years of Covid postponements, Ginni and Frank, two experienced retreat leaders in the Zen Peacemakers tradition whom I had met in 2014, had been holding Zoom Council meetings for the registrants of *their* Auschwitz Retreat. They did this to hold the "retreat space" of reflection, investigation, and sharing until everyone could be together on the ground at Auschwitz. In June of 2022, at Ginni's invitation, I attended one of their Zoom Council meetings. They invited a guest speaker to report on the status of the refugees pouring into Poland from Ukraine due to the Russian invasion of that country earlier in 2022. The speaker said, "We need therapists here." I sighed to myself.

My internal reaction was an immediate private protest lasting eight nanoseconds. While the meeting was going on without me, my thoughts were: *God damn it. I hate Ukrainians* (referencing the country's long history of vivid antisemitism). My internal dialogue continued: *But, since I am going to be in the region already* (attending the next Buchenwald Retreat in Germany in a few months), *I cannot ignore this plea.* Rejoining the meeting, I was launched again. My plans were revealed to be irrelevant—this time I (gracefully) let myself be taken by the thought: *So, go to Poland, and help the Ukrainians—this is where the good stuff is.*

I realize that, in moments like this, my reflexive reaction is to feel hate. You have heard this from me before—a reflexive hate for Poles, Germans, Austrians, Ukrainians, Lithuanians, Russians, and on and on and on . . . until we've covered the large list of persecutors and perpetrators who have figured out that thievery of Jews is not problematic—nor is their removal and murder.

Although the reflex within me is to start from hate and fear, *I hate Ukrainians* did not stop me from arriving at compassion for people in trouble. I immediately knew what *right action* was for me and pitched to Reiner that we alter our plans (we had planned to do some touring together after the Retreat) and instead go to Krakow so that I could (*God help us all*) offer my services as a therapist to the Ukrainian refugees and he could volunteer his time and expertise as well. He was unhesitant in his enthusiastic agreement.

Paszkowka (Pash-koov-ka) and the Jewish Community Center of Krakow

Meeting in Krakow, Reiner and I rented a vehicle, which allowed us to split our time between volunteering at the Jewish Community Center (JCC) in Krakow and being with sixty or so refugees who were living as a supervised and supported community at Paszkowka Palace—a large hotel with open grounds approximately a forty-minute drive west of Krakow. But the first place we visited was the old Jewish cemetery in Krakow. As we began walking, the first headstone I noticed—and I swear this is true—said STERNBERG. I was a bit taken aback. As we walked around, we noticed how unkempt the cemetery was and started gathering trash. Then we drove off to Paszkowka.

The Palace was rented for the refugees by the JCC, which also provided them with food and supplies. Most of the sixty people there were women and children. The community did their own cooking, cleaning, and maintenance work. Teachers, a translator, and the services of a Ukrainian psychologist were provided. Everyone living there had fled from the Russian shelling of Eastern Ukraine. Many knew a credible amount of English and were trying to acquire more. The children ranged in age from one through adolescence. People lived there for an indeterminate amount of time. They were all trying to sort out their next moves, as were the governments and refugee-support organizations. Because of this, the population of The Palace changed over time.

Reiner and I were immediately taken with the refugees' situation—living in an ongoing state of *Not Knowing*. They didn't know how the war was going to turn out, they didn't know how the men they left behind were going to be on any given day, they didn't know if they would ever be able to return home or even if their homes still existed, and they didn't know how much longer they could remain at Paszkowka, as the lease kept getting renegotiated for six months at a time.

Jola, the guest speaker in the Zoom Council meeting, volunteered her services to supervise the Palace. Meeting her at the JCC, we received our orientation. She encouraged us to go to Paszkowka to "interact" but *not* do psychotherapy or crisis intervention. She explained the change from her original request for therapists by saying that, very recently, volunteer therapists had done psychological harm to the refugees. They had encouraged them to open up about their traumatic experiences in a way that the therapists were not able to follow up, leaving the refugees hanging with (and reacting badly to) that very heavy material.

"Completely understood," I said and shuddered at well-intentioned harm done.

So, armed with our wits and the four Frisbees I brought, Reiner and I showed up in the waning days of summer vacation 2022 and were introduced to the kids and adults of Paszkowka.

In the beautiful and massive yard, the Frisbees started to fly. The children were the first to engage, under their mothers' watchful gaze. When we first played Frisbee with the children, the mothers sat on the sidelines, watching their children be happy and enjoy themselves. They said afterwards that it made them happy to see their children laughing. We felt very gratified to be part of a light and beautiful moment in their lives.

It was instructive to us to watch what happened when a plane flew overhead. As soon as the plane could be heard in the distance, the children all froze and looked up. They stood like that until they could determine that it was a civilian plane, and then play resumed.

After a bit, the mothers came out and began to participate. The very few men on the premises at times observed our interactions but, outside of greeting us, did not interact. Frisbee-playing turned into some soccer-playing, and, after a few hours, with the help of our twenty-three-year-old translator, we were able to introduce Qigong and Tai Chi to the group.

Reiner and I described the background and intention of the art of Qigong to some of the women who were interested. They asked me how old I was. Seventy-two, I replied. This was received with incredulous looks. They said I ought to state my age at the beginning of my introduction of the practice as a personal testimonial to its usefulness! They asked, "Where does one put their mind in the practice: clear mind or on the body?" I explained it can be either. I talked about the advantage of focusing on the hands. I mentioned I can feel energy there during these practices. I extended my arms and hands at a forty-five-degree angle out and up in front of me and said that, for me, it is as though my hands are resting on a shelf. I said others can sometimes feel the energy as well. They said, "Show us." So, I stood up and did a dozen repetitions of two moves. I sat down and asked what they experienced. "Well," one said, "the headache I had before you began went away." Another said, "I felt energy in my legs running down to the ground." Another said, "The heaviness and pressure in my shoulders lifted." The last one felt nothing.

Then, seemingly out of nowhere, someone asked, "How do you deal with blaming yourself?" I was taken aback; I said, "Oh, this is a big topic," and paused in thought. Reiner came in and talked about the lifting of blame that we both experienced through the Zen Peacemakers Retreats we'd been on, which led us to Bernie Glassman's profound teachings about *Not Knowing, Bearing Witness,* and *Right, Loving Action* arising spontaneously. And this was the way, without doing psychotherapy, that we were able to offer a useful response to this spontaneous sharing and heavy question.

At one point, a one-year-old boy who was walking around on the patio holding onto his mother's fingers looked right at me as I was about to pass him on the steps leading into the building. Of course, I stopped and looked at him. He directed his babbling at me. I returned the conversation and squatted down. He picked up a piece of chalk and made some random marks. He reached for me, and I extended my hand so he could touch it. More conversation, and then he took my finger and let go of his mother's. I looked at her, and she appeared to be fine with this development, so I rolled with it. He directed us up the stairs. Then he directed us across the patio, out into the grass, and over to a ball, which he attempted to kick. He moved the ball, and I joined in moving the ball with my foot. Next, he spied a bucket which he promptly put on his head. When it fell off, I picked it up and put it on my head, which he found to be a show-worthy move, laughing his tiny butt off.

Day after day, Reiner and I were overfed at lunch as our hosts were determined to take care of us with their food. We were not allowed to go through the buffet line. Instead, platters of food were brought to our table. We knew implicitly how important their offering of food was to them, how normalizing it felt to them. We could see the pride they took in their offerings and in our enjoyment.

We took a group through more of the twenty-four-step Tai Chi I had introduced. We were watched by a group of men sitting at a table on the patio. One of them got up and recorded the lesson on his phone, which we took as a sign of acceptance by them. The men remained the hardest to connect with.

Jola asked if Reiner and I would do volunteer work distributing food at the JCC—the community center that, at the outbreak of Putin's invasion of Ukraine, transformed itself into a relief organization. It is a testament to their director and to the funding that has flowed in from Jewish charities in the United States that the place is able to obtain and distribute six to eight thousand dollars' worth of food each week. The building has been transformed into a child-care center, a warehouse, a distribution center of food, toiletries, clothes, a community kitchen, and administrative offices for volunteers and numerous paid Ukrainian and Polish staff. I pondered the assembly of this operation: the ordering, obtaining all the equipment, obtaining the supplies, organizing the office staff, the creation of a Human Resources Department, the accounting, the fundraising, the public relations, and keeping track of the many people "knocking on the door . . ." Wow.

Reiner and I were quickly absorbed into the volunteer group, breaking down bulk sacks of beans, rice, coffee, tea, sugar, cereal, macaroni, lentils, sunflower seeds, and peas into four-hundred-gram plastic baggies. The baggies were placed in a bin, and once the bin was full, it was carried down a short hallway into a room that served as a market where the refugees shopped. There were restrictions on the frequency of their shopping (every other day) and on the amount they could take. The line formed on the street and ran through a courtyard to the entrance of the building, where each person's papers were checked.

Women. Women holding their children's hands. Women with babies in strollers. This is the line that, for five hours, six days a week, snaked through the courtyard, the entryway, and, finally, the front-room-turned-market. The market room was crowded. The staff was kind and helpful. None of the women smiled as I passed them.

As Reiner and I did this repetitive work, my mind traveled . . . to my father's parents' grocery store and how, during the Depression, my grandmother, the immigrant from Poland/Ukraine, would not turn away people who could not pay for their groceries, extending credit she could ill afford . . . and to Bernie Glassman, speaking of the Zen practice of hearing/feeling and feeding the "hungry ghosts," and to stories from World War II of strangers throwing an apple or some bread to a prisoner tramping back to camp after a work detail.

In this work I am doing today, I appreciate my grandmother in a way I hadn't before, and Bernie, always pointing at the universal, and me wondering if there was some way my work could pay a karmic debt. From time to time, I glanced down the short hallway separating our work area from the shopping area to observe the line advancing slowly. I found myself smiling frequently, thinking of how good it felt helping feed hungry, desperate people. Those people don't know me and never will. I am fine with that. Their gratitude would be a distraction.

———

Not Psychotherapy: Manhood Acknowledged

Reiner and I were about to spend a day touring, but both of us felt our time with the children slipping away, and we wanted to be with them. So instead of touring, we went to Paszkowka. When we arrived, things started out slowly. There weren't many people around the dining room and patio. Reiner and I went into the yard to show each other Tai Chi forms from our respective practices. Some kids came out and wanted to play Frisbee. We found one Frisbee, but where were the other three? Seems they could not be located.

The group of kids playing with us grew to five. I noticed a large hole in the yard, likely the work of moles. There would be a severe injury if a running person's foot found the hole. I left the game and went over to where a couple of the men were trimming bushes. I asked for a shovel and pantomimed that. "No shovel," I was told. I found that unlikely, as there were raised mounds of loose dirt where someone had filled other mole holes. Undeterred, I found an empty flowerpot to scoop some of the excess mounded dirt off the top of the filled hills and used that to fill in the hole I had discovered. The men watched me. I returned the pot, and one of them said, "Thank you." I indicated the injury to the leg that would have surely taken place, and he nodded *Yes*. As I returned to the game, I noticed that one of the men had produced two more Frisbees. Noted.

Later, when Reiner and I talked about this experience, we shared how we both wished we could have gotten more connected with the men, but they seemed unapproachable. We wondered how they felt being safely ensconced in Poland while their comrades were engaged in brutal warfare back home. Did our eyes, our presence, somehow shame them?

Manhood. So complicated. I did not know how to help them or us with them. Our help, even our presence seemed like it could be an affront to them. There was no clear pathway for us to speak to them about their experiences as refugees, their histories, or their hopes for the future, at least none that we found. I checked in with Reiner on this perception, and he was thinking about it similarly. And so, Reiner and I settled for signals that indicated acceptance by them: a warmer greeting, their thanks, and their small contributions (finding the other Frisbees and recording the Tai Chi).

Many months later, while I was having a conversation with Reiner, it occurred to me that all the men smoked. Reiner and I would often see them after their work around the grounds, sitting at a table on the patio and smoking. It is only then that I realized the way to approach them: show up with a carton of cigarettes and a box of cigars. I can picture taking a cigar out, asking for a light, motioning to a chair—"Can I sit?" and imagining their invitation to do so. There it is. No conversation, no playing a game. An old-fashioned smoke. I'll know for next time.

There were now three Frisbees flying around a circle of four adults and five kids. Mercifully, some kids had become tired, and

I gladly accepted the request to stop. As we gathered on the patio, one of the mothers who had been in the Frisbee circle began to show Reiner photos of her daughter's artwork. When her daughter saw that, she and her friend ran off, returning moments later with works of theirs, which were given to Reiner and me as gifts. Then the girls took us by the hand to the art room, where we were shown in detail the rest of their productions. They printed their names and ours on the backs of the gifts. I noticed handprints on the mural hanging in the art room. It occurred to me to ask if we might be able to have our handprints added. They jumped at that idea, and the paint came out. The girls each took one of our hands and painted half our palm yellow and half blue. They walked us to the mural, pressed our hands onto the mural, and then printed our names above. I watched the mother observing and taking pictures. In the preceding days, I had not seen her smile. Now she was beaming. After the cleanup, we were again taken by the hand into the dining room, with one of the girls placing herself in-between me and Reiner. Her hands in ours, she declared, "Mine." Lunch rescued us from her taking full possession.

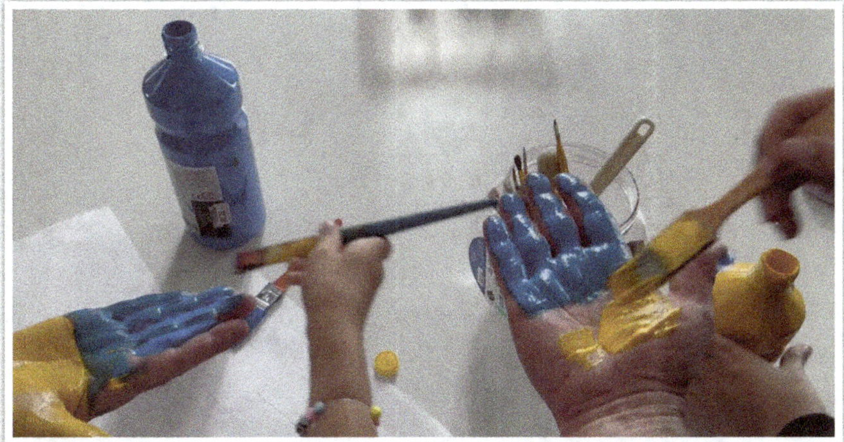

Photo credit: Ira Polikarpova

Perhaps these small interactions deepened the complexity of us, two male strangers, coming into the group's space—the men could easily have taken us to be interlopers. If this was an unspoken injury to the men, it was well concealed by their warm greetings to us. But inadvertent harm is easier to produce than one thinks . . .

After our compulsory overfeeding at lunch, Reiner and I said our goodbyes for the day and walked to our car, full of food and full from our interactions with the current citizens at The Palace. With our handprints on the mural and the children's gifts in our car, we smiled at each other to share how touched we both were.

Not Psychotherapy:
Leaving Them

Volunteering with the Ukrainian refugees in Poland provided an opportunity for Reiner and me to do some touring. Although we both had previously been on a Zen Peacemakers retreat at Auschwitz, neither of us had seen the old *Judenrampe*—the original site of disembarkation for the trains-of-horror before the rail line was extended into Birkenau. The *Judenrampe* is close to Birkenau but easily missed unless you know to look for it. The plaques telling the story of the place included photos of the first prisoners disembarking and being sorted. Seeing this was invaluable to me. I could see so much on the faces of the predator and the prey as they briefly interacted. The utter bewilderment on the face of a Jewish man reveals his total incomprehension of his or his family's situation. On the face of the nearby SS man, there was a look of acquiescence. That is different from the look on the faces of the SS in photos taken after transports had become routine—those were faces of people who had become brutal or who were "gone."

Reiner and I did Tai Chi to ritualize our presence for every being that had been present at the Ramp. I realized these were the correct words all along: Tai Chi was my ceremony of reckoning and remembrance, our effort to realize, to take in what happened on this ground: madness, fear, and loss. And it was an effort to extend humanity to the poor souls dressed in German uniforms. I write words that amaze me—they are surreal to my mind and my ear. They convey—shall I call it *empathy?*—to people engaged in an obscenity. It feels natural and bizarre at the same time. I can't explain myself beyond that.

We left memorial stones in one of the two red boxcars sitting on the siding after Reiner lit incense and said a prayer for those who had once been in and those who had been outside of the boxcars.

Together, we read the credo of *The Days of Peace* from the Buchenwald Retreat.

"Our Vision:

We feel the need to turn to our personal and collective wounds. We see this turning as loving action on the way to inner and outer peace.

We feel called to acknowledge the wounds of our time, to learn from them and to heal them where possible. This strengthens our determination not to cause new wounds.

We recognize our fears, defense strategies, and indifference and let arise from this the strength for acting courageously.

We commit ourselves to embodying the insight that the recognition of differences and diversity makes interconnectedness possible.

We want to understand what causes war and what causes peace, so that we can act peacefully.

*We see ourselves as part of a learning community and are
ready to contribute to peaceful vividness.*
*If this vision inspires you, you are welcome to share the Peace
Days in Buchenwald with us."*[44]

We moved just down the road to Birkenau, where we pulled
out the photocopies I had made of David Olère artwork from his
book; *David Olère, The One Who Survived Crematorium III.*[45] Olère
was an artist who, as a prisoner, was presented with the choiceless-
choice of functioning as a *Sondercommando*—one who attended to
the herding, undressing, murder, and disposal of victims at the
gas chambers/crematorium. His drawings and paintings, done
after liberation, captured scenes and images he had personally
witnessed and participated in. His art powerfully brings to life
the destroyed crematoria of Birkenau, providing the visitor with
a way to visualize what the ruins of today once were. I believe
his book is necessary for encountering the Holocaust and is a
necessary accompaniment for visiting any camp. It provides what
one's imagination cannot.

Reiner, in German, and I, in English, read out loud his friend
Susanne's reflection piece written by her after she visited the
Neuengamme Slave Labor Camp near her home in Hamburg in
2010. She had asked that I read it in English when Reiner and
I were performing a ceremony at the ruins of a crematorium
at Birkenau.

---

44 *Credo of The Days of Peace* for the 2022 Buchenwald Retreat, Kathleen Battke, Reiner
Hühner, Dorle Lommatzsch, and Judith Beermann Zeligson (2022), used with permission.
45 Olère, David, *Crematorium III* (Oświęcim, Auschwitz-Birkenau State Museum in
Oświęcim, 2018), 23–175

"MALEDICT PLACE
(At the former Slave Labor Camp Neuengamme, near Hamburg)

There are no words in this place.
All I can do is keep quiet and walk the
soil of pain and sorrow like
walking on hot stones.
The very soil their mistreated feet have
marched upon and stumbled.
The very soil that is deeply soaked with blood, sweat, and tears.
To walk this soil is the only thing we
can ever have in common.
Its breath rises through my burning soles, up the legs into my
smoldering bowels and further into my
heart that contracts with pain.
Up into the throat creeps the pain and
chokes me, the sweating palms of
my hands dangle on helpless arms.
My soul is screaming, and my brain is
struggling with what my eyes see.
Want to let the old grief flow through me like a stream,
want to surrender to their sorrow and
be one of them in the end.
Want to weep the tears that mother and
father did not dare to weep.
They sealed their hearts and turned into stone.
Silently they passed on their stony load
to me and silently I took it.
Today I am not silent any longer."
23.08.2010—26.08.2022/Susanne Behrendsen[46]

---

46 Behrendsen, Susanne, *Maledict Place*, an unpublished poem (2010), used with permission

I felt very touched and honored to have been asked to be the voice for her reverent heart and soul.

Having concluded our business at Auschwitz-Birkenau, we made the long and now familiar walk out of Birkenau. Two things struck me: that Auschwitz-Birkenau felt familiar to me. That is a mind-boggling sentence to write. I had accumulated enough time there over the course of the five-day retreat in 2014, and now this visit, that the place was familiar. I pretty much knew where things were and how to get to different locations within the vast camp. And then there was the experience of *walking out* of Auschwitz-Birkenau. Walking *in* was a staggering moment when I first did it in 2014. Walking in this time did not have any of that impact. But walking *out* . . . walking out remains powerful—that I can and that I am "leaving them" when I do. And it occurred to me, I don't ever quite leave them—which is good. It feels like bringing dignity to them.

———

A conversation Reiner and I had with Jolanta over dinner that evening turned to sites she recommended we visit. We told her we had just gone back to the *Judenrampe*. This launched a conversation about Auschwitz as a museum. She said something I had not heard anyone articulate before: she believes the museum does not accomplish what it purports to—most visitors cannot grasp what they are being shown. I agreed, because most visitors have almost no means of visualizing or processing what Auschwitz is there to show: an industrialized version of our common capacity for null humanity—our common, mundane capacity for madness. Anyone attempting to grasp the place and the history must have support and aids for visualization, for encountering, and processing that which staggers the mind and imagination. Jolanta also pointed out that, for some visitors, going there is an act of bravado and voyeurism such as we would see when we gaze at a horrific multi-car crash with bodies lying around. She believes that place ought not be propped up but left to nature and the hundreds of years it will take for the earth to un-defile itself.

Reiner and I countered by talking about the life-altering experience we each had spending five days there with people who were frightened to encounter a place that held such horror. We felt the place-as-museum had value because of the unique transformative possibilities it held. We illuminated that point with the fact that, but for the Auschwitz Retreat, we would not know each other and would be the poorer to have missed out on our healing relationship. However, in less than twenty-four hours, I would be deep, deep into Jola's point.

Reiner said he was ready to encounter Plaszow (Pla-shou)—the camp portrayed in the movie *Schindler's List* with its monstrous Commandant, Amon Göth. After correcting numerous missed turns, we parked the car along an expanse of fields, brush, trees, and some ruins, with barely an indication that we had arrived at a site of atrocity—tucked away as it was in close proximity to apartment buildings and the bustling "regular life" of a suburb of Krakow.

Eighteen billboard-style markers explained what occurred at various locations around the acreage. We were jolted to be in Jola's vision of how the places where evil prevailed ought to be handled—nature *was* absorbing what had been Plaszow and before that, what ironically had been a Jewish burial ground. At first, I was deeply troubled, as this felt like a sacrilege to what had occurred there. But after I deposited a remembrance stone on the wreckage of a synagogue that had once been used for burial rites before the *Shoah*, I had an unsettling sense that maybe Jola was correct. What had felt so wrong began to form in my mind as the only way to allow this place (devoid of any buildings from the era of the camp) to be. At first appalled to see joggers on paths, mothers pushing strollers and kids romping around in the brush and forest, I thought, *Maybe normal life could be the antidote to the abomination of the earlier time.*

Reiner and I walked the acreage. We read the billboards and took in the towering, powerful memorial sculpture. Several times, Reiner spoke with tears of powerful shame that his people had done evil here. We were very somber.

I had been receiving and acknowledging his feelings, and then, at one moment, I said, "Reiner, this time it was your people. In the United States, it was/is my people. It seems to me that evil is like a volcano. It erupts from time to time. The lava obliterates what is in its path. The volcano does its work: it creates a new place. Doesn't evil do its work, also? It, too, creates new places. Could it be that we are here witnessing the awful, destructive horror that is creation?"

My question hung in the air—it hangs there still. We agreed that nature and regular life seemed the appropriate way for this place to slowly shed the screams of its victims and the maniacal, sadistic laughter of its deranged master of ceremonies—Göth. It is a very powerful image for me to imagine both of those sounds: the screams and the maniacal laughter, slowly, very, very slowly, fading, continuing to fade, long after my lifetime.

At the end of our exploration, we walked into the entrance of a cave that was a tunnel leading to the quarry. There, we put our packs down and did Qigong into the madness and the mundaneness of Plaszow. The Qigong at Plaszow felt especially connected to the earth because we kept encountering openings into the ground, the actual wounds into the earth itself. An energetic experience emerged: the feeling of Qi moving out of the earth, through us, into the atmosphere, and then, from the atmosphere, through us, back into the earth. I felt like a conduit. Ultimately, viewing Plaszow as a nature preserve felt like letting go of history in a way that did not strike me as a travesty.

Finished with that effort, we lumbered back to the car and made more wrong turns trying to get back to Krakow in 2022.

I had on my agenda a visit to the town of Tarnow and the Buczyna (Boo-chen-awe) Forest, the site of a number of mass graves that unfortunate Poles and Jews had been shot into. One contained eight hundred Jewish children ages infancy to eight years old who, prior to being released from this life, had been kept in a locked house alone without water or food for two days and then thrown alive into the grave where they were disposed of with hand grenades. And I wondered, through the haze I entered, how to write about this day.

Our guide told us there were reports in the immediate aftermath of those murders; locals complained to the Germans about the stench emanating from the ground. The Germans provided lime to prevent such untoward results in the future. And there were reports of sounds emerging from the ground and the dirt shifting—as those entombed below worked their way into becoming deceased.

The forest itself is beautiful. Time and again, I encounter this irony: sites of abomination today are beautifully forested and lush. Indeed, there are trees growing out of a couple of the mass graves. Perhaps, like my encounter at Plaszow, the incorporation of abomination into the natural world—the overtaking of abomination by the natural world—is fitting and necessary. How else would this energy and its victims' remains become transformed? This implies something very interesting to me: where and how does the residual energy of the *perpetrators* become transformed? In the very same place? The clearing and resolution of destructive or evil energy is not simply to benefit the victim. The clearing and resolution of destructive energy affects the lingering radiation of the perpetrator energy into the world. It comes through as thoughts, feelings, actions, inactions, and the vibrations of guilt and shame. Reiner and I encountered this point later.

I was no longer content to run for cover by hating Germans, and, here, Reiner's loving and grieving presence was so helpful to me. I felt drained by the enormity of the mass graves and became quiet within the haze that still enveloped me. My daughters had given me a memorial stone to place on the children's grave. I contemplated the pictures of the children placed there, along with various other shrine-like memorials on the grave. I placed the memorial stone among the other stones that had been left. It was a comfort to me to think of a link between my children and these children captured by the presence of that stone. But the comfort was small in the face of the almost ineffable sense of loss, horror, and dark wonder of it all.

Objects sitting on the Children's Mass Grave.
Photo credit: Peter Sternberg

Reiner performed a Zen ceremony with incense. We looked at each other and then wordlessly, with great heaviness, began walking out of the forest.

We had not gone far when it occurred to me that I needed to stay a bit longer. I asked Reiner to wait for me at the car. Alone for a few minutes, it finally dawned on me I had forgotten to do the practice I had intended. I was standing on a small hill next to the children's mass grave. In this stark scene, I was a visitor to an epitome of null-humanity for a few minutes more. I wished those children could sense, could feel my presence as their witness. I wanted them to know I was willing to feel the gaping hole in what we call "humanity" that had swallowed them.

I was pushing beyond emotional exhaustion. I was hearing Pink Floyd's *The Great Gig in the Sky* in my head; Clare Torry's otherworldly riff and the chord progressions in that song seemed made for the moment—it opened my tears as I began Qigong. My hands to my chest, slowly exhaling, I extended my arms out at a 45-degree angle to the side from the midline of my body, fingers upward. Then, with fingers flattened, I retracted my hands back to my chest as I inhaled. My body again seemed to be operating like a pump. My knees straightened as my hands came in, pulling energy up and in. With that energy concentrated in my torso, I released it through my hands as my arms extended and my knees bent. Over and over. Mindfully, mindlessly—it did not matter . . . moving with that music, feeling the gaping hole of null-humanity existing within our humanity, remaining in the rightness of Bearing Witness—until my body and brain felt fried.

Having wrung out what I could, I stopped. Not numb, but in a place of acceptance beyond tears, I slowly turned to leave.

That is exactly how it felt—I turned and left them. I had to leave them. Yes, the sense of having them with me always was still in place, but at that moment, it was the terrible feeling of having to leave them behind. This was the saddest moment, as I said out loud, "Oh, children, I must go . . ."—slowly stumbling away, leaving them.

Not Psychotherapy:
The World Sucks, and We Played Frisbee

And now for a fresh approach to peacemaking—captured in this exchange between Reiner, the German (navigating) and Peter, the Jew (driving):

The Jew: (expressing consternation about two upcoming possible right-hand turns that were rapidly approaching) There?!

The German: (expressing firm clarity about the correct course of action) *No!* Not there!

The Jew: (Expressing doubt) So, you're saying, not there.

The German: (Expressing exasperation) That is correct, not there! We turned down that road twice before, it is not the correct road.

The Jew: (Having trust issues) You are certain?

The German: (Not having trust issues about his navigation skills) Yes, I am certain!

The Jew: (Expressing reluctance as the first road is being passed) OK, not there.

The German: (Wondering why this was so difficult) Good! Not there.

The Jew: (Swerving into mistrust again) You're sure?

The German: (Not bothering to camouflage frank irritation) *Yes!*

The Jew: (After a pause, expressing acquiescence if not trust) . . . I want you to know . . . I will never turn down that road again.

The German: (Expressing encouragement and doubt simultaneously) Good!

The Jew: (Feigning certainty) Ever!

The German: (Trying to make the best of it) Good! Me, either.

The Jew: (Expressing an effort at goodwill) For me, that road does not exist.

The German: (Demonstrating undeserved goodwill) I join you in this. The road is gone.

The Jew and the German collapse into the laughter of the ridiculous, hands moving up to block out the wrong road.

We laughed harder, calling our exchange *peacemaking.*

It turns out that Reiner and I had been pondering the same question: "Why do we do these encounters?" As I prepared to write my notes for the day, I came up with this: "Because it is very difficult." Sounds egoic, at first. But, to simply call *confronting the difficult* an "ego trip" would miss this: in the difficult, in the extremely difficult, there is a naked confrontation with reality.

I found it vital, especially in the heaviest parts of this journey, to notice the fullness of these facts: the world sucks, and the little boy at Paszkowka wanted me to toss him in the air so he could fly, and the kids wanted to play Frisbee, and some of the adults wanted to learn Qigong and Tai Chi. And, it felt good to help feed people who needed that help right there and then.

Ugly, ugly—I mean *fucking ugly*—feelings were triggered in me as Reiner and I stood on ground desecrated by perversion in the extreme. But then the ugly was validated, received, and defused with and through another . . . through Reiner, and for him, through me.

In subjecting ourselves to encountering what is ugly outside and within, to look deeply at it, to see how our worst selves pop into existence anywhere and everywhere, we then look deeper still so we can break, or release, or diminish the spell that had created the worst. The simplicity of giving and receiving that compassion, in the midst of obscene perversion—how could I possibly stay away from the richness of that?

———

Not Psychotherapy:
Who Sent the Purple Bicycle?

We spent a day at the JCC, breaking down sacks of wholesale foodstuffs into baggies again. This time we were situated on the third floor of the building, using the glass elevator to move the packages of food to the first floor. I took this elevator ride a few times as I brought bins full of baggies to the "market," where the women who had been waiting in line "shopped." Their faces were grim, and the children with them looked blank. On one trip, as quickly as I put bags of sunflower seeds on the shelf, the women were taking them off. I knew there were two more hours of women in line waiting to come in, and this was the last of the sunflower seeds. It was for me a hard, up-close, and personal encounter with others' reality.

On my way back up to the third floor, I looked out of the glass elevator and saw the people having their passports and other papers checked before entry. As the elevator slowly rose, I watched them receding as though I were taking off from their reality. It was a short yet powerful elevator ride—an unintentional choreography that struck me as cinematic in its visual power.

Here is another version of taking off from their reality: I went out to lunch and needed to make it quick because I had to leave in two hours, and another load of goods had just come in. In the square of the Old Jewish Quarter just two blocks away, I walked around, looking for street food, and found a Turkish falafel vendor. The smallest sandwich was so large that I could not finish it. The last quarter of it ended up in the garbage. As I weaved my way through the line of women waiting to get into the building, I thought of being able to easily afford that sandwich—and not being able to finish or save it.

How to have gratitude for my circumstances and not have guilt? I do believe survivor guilt invaded my childhood (and not only at mealtime)—as though my family were in a position of want, as though we didn't know where our next meal was coming from, as though finishing every morsel on my plate had survival value for anyone or made some hungry person's lot better. Somehow, to honor my ancestors' impoverishment, fear, and want, along with my parents' living through the Depression, it was incumbent on me not to intensify some starving child's experience somewhere in the world by not finishing food on my plate in our Chicago home.

The conditioning worked. I operate way beyond a gratitude for the availability of food and, as my wife will attest, have a very hard time letting go of food that, how can I put this . . . ought to be released. "It's okay; this discarded food is not leaving someone else hungry. You don't want it; let it go"—her voice, and even a sane voice within me, will gently say this. I watched my children be easy with food and know this is healthy. I marvel at their sanity and try to emulate them. There is something about want, guilt, and fear in association with good fortune that has very deep roots. Is it really about food at all? "Survivor guilt" can be spoken of as an *embarrassment of riches*. Oh, yes—embarrassed by good fortune. This is a very familiar stone I carry.

This eating business is complicated for me. Recall my early memories as an infant of *needing to eat until my mother was full*. You won't be surprised to learn that, as a growing boy, I had a reputation in the family as a good eater. That behavior brought the women in my family much openly expressed joy. . . .

I was glad I could afford the sandwich. I was glad I could stop eating the sandwich. I was glad I did not feel guilty walking among the unfortunate people. I was conscious of my good fortune, which did not require atonement. And I realized that, at that moment, *at that moment only*, I simply was not one of them. I knew, from a deep place, that at some as-yet-unidentified moment in the future, my not being one of them could turn out to be no longer true.

My shift over, I walked back to my hotel. I was exhausted at every level, so I pulled out my phone and opened one of my playlists on Spotify. Quite randomly, "Start Wearing Purple," by Gogol Bordello and the Gypsy Punks, was queued up to play. It is the end song of my favorite movie: *Everything Is Illuminated*. (I urge you to listen to the song as you read on.) As I walked down the sidewalk, from my shirt pocket, the chorus, in Russian-accented English, began (yes, the chorus is "start wearing purple"), and I swear this is true; I looked up, and, in the distance, I saw what appeared to be a red-haired woman riding a bicycle toward me. But then, as she got closer, I could see she was wearing a loudly decorated *purple* over-blouse, *purple* shirt, and *purple* pants, riding . . . **a purple bicycle**. She was moving steadily toward me as I stood still on the sidewalk. ". . . start wearing purple for me now . . ." coming out of my shirt pocket.[47] My mouth fell open. I had never encountered purple moving toward me on two wheels before—let alone to music. As I stood there, I adjusted my mouth, pressed my lips tight to keep from bursting out laughing. She rode past me—with the song still going, I turned and watched her ride away from me down the sidewalk. Yet again, I was in the surreal world and found it so funny that I thought, *Shouldn't the director yell 'Cut' right about now?*

The next day I told Reiner that I was going to make another stop at the Jewish cemetery to do more cleanup before we took off for the Palace. He asked to join. We filled two huge bags with debris. We were sweating mightily hauling those bags the length of the cemetery to a trash bin. Walking back to the hotel to get the car for the drive to Paszkowka, I recounted to Reiner the story of encountering the woman on the purple bike and, well, you know I had to do it . . . out came my phone.

Our laughter flowed easily, and I wondered what the hell was happening; a German fellow was feeling like one of my closest friends, and we were laughing about the spectacle of *two-wheeled purple* moving down a Krakow street—to music! It felt like a nod to the sense that our time together had a life of its own.

We went to the Palace for Reiner's last day. Since he was leaving and I was staying in Krakow for a few days more, on the drive out, Reiner took great pains to reaffirm for me the-road-that-does-not-exist-and-therefore-cannot-be-turned-upon. I assured him his implored rhetoric was not wasted on me—although yes, I admitted, there was some chance I would be ringing him up from Gdansk (the other end of the country) and requesting his help.

---

47 Hütz, Eugene, "Start Wearing Purple." *Voi-La Intruder*, Gogol Bordello, 1999

We had done a good job of letting the folks at the Palace know when we were leaving. One of the adults gave Reiner some art she had made of the Buddha, and he gave her a T-shirt with the image of Thích Nhất Hạnh on it. She was delighted. She said she was going to miss him and asked if he might return in the future. Indeed, he said, he might. After warm hugs for him, off we went. And with the self-assurance of a native taxi driver, I deposited Reiner at the train station in Krakow. We would be meeting up in a few days in Leipzig, Germany.

———

Not Psychotherapy:
This Is How the Wheel Turns

worked at the JCC breaking down cardboard boxes and cleaning out their garbage area. It was nasty work, but it provided me with a great sense of satisfaction. It made me laugh in the moment. I came to Poland and cleaned.

There were five of us breaking down the load today, and three of us would be leaving next week. We were concerned about how the work would get done once we left, and, just then, we were informed that there was a Polish-American woman downstairs who wanted to volunteer. "Bring her up here," we said, and then taught her the few ropes anyone needs to know to do the work. We were heartened that she and her three friends were going to work there for a week or more. And that is how this place operates! People come, and they go; others come in, and then they go. Somehow the work that must be done gets done. Somehow. Just that was such a great experience for me to take in.

Successfully driving past the road-that-does-not-exist, I arrived at Paszkowka to teach Qigong and Tai Chi. Everyone knew that tomorrow was my last day. I did a final art project with the kids. I had a very large sheet of paper and drew the outline of the Eastern United States on the left side, and indicated Chicago. On the other side of the sheet, an outline of Europe indicated Kyiv, Krakow, and Bonn. Then I drew arrows running back and forth connecting these places. In the middle of this, the twenty-five-pound bowling ball of a child found me and had to get in my lap for beard exploration, the sharing of some of his red pepper, and an animated conversation. My handprints in yellow and blue appear above the United States, and the kids' handprints in red, white, and blue appear above Ukraine. The drawing was hung in the dining room. And again, what a deep sense of satisfaction I had: the art and its importance to the children and the adults, reflecting the gift of connection.

The next morning in my hotel room, facing my last day at Paszkowka, I wondered what gift I might bring. And then I spied a small book of Wendell Berry's poetry I had brought with me called *Leavings*. I knew at that moment that this book was my gift. This was my inscription:

To my friends temporarily at Paszkowka,

Thank you for welcoming me into your space, where I had the opportunity to get to know you and your children. Spending this time together has enriched my life. Through the stories I will tell, our time together will enrich the lives of others.

Please know that there are a great many people who think of you and carry you in their hearts. I am one of them.

When I was packing for this trip and decided to bring this book, I did not know it was for you.

It was. It is.

With love,
Peter Sternberg, 11 September, 2022

My final arrival at Paszkowka was announced, and thus began a round of picture-taking with the kids. There were four children who decided to try Tai Chi today, so the class was large. Two of the participants were very close to having a good grasp of the twenty-four-step form, and so we repeated it many times to give them practice. I then presented my gift and read the inscription, leaving all of us visibly touched.

Sunday lunch was less formal than other midday meals—I was permitted to make my own plate—thank God. After lunch, I worked with the three adults who pretty much had the Tai Chi form memorized, and we did it another four times. I congratulated them on their achievement, and they warmly thanked me. They sat on chairs, facing me, and then one of them began a conversation (of course, this happens in the final minute), asking me how one calms the relentless "monkey-mind" voices in the mind. "You don't—you observe them."

This led us into an hour-long conversation about meditation, the Three Tenets of Zen Peacemakers, the *True Self* and the *False Self*, the care of the child we once were that resides within us by our competent adult Self, what Reiner is doing with his time now that he is retired, and the course of my reconciliation journey to various places of atrocity over the last eight years. We talked about Germans and Jews, Reiner and me, how we help each other face what has to be faced/owned, the Americans and their failure to take responsibility for the genocide they have and are perpetrating with Native peoples, and the World War II

German atrocities that occurred in Ukraine. They told me about a memorial in their hometown of Kharkiv—the massacre site of *Drobitsky Yar*, a ravine outside the city. There was no mention of Ukrainian antisemitism having any role in these historic events, and I did not bring it up. Rather, after they told me that Kharkiv is a multicultural city and has Jews living there, I inquired how that was working out. "Good," they said, emphasizing an ecumenical spirit of acceptance of diverse cultures and houses of worship. And that is where we ended—with me being welcomed to continue our study together once they are back home, and I am making my first trip to Ukraine.

I thought of this curious story from when Reiner and I first arrived at the Palace. I noticed that the young woman who'd been introduced to us as our translator wore a large Star of David on a chain around her neck.

I said to her, "I, too, am a Landsman," identifying myself as a Jew. She looked at me curiously.

When she introduced us to the rest of the refugees, I could tell from her language that she referred to me as being Jewish. Shortly after that, I asked her if she was Jewish.

She said, "No." I pointed out that she was wearing a necklace that identified her as being Jewish.

"This is my lucky talisman," she said.

I shook my head in disbelief and said, "Do you know that, at a not very distant time, walking around Ukraine wearing that could have gotten you accosted, raped, or killed?"

"No," she said, "I did not know that."

I made an effort to speak in a neutral way, not wanting her to feel uncomfortable with me, as I sought to understand how she understood her country: "Are you aware of the history of fierce antisemitism in your country, including many from your grandparents' generation, who participated with the Germans in exterminating the Jewish population?"

There was some shock that registered on her face as she again said, "No."

Moving it out of Ukrainian history, I asked, "So, how did this come to be your lucky talisman?"

She explained: "When it became clear that me and my mother had to flee from the Russian shelling, we asked our relatives, who were also leaving, if we could join them in their car. They said, 'No,' because there was no room for us in the car. It was fully packed with their possessions, and they would not remove any to fit us." She went on, "These people, like me, are Eastern Orthodox Christian. Me and my mother made it to Poland. When we got to the border, there were the Jews to take care of everyone with food, medicine, and shelter."

She was struck by that ethos and wanted to symbolize (and hold onto) her good fortune in having encountered it, and that is why she had taken the Star of David as her lucky talisman. She said, "Now I feel drawn to Judaism because of their generosity."

I pondered her story alongside what I had heard of the current ecumenical spirit of acceptance in Kharkiv. I pondered how unencumbered these people were by the recent sordid history of relations between their people and mine. I noticed that Peter-the-Bombardier, the enraged one, was not present. I would have expected a burst of anger within me at the perception of their casual ignorance of their country's ugly history. Instead: "Let it be," a voice inside said. The voice went on, "This is how the wheel turns." I was reminded of nature reclaiming the defiled ground of Plaszow. My knowledge of what was ugly was irrelevant in the face of what was lovely—being in an unexpected connection with these people. That fact made me smile.

There were hugs all around. Before I left, I had already received emails of pictures from two gmail accounts with names in the Cyrillic alphabet. And with that, I bade everyone well and walked out of the palace with deep satisfaction, wonder, and sadness at leaving these folks.

Months later, in a Zoom meeting, hearing Reiner's and my stories, Jola described our interactions this way: "This is Healing History." It was that simple. *Healing History* is what I now understand I had been doing there. It is exactly how it felt. It feels like a most worthy thing to be a part of.

<hr>

Sitting on the green couch (in what I am inclined to call "The Book Torture Room") nine months after my return from Poland, I asked my daughter Maura to review this last section of writing. In noticing the Peter-the-Bombardier thread throughout the piece, she asked me more precisely why I went to be of help to the Ukrainian Refugees.

Maura: "So you're in the Zoom Council meeting, all set to go to Germany, and then, boom, another catapult. And you're going to Poland to be with Ukrainians. Why?"

After a thoughtful pause, I felt a smile breaking. "Because I suck as a Bombardier."

Maura: "What do you mean?"

Peter: "In order to be a good Bombardier, if you are carpet bombing (which is preferred in my revenge fantasy), you must obliterate the humanity of the people you are bombing."

Maura: "And . . ."

Peter: "That's a small failing of mine. I would like to be a good Bombardier, but I have trouble."

Maura (writing furiously, barely concealing her own smile): "What kind of trouble?"

Peter: "I see myself in the people I am to bomb. And them in me."

We paused, looked at each other, and smiled. And what was it that passed between us? Very simply, an acknowledgment of the ironic truth of my statements. But that wasn't all. It was a moment of transition, hoped for but not always achieved, when the parent allows transparency to the child at the same time the child is willing to accept him in his complexity, confusion, contradictions, shortcomings, heroics, and even in his idiosyncratic brand of madness. So that smile was special, a treasure, because it is one of those smiles that travels on and on in time, backward and forward—through the generations and rebirths.

Maura broke the silence. "So, that's why you said, 'Yes' when you heard that the Ukrainian Refugees needed the help of a therapist?"

Peter: "Yes. Because it seems," continuing with a pause, a smile, and a wink, "that just now, I suck as a Bombardier . . ."

———————

Peter

Zen Boy

Zen Boy:
The Steam Room

left Poland and linked up with Reiner in Leipzig, where we began our moving retreat across Germany. One of the places I wanted to visit was a small slave-labor camp called Leipzig-Thekla, a subcamp of Buchenwald located in the Leipzig suburb of Thekla. The camp was not easy to locate, but we were determined, and Google Maps got us close. We parked the car and trudged on a path by the side of a busy road. Amid overgrown brush and forest that had been steadily reclaiming this small camp, we finally came upon a clearing that held the memorial to its victims.

What is noteworthy about this work camp is the two massacres there that caught international attention. The first was a massacre of some sixty partisan fighters, who were burned alive. The second massacre was discovered one day after it occurred, when the United States Army liberated the camp and recorded what they discovered with photographs, including soldiers weeping next to burned bodies.

With the end of the war closing in on the Germans, they had to steadily abandon the camps they operated. Prisoners who could walk were force-marched to other camps. In Thekla, on April 18, 1945, the Gestapo, along with members of the SS and *Volkssturm* men set out to burn alive the approximately three hundred and four prisoners who could not be moved. The *Volkssturm* men were a militia of males aged sixteen years old and those older than sixty, who were drafted in the waning days of the war for the purpose of carrying out "Total War"—those who resisted this service were killed. Only sixty-seven or so of those camp prisoners survived the Germans' closing effort, in all likelihood because the Germans ran out of time, fleeing the advancing Allies. The memorial area addresses both massacres.

After reading about the history there and placing stones at the memorial, wordlessly—and with great heaviness—Reiner and I retraced our steps to the car through a lightly falling rain. Back in the car, with a heavier rain falling outside and the weight of Thekla upon us, Reiner initiated a conversation. His parents had been "adamantly silent about the war and the Holocaust." Speaking with anguish, he maintained that they *had* to know about the horrors perpetrated—certainly his father knew of the horrors of the siege of Leningrad, because he was there for the nine hundred days of the siege. But there was only silence from them both. His father made a concerted effort to cover up any sense that anything had been amiss during the war. Reiner said his father became a "great performer" and threw himself into "gregarious frivolity." His parents' silence has vexed Reiner to this day because their silence—and the silence that permeated the family—intensified his sense of shame and guilt.

After hearing him say that, I turned in my seat to face him and spoke something I had not considered before. "Do you think their silence was a moral failure, or was it a matter of survival?" Upon hearing me say this, Reiner exploded into racking sobs. We clutched each other's arms while his body heaved with the sudden release of great pain, and we waited patiently while the tsunami of moaning and sobbing moved through his body.

After some minutes, the convulsion of grief passed. I asked if I could go on, and Reiner emphatically said, "Yes."

"When I think about the things I am ashamed of in my life, I realize that my immediate reaction is to hide them from others. I am not inclined to speak openly about shameful things, irrespective of whether these things warrant shame at all." Expanding on that, I said my impulse has been to try to preserve my damaged ego, my pride, my image at all costs, since I could not tolerate the vulnerability of exposure. Exposure felt like the absolute worst thing that could happen. Consequently, I was left with no way to handle "the vulnerable (shameful) thing" and to bring it into the "regular world."

Even as a therapy patient, talking about "shameful things" with my therapist did not completely bridge the shameful events back into the "regular world." For most of my life, those shameful events retained much of their status and harmful energy. A major shift occurred for me in 2014 when I took my turn reading names of victims on the selection site at Auschwitz-Birkenau at the Zen Peacemakers Bearing Witness Retreat. I had resolved to—and did—speak the names of the monkeys and other animals I had done brain research upon as a student more than fifty years earlier.

Reiner immediately and emphatically related to the point of survival and pointed out the very different way his parents lived this out. His mother was depressed, and his father played at being a man of importance. And he emphasized this sad, sad fact: that, because of their need to survive, neither could emotionally, relationally, show up. The pain of that was palpable to us both at that moment. There was more sadness for Reiner,—but it arose now from deep clarity and releasing.

And in that moment, he and I pushed beyond the ego-shoring his parents deployed (depression and aggrandizement) and restored dignity—we did that for us, and for them.

A BRIEF DIVERSION INTO SHAME

Three months after sitting in that car near Thekla with Reiner, I was in a hotel, relaxing in a steam room. I was immediately transported to an earlier time in my adult life when I was in a very rough encounter with shame. I was thirty-two years old, just out of another failed romantic relationship, in therapy again, and I was a participant in a five-year training group for psycho-therapists. Twelve of us met with Lenny Hochman, a psychologist from New York, five times a year for two days at a time. Lenny was a no-nonsense trainer with X-ray vision: a unique ability to know you, whether you thought you were revealing yourself or not. In fact, this was the exact purpose of his training: to teach us how the person's body structure, way of moving, way of speak-ing, taken with their behavior, provided a clear insight into the formative experiences in that person's life. Lenny understood and practiced the therapeutic process in an old-school way. He also understood infant and early-childhood development and was able to suss out the roots of the damage the patient was carrying. He used the twelve of us to demonstrate the points he wanted to make. In short, at any moment, he could turn to any one of us to demonstrate the teaching, e.g., "When we look at Peter, we see someone who experienced intrusion. We see that in the shape of his jaw and in his manner of hiding himself, right here in this group." It was that rough. I learned a lot about myself and my craft, even though I was always a bit nauseous in the days leading up to and during the training.

I developed a ritual for the end of the training weekends, which I expanded into a regular ritual at the end of my work week on Saturdays; I went to a steam room and hunkered down in there for an hour or two. The benches were tiled and wide enough to lie on comfortably, and, when the steam came on, it descended from the ceiling as though a cloud of thick fog was enveloping the world. I would watch it coming down and watch the room disappear; I, too, soon disappeared into the cloud. This was solace; this was refuge for battered me: I could not be seen! I was in a process with my training and with my therapy that was exposing every troubled, ugly, embarrassing, messed-up, needy, hidden, false, prideful component of my psyche—known and previously unknown to me. I can sum it up this way: I had come into my thirties thinking I had outfoxed, outmaneuvered the damage that had been chasing me. I thought I had outfoxed vulnerability. I was, by many accounts, successful at my undertakings. Even my failed dating relationships could be made to seem innocuous, since another was just around the corner.

But I had finally met two people who, unlike my previous three therapists, understood the severity of the damage chasing me and knew that there would never be a substitute for openly facing that damage. I wanted the encounter with my damage to remain private for this reason: *exposing any vulnerability would further undo me.* I had already lived the experience of not having adequate protection, of feeling openly mocked for my vulnerability. My history was that exposure was only going to make me even *more* afraid, *more* paranoid, *more* alone . . . *hurt more.* Vulnerability was always going to hurt me—it always had; being defenseless, being needy, being exterminate-able, being a despised outsider, each one and, surely, taken as a whole, felt exquisitely intolerable. I liken the experience of vulnerability to touching an electrical wire that has a short in it. Ergo, the self-admonition, "Hide! Hide! Hide at all costs! Keep your needs and your blunders to yourself." If someone used a word I did not understand, I would not ask them what it meant—I stumbled along trying to understand the word through the context of speech. I could not admit I didn't know it. Yup, not knowing the meaning of a word and asking revealed too much vulnerability.

And when the blessed steam descended in that room, and I was gone, I had an hour or two of peace. I could relax because I could not be located, could not be seen—because I was gone.

Not stopping there, being gone took on a new proportion. I was so disgusted with the realization of how my needs had been used by others to hurt me, how my needs had opened the door to my undoing, that I began to abjure the needs of my body. I ate just enough to not be lightheaded and dropped fifty pounds. Hunger did not bother me. I mastered it. I took on the mind of the ascetic to get away from my needs and to get away from my capacity to use others' needs of me to prop up my sagging, damaged ego. I would not date. To make matters worse, I had co-opted my martial-arts study to support the false sense of strength and invulnerability I sought through this rigid asceticism. And ironically, during this time, my capacities as a martial artist were greatly expanding.

Lenny made it clear to me, and I could follow him conceptually, that I would never be able to experience love and leave depression and rage behind, unless I could come to accept that I was, like every other human, full of shit and full of vulnerability as well as being the nice guy, the sensitive guy, and the strong guy I held myself out to be. Yes, I understood him, but I could not tolerate what I understood. So, I steamed and starved. I tried to steam clean my psyche and soul—and if cleaning didn't work, at least I could minimize the damage I believed I embodied—those parts of me that I detested and could not get away from without actually killing myself.

My poor therapist lovingly stood by me while I went through the hell I had to live. Although much later, she said she was frightened for my well-being, in the thick of it, she was steady and unflappable. And for the second time in our sixteen years together, my beloved dog Casey had the job of taking her end of the rope in her mouth while I, at the other end of the rope, flayed and flopped about, barely managing to hold on for two years. Finally, unable to hold it back any longer, out like vomit, came the rage and pain I had sought to control and obscure. Photos, a tree stump, and my ax; Chinese throwing stars, photos, and a plywood target in my basement; a heavy bag that said it couldn't take much more. Vomiting the various sicknesses of my psyche that had accrued from my very beginning until the current moment—all made manifest in the damage seen in my intimate relationships and in the faulty construct of who I took myself to be. One round of it after another, for days on end. Finally, it was my ax and a paneled wall in my basement because *something had to be destroyed.* Paroxysms of awful pain and rage emanating from my childhood home, my experiences with peers as a child and adolescent, my vulnerability to false professional mentors in my twenties and thirties who used me, the recent and distant history of the despised people I came from—all of it amplified by the sickness of humans: persecuting and tormenting one another, and, for all I knew, the sickness of my karma, topped off with the treachery of a loving God that had obviously blessed it all, had coalesced into an enriched nugget of loneliness and rage that cracked open—its howling energy spewed out in my basement and with my therapist in my sessions.

With each go in the basement, Casey, the tether dog, lovingly waited for me to drag myself upstairs after the emotional retching so she could lick the tears from my face—which of course, opened my raw, rageless, convulsive sobbing.

I don't believe I would have made it without her, without her love.

I call it my black-and-blue period.

───────────

When I said to Reiner, I understood wanting to, needing to, being desperate to hide what is shit about us, what is horrifying to us about us, that which gets revealed to us in the terrible instant our eyes open to some reality about ourselves, before our eyes can squeeze shut tight against the truth of us, seen and now sickeningly known in that instant—yes, oh yes, I understand shame and how, in order to survive that glimmer of what is real, we make the truth and ourselves not be what we know we are. Instead, in that exquisitely awful moment, we make the truth—and us—*not be so.* And with that, the Self is split.

Can I grasp Reiner's mother becoming lost in depression as she blocked out the truth of what it meant to be a German citizen at that time? Oh, Yes. Can I understand Reiner's father creating a charade for himself to block out what he saw, did, and knew? Oh, Yes.

In a moment of compassion for them, it occurs to me to say: "Come. Join me in the steam room. It's peaceful here, at least for an hour or two."

───────────

Zen Boy:
Reiner Returns

From Leipzig, Reiner and I traveled west to the Buchenwald
Memorial. You read the story of Janice and me discovering
Soviet Special Camp No. 2 in *The Clearing*. At the end of the
first Buchenwald Retreat, seven Germans went with me to
encounter that place. Reiner was not one of them. He told me
later he could not bring himself to do it, and he deeply regretted
not going. He spoke of his father, who'd served in the *Wehrmacht*
and was involved in the nine-hundred-day siege of Leningrad.
That experience and much more had remained unspoken within
his family. His parents' silence and denial were like a corrosive
agent in Reiner's life. He explained it was that freight that had
held him back that day at Buchenwald.

I spoke about my troubled relationships with my father and
my mother. We agreed on how hard it is to shed all that we have
been given. Like pack mules, we carry others' loads into and
throughout our lives. We confirmed that we both had business in

that forest just outside of the camp. We each had father-business to release, and we had business between us—to symbolize and affirm that we are brothers on the same path and support each other in the encounters that must be had.

As I prepared for the outing, I realized that, as wounding as my relationship with my father was, I did not carry a sense of shame about his behavior in the world. Oh, would that have made being his son even harder than it already was!

Now, four years later, Reiner and I drove west out of Leipzig and arrived at Buchenwald. We walked quickly through the entry gates, past the Singing Tree, where truly unfortunate prisoners met a more cruel death—hanged by their arms from behind their backs. We walked past the gas chambers, past the medical-experimentation area, across the camp, past the art installation, and out to the exterior guard path, where we found the exquisite birch forest that held the mass grave.

In the clearing, among the memorial markers and headstones, Reiner shared photos of his father: as a young man, a soldier, and in his later years. I had pictures of myself in uniform at military school and pictures of my family. In the clearing, through the exquisite forest, the sun flickered on us. It was another sublime day in a-forest-that-holds-atrocity—the warmth of the sun released the scent of the earth and trees.

Reiner performed a Zen ceremony with incense to acknowledge and release the shame and pain for all associated with this place. We remembered our friend Janice, who died within two years of the retreat. And we remembered two others who died, one of whom was Reiner's friend who "left this world by his own hand." Reiner performed Tai Chi in the clearing where I had done it in 2018 and where I had orchestrated the group into a circle for Qigong both toward each other and then outward, into the forest. The flow of Qi then and now was very much like the pump experience I'd described at the children's mass grave in Poland. Reiner and I, by this time, were very naturally in sync, moving together as though we had been practicing for years.

After that, Reiner meditated while I walked around the forest. We closed our long-awaited outing and silent processing by throwing the memorial stones we'd brought for this purpose into the forest, and then Reiner placed another at the memorial site.

Atrocity acknowledged. Check.

Perpetrators caught in revenge acknowledged. Check.

These deaths as the natural culmination of unchecked madness acknowledged. Check.

The damage that flowed from all those stories into Reiner's life acknowledged. Check.

The damage that flowed into my life from the madness that created these stories, and from the madness of religious persecution over two millennia that rolled through my family, that rolled slant into my life at military school and showed me the precariousness of my place in society—acknowledged. Check.

Together, we had well attended to our business at Soviet Special Camp No. 2.

Zen Boy: Mercy at Bitburg

In May of 1985, after attending a G-7 summit meeting in Bonn, President Ronald Reagan, at Chancellor Helmut Kohl's "suggestion," visited a cemetery in Bitburg, Germany, where German soldiers are buried, including approximately fifty-nine (there is uncertainty as to the exact number) *Waffen* SS. At the time, there was enormous pushback about this plan from many sources, none more outraged than the world Jewish community, which protested loudly. I was one of those loud protesters naming his actions as a desecration to the memory of the victims of these individuals. Reagan believed his actions "helped strengthen the European Alliance" (read as *appeasing Helmut Kohl*) and "helped strengthen our European alliance and heal once and for all many of the lingering wounds of war."[48]

---

48 Reagan, Ronald, *An American Life,* 1990, New York, Simon and Schuster, 409

I thought this was bullshit. Then, in 2022, as I was preparing myself for a moving-retreat across Germany with Reiner, this thought came to me: "Hey, Zen-boy, witness-to-atrocity, are you willing to acknowledge the atrocity visited upon the poor fuckers buried at Bitburg?

. . . Well?"

So, I pushed the envelope and told my friends Reiner, Kathleen, Vicki, and Dorle, I would be visiting Bitburg Cemetery to encounter the SS "men" buried there. None of my German friends had been there before, and, when they heard of my plans, they wanted to accompany me. Could I go there and preserve the channel I had been working to open—to take in "the full catastrophe" without splitting myself from those I had spent a lifetime hating and would have gladly burned to death? The Bitburg Cemetery was going to be a challenge.

Leaving Bonn, Reiner drove through the bucolic country-side. I had a hard time staying awake during the drive. Bitburg is a quaint-looking town. We found the cemetery and walked to the military section. I took a deep breath and walked in, placing myself among the SS resting in neat, well-kept rows of graves. As I walked the rows, I took particular note of the ages of the "men." So many of them were not *men* at all; they were in their late adolescence. The cemetery was beautiful in the way cemeteries can be. Being there felt surreal to me, but that faded as I emotionally and mentally acclimated. "Zen-Boy" felt the rightness of my being in attendance.

I had prepared something to read. I didn't know if I would read it, but once on the ground of the cemetery, the impulse I had was to follow through, so I did. Standing at the memorial that overlooks the military section, with Reiner, Dorle, and Vicki beside me, I disturbed the rest of the dead and spoke.

Statue outside the military section of the Bitburg Cemetery.
Photo credit: Peter Sternberg

TAI CHI AT AUSCHWITZ

Bitburg—September 2022

My grandmother sent letters and money to her family
in Poland
—or was it Ukraine then?
Until the letters came back stamped,
"Undelivered."
The **addressees**—they had already *been delivered,*
and the entire village vanished.

In Bitburg,
I visited the well-festooned section of the cemetery
where fifty-nine SS men were currently resting.
I disturbed their rest with my presence.

A searing sculpture just outside their area,
was the only indicator of what
the resting men had done
back when they had been . . .
active.

"SS men—listen up! There is no hiding now.
That is over.

I know what you did in the forest.
I know what you did in the camps.
I know what you did in the ghettos.

I know about the singing tree and the standing cell.
I know about eradicating the 'defectives.'
I know how you used fire, bullets, clubs, torture, and gas.

I know how you used fear, slavery, starvation, and disease.
I know how you used 'experimentation.'

And yet . . . the truth is . . .
God Damn Me!—it is visceral, isn't it?
I can feel the mystique that lifted me up
when I wore a uniform as a would-be young man welling up.
And how handsome you must have looked in *your* uniform.

I sense what most of you were after,
probably the same as me,
glory, pride; finally, your rightful entitlement.
You thought that was respect.

I, too, thought glory and pride were respect.
I recall the yearning,
I was so close to giving into it
by choosing to go to Vietnam.
The slightest push of the wind and . . .

Enough now. Go back to your rest,
a deeper rest because your secrets are out.
Someone knows."

Then, Reiner and I read that piece together. Afterward, I led the four of us in what had now become a ritual, sending the energy of Qigong into the place. We walked off the memorial in silence and took a last stroll among the Nazi dead.

We were all moved by the experience of being there. I was glad for the way I encountered the dead SS and the way I was with my friends. I was so grateful for their helping me present myself to my most notorious enemies. This outing was powerful for us all.

I re-contemplated the story of the dying SS officer Simon Wiesenthal writes about in *The Sunflower*; the one who begged him for forgiveness so he could clear his conscience as he lay dying of his wounds. It has taken me all my seventy-two years to figure this out, but I think I know how I'd answer Simon's question: "You, reader . . . mentally change places with me, and ask yourself the crucial question, 'What would I have done?'"[49] I find I am inclined to say to that dying man:

I am luckier than you.
My madness wrought harm that so far has been *forgivable*.
I could have been you—pulled into, seduced into, forced into
the *unforgivable*.
I am sorry for you—for all the suffering you wrought
that goes on and on,
flowing out from the collective Madness into everyday life—
even all these years later.
I am sorry. I am so sorry,
so very, very sorry . . .
for you.

In silence, we walked back to the car and then applied ourselves to finding a café in the quaint town of Bitburg, Germany, all of us of one mind: that reconciliation and restoration, at this moment, involved pastries and coffee.

----

49 Wiesenthal, Simon, *The Sunflower*, 1976, New York, Schocken Books, 98

Zen Boy:
No Way Out

Remagen *is the place* where the Allied advance in March of
1945 crossed the Rhine into Germany. Long before this crossing,
it was clear to any rational person that the war had been lost.
But Hitler was not finished with his rage at the people who let
him down. There is a cemetery close to Remagen. So many of
these graves are of *Volkssturm* "men"—the militia composed of
teenage boys and old men who were to fight to the death for
Hitler's mad glory. I was there to honor the poor souls caught
in a "choiceless choice"—facing a death whose only point was
to feed that mad glory. Those who resisted this service to the
Führer were hanged from streetlamps. Or shot. Ironically to me,
this cemetery is revered by Neo-Nazis who hold a yearly com-
memoration to the glory of National Socialism. Dorle, Vicki,
Reiner, and I dedicated our presence in opposition—acknowledging the people caught in "No-Choice" and wasted.

Nearby, we visited *The Golden Mile*—so named because the surrounding fields had turned golden in color during the summer months of 1945, when the site was a camp of open cages that held German POWs exposed to the elements for months without adequate food, water, and sanitation. At The Golden Mile, approximately 1,247 out of 200,030 POWs died. Zen-boy, erstwhile bestower of dignity, bowed in compassion for "no-choice" young boys and old men who were chewed up. *Chewed up and wasted.* And writing that I hear Peter-the-Bombardier, chiding the Allies: "**Only** 1,247?? What the hell is wrong with you guys? It should have been 1,247 **left**!"

From there, we traveled on to the EIAB (European Institute for Applied Buddhism), which was a *T4* facility during the war. After the war, it was repurposed as a hotel, and then it was acquired by Thích Nhất Hạnh to become a Buddhist monastery and retreat center. There, we met Kathleen, another Zen Peacemaker Retreat veteran. The five of us conducted a ceremony of remembrance. I asked for access to the basement because it was in the basements of these institutions that the gas chambers and crematoria had been set up. We left stones in the basement and at other locations on the property *in memoriam*. What an odd, yet very purposeful juxtaposition. Deep bows to Thích Nhất Hạnh for bringing the healing energies of gardens, meditation, and peace into a formerly desecrated space. That was a true Zen move.

Germany is disorienting to me. So cultured and civilized. And for all that, they were unprotected from madness—stark, frank madness. They became ruthless, savage, and impotent to affect their trajectory. The mad ones later claimed they were victims. Can we be a victim when we are the perpetrator? I don't want to answer myself, but I must: *Yes.*

I *hate* my answer. It looks and sounds like a loophole, an excuse. It drives the Bombardier and the Jew in me mad. But the horrible truth is . . . Yes.

I think again about shame and the exquisitely intense moments that follow *being stopped* when we have gone terribly wrong. Being stopped and forced to see ourselves through another's eyes. What an interesting moment. We can wake up and realize where we have been and what we have been doing. Or we can close down—hard.

If we open ourselves (wake up), judgment comes, and it is a judgment that what we are doing, who we are in this moment, is considered by another (and perhaps ourselves also) to be wrong, or harmful, or sick.

The experience of getting a glimpse of our true selves that comes from being stopped can last for a millisecond or a lifetime. The hard truth is that the only antidote to living with the radioactivity of the truth-of-ourselves (shame) is to open it and discover acceptance about *one's horrible self.* Openness and acceptance neutralize the secret and hence the radioactivity of shame. The power of judgment to endlessly sear us becomes neutralized. This is what Lenny and my therapist were trying to get through to me. And, through loving acceptance and example, to a great extent—did (I put the weight back on).

What my journey into PTSD showed me is that there is no substitute for the healing that can occur through an encounter with people, when there is *authentic reckoning* (about what was done or not done) and *when there is responsibility-taking.* These are the necessary ingredients for *reconciliation* within oneself and with another. I have felt this healing myself and have observed it in others. The healing potential is strong, and it is there for us as individuals, there for us in relationships, and there for our societies. You can see how the encounter process works by looking at the work of

The Truth and Reconciliation Commission in South Africa after the fall of apartheid, in the work of the *Restorative Justice Initiatives* in this country, and in the easing of Moral Wounding symptoms among veterans who have attended the *Elderwarriors Healing Journey*, where they encounter civilian attendees who take responsibility for the veterans being exposed to physical, mental, and moral damage. And you can see how it works in the stories I've shared.

Healing encounter is exactly what Reiner and I accomplished with each other as we made our way across Germany. But at the Soviet Special Camp and at the Golden Mile Camp (where German soldiers, seventeen and eighteen years old, were exposed to the elements after surrender, with much suffering and many dying) and again at Bitburg, a cemetery where fifty-nine SS boys/men are buried, I was challenged. Can I hold the Zen stance of acknowledging *all the hungry souls?* All those "in trouble," all those "once-upon-a-time-not-evil" drafted boy-soldiers, lying right alongside the sadists? (The sadists, the ones I want to hang by their arms from behind their back, the SS way, trussed up on the "singing tree," so named by the Germans to mock their victims' screams—but only after I shatter some collar bones.)

Well, Zen-boy, shattering collar bones? Can you acknowledge *all the hungry souls, even the sadists?*

Yes. I'll say, *Yes, I can . . .* as long as you look past the small, small matter of retribution.

So, no. Fuck it—no. Not yet. Not *all* the hungry souls.

There I am, extending compassion for my enemies, from a place of non-judgment and equanimity, I'm on my third grounded inhale and . . . *FUCK, who let the sadists in?!* Maybe I can get past retribution for a bit, but then the fucking sadists show up and, *poof!* Zen is . . . *gone.* Gone!

Then, I have to start again, to get it back, to push past instinct, so that, at least for a while, or a moment, or a blessed passing second, I can have acceptance for the full catastrophe—mine and everyone else's.

———————

Zen Boy:
German Soup

Having finished our Moving Retreat and come to the end of my
time in Germany, I said a difficult goodbye to Reiner, who had
to return to work. He and I had deepened our friendship and
brotherhood through the intimacy of sharing our histories, our
grief, our rage, and our laughter. The feeling of deep respect
as friends and as men is special to us both. Our time together
had been enriching in ways we would continue to realize in the
coming months of processing and debriefing.

I remained in Bonn with Vicki, Dorle, and Kathleen for my
last full day in Germany. We were all going to meet for breakfast
and then send Vicki off to the airport. Dorle and I had planned
to visit *The Beethoven House* for a tour before I boarded a train to
the airport hotel in Frankfurt.

The night before, I had started to feel ill with what I thought
was a sinus infection. My Covid test was negative, but feeling
worse, I canceled the tour, wanting only to rest. I said a warm

goodbye to Vicki, both of us in deep gratitude for our relationship. At this point, Dorle and Kathleen asked me to go with them to Kathleen's community and hang out there until I had to go to the train. Wanting only to sleep, I marshaled some strength to reluctantly go along with their offer. Once at Kathleen's, it was clear that I had a fever. I occasionally erupted into deep coughing.

While Kathleen was heating some of her husband's homemade vegetable soup for us, Dorle asked me if I wanted a foot massage. I said, "Sure." She did a gentle reflexology massage. As Dorle's massage went on, I became more and more emotional. I began to cry softly. She looked up at me and inquired about my tears. I said, "There's a lot going on, and I want to speak of it when Kathleen is in the room."

Kathleen returned and served the soup.

I said, "This illness has turned out to be an unexpected, last deep dive of the trip for me." My tears returned. "The tears have to do with your tender caretaking and nurturing of me. Becoming friends over the last few years out of our deep shared experiences of peacemaking and self-exploration felt stunningly natural to me. But this tender caretaking and nurturing is something else. I could not have conceived of this experience!"

Taking pains through my strong emotion to be very precise, I said, "Here I am, sick and vulnerable, and I am being tenderly, lovingly, *taken care of in Germany, by Germans!*" And with that, I broke down sobbing. Dorle came over and put her arm around me as that emotion took its release. Through tears, the three of us looked at each other with such presence and love.

After we finished the soup, I said, "I will be telling Maggie about this tonight, and she will want you to know what it means to her that you are caring for me while I'm ill." That brought more tears. They were very touched.

I had to get to my train, so Dorle and I had our hard goodbye, acknowledging our healing connection now over nine years and the deep friendship that has enriched us so much. I was becoming more ill by the minute. Kathleen took my suitcase, and I took the smaller packs. We walked a couple of blocks to the tram. Kathleen escorted me to the central train station, where she helped me buy my ticket to Frankfurt. Then she took me to a nearby pharmacy for a decongestant and a cough suppressant. As if taking some cosmic cue, the pharmacist, who did not speak much English, gave me some lozenges—gratis. Then Kathleen took me back to the train platform. As I followed her down the platform, a vision of the Track 17 platform flitted through my mind. That was four years ago—when, according to my wise daughter, it was not the right time for me to connect in reconciliation with a German, when the invisible wall, only microns thick, could not be pierced by me. And here was Kathleen putting me on a bench exactly where my train car would stop. *I felt so well seen to.* We said goodbye with a lot of love for each other, and she asked me to let her know that I had arrived safely. I said I would. And when the following thought formed within me, it seemed as surreal as anything that had happened to me so far . . .

Is it possible for a person to feel tucked-in on a train platform? **Is it possible for a guy like me to feel lovingly tucked-in by a German woman *on a German train platform?***

It is.

I did.

Once *home, Reiner and I* went back into our *Encounter* exchanges again—this time over email and Zoom meetings. One of the points we were quickly into was victimhood. This grew out of a magazine story Vicki shared with us all about the number of Nazis who were knowingly brought into the German government after the war: how crimes were routinely overlooked, how deals were made, how resisting communism put off war reckoning, and how many victims of Nazi crimes were excluded from any sort of compensation—the Sinti/Roma, the forced laborers from Eastern Europe, to name two. My German friends were appalled by this fact: criminals getting away with it—so many of its victims unacknowledged, their claims for restitution repudiated.

I wrote to Reiner: "That Germany came to any reckoning *at all*, that some leaders were able to advance the idea of restitution, that there were laws passed in Germany outlawing the denial of the Holocaust, that authors began asking questions and writing, that therapists began paying attention to intergenerational trauma and collective shame and guilt—are all miracles in themselves. Miracles! That you and other members of your generation clawed your way out of cultural denial and went into the moral abyss to examine it and sort through it is nothing but a miracle! That is precisely how I see it and precisely how I see you and the other Germans I have met through retreat experiences."

Reiner told me he was quite touched and felt strengthened reading this.

———————

And there is more . . . In another conversation with him, I spontaneously brought up my history of contempt for the Jewish victims of the Holocaust who, in my previously held view, went to their deaths like sheep to the slaughter. Among the in-line-to-be-dead were people in denial, in passivity, in prayers to a loving God to save them, in an understanding of their suffering as grounded in sin against that loving God. All this sheep-like behavior inflamed my rage at "the sheep." From age eleven, I asked, "Why didn't they fight?" They could have overwhelmed their captors. I was tormented by what I took to be their impotence. This led me to the following piercing acknowledgment. For those victims, the following description from Rita Gabis's memoir *A Guest at the Shooter's Banquet: My Grandfather's SS Past, My Jewish Family, A Search for the Truth*, was true:

> "'History is by its nature retrospective,' Boyarin said at one point.
>
> So obvious, but I'd never thought of it before. His words utterly changed the way I considered the past.
>
> 'We give order to it, as if it was orderly. But the people who lived it or died during it—there was nothing retrospective about their experiences, about what they thought would come next, how

they interpreted, for instance, a day of brutality. How could they know, the way we know, what would follow?'"[50]

Of course, it was me who felt like a helpless, impotent sheep. Contemplating this passage raises within me a need for another ceremony at a camp: this time, the ceremony will be for me to approach the ghosts of the stunned, the shattered, and the desperate soon-to-be-dead with a deep apology for my arrogance and contempt. These are the words that followed that thought:

To those in shock, disbelief, incomprehension,
Those who made deals, cooperated, collaborated,
Those who pleaded and begged,
Those who were compliant,
Those who took bread from others,
Those who gave bread to others,
Those who prayed,
Those who went insane,
Those who killed themselves,
Those who resisted, in all manners of resistance; by educating others, celebrating holidays, maintaining dignity, performing acts of sabotage, saving others, fighting, hiding, preserving humanity and love . . .
To those who were in acceptance of their fate . . .

I, the man who was never in your shoes, never starved, never so threatened, never in a world that mad—not even close—beg for your forgiveness. What would I have done—big shot that I wished myself to be? Would I have had a shootout with the bad

---

50 Gabis, Rita, *A Guest at the Shooter's Banquet: My Grandfather's SS Past, My Jewish Family, A Search for the Truth*, 2015, New York, Bloomsbury Publishing, 298

guys? When? How? Or would I comply to live another day? It is absurd to think I can say. Of course, I cannot say. And that is the point.

To all who were in it, no matter how you were in it, no matter where or when you were in it, my arrogance chastened, I deeply beg your forgiveness.

———

Zen Boy:
Post-Traumatic Treasure

In the months following my return from Germany in 2022, I had opportunities to process the events with Reiner, Kathleen, Dorle, and Vicki. Over the course of several conversations with Dorle, reflecting on the tender care I received from her and Kathleen when I was ill, we unexpectedly arrived here:

Dorle made clear that, when I perceived myself as a Jew being cared for by Germans, she was instantly brought into an encounter with her *Germanness*. That challenged a long and deeply held attitude she had. She said she had regarded her Germanness as something "to be studied." Aloof, she looked at it studiously—while maintaining a necessary distance from it. My speaking of feeling lovingly cared for by Germans put her in the moment of *encounter with herself as a loving German*. This, she said, was a challenge to her lifelong view of herself. She had left Germany as a young adult because she could not live in the cultural denial of Germany's recent past. This conflict was most acute with her parents and other family members and remains so with some of them. Hence her statement to me—that her Germanness was something she wanted distance from: to be observed and studied. It wasn't her.

I took what she was saying to be a profound extension of my experience at Kathleen's: an opening in which Dorle claimed a split-off part of her identity; that, as a German, she could love, have her love, express her love, her tenderness—easily and naturally, express it as a German, for me, a Jew.

We reflected on the other extraordinary opening moment, back in 2018, when, at the Days of Peace Retreat, she asked me if I'd allow my Yellow Star of David to serve as a "talking piece" for the group. I told her how that moment held such extreme vulnerability for me that it was hard to breathe. She recalled that she asked me directly if she could use the Star as her talking piece. "Your consent gave me back my dignity in a sea of guilt—therefore protection was not necessary anymore."

She went on to explain that my vulnerability, tears, and speaking that September day in 2022 at Kathleen's place in Bonn, brought out and amplified her experience of **dignity restored**. In her offhand way, Dorle smiled and continued with this simple statement: "Yeah, trauma was transformed into Treasure."

And with that, she introduced me to a term I had not previously heard: *Post-Traumatic Treasure*. I implicitly understood that trauma contains the seeds of treasure just as transformation is embedded within every journey into darkness. So simple and elegant, and yet, despite knowing it, I had not seen or realized or applied it until now.

Dorle's comment rejiggered what the past nine years had been. In just a few nanoseconds, the angst of it all rearranged itself so I could appreciate it as a whole. The sudden launch off the catapult;

this unexpected, unplanned-for, serendipitous journey-with-a-life-of-its-own had always been, and remains, a Treasure—waiting for me, a man walking around with an *Inner Hitler,* to see it.

Post-Traumatic Treasure . . . in its enigmatic simplicity . . . the perfect container for this journey . . .

So far.

Maura

Interlude #5

Miracles at Yellowstone

My *sisters and I* weren't raised in any particular religion. For much of my life, my Jewish father tended toward an atheistic worldview. And while my Irish-Catholic mother had deep reverence for the Divine, she also had great disdain for the misdeeds of the Church.

We benefited from their openness, learning about and exploring different spiritual traditions, still opening presents every Hanukkah and Christmastime. But I never went to Hebrew school or Sunday school or prayed before bed, so it's not like I know God through the lens of an organized religion.

I can't quote a holy book or pray the rosary to prove that God is alive in those moments my father was meditating at

Auschwitz, the Pine Ridge Reservation, the Lynching Memorial, or Buchenwald. I have no great command or any formal authority over where God is, or who built the catapult that flung my father into reconciliation in the first place.

And, when I read about my father speaking the names of his beloved, tormented monkeys, or the pain of the *klezmer* music, or befriending the descendant of a Nazi, or playing frisbee with Ukrainian children, I can't quite fathom the power of it all.

I could see **It** etched in my father's face: the awe of taking a horrific nightmare and turning it into a place for a wedding, of taking the profane, dark stain of evil and transforming it into love. I thought I knew about love, weddings, and forgiveness. I had gotten married—I thought forever—and I had faced an inner demon here and there. But before I read what we refer to as his *godforsaken essays*, I had no idea what real power was or what God actually *felt like*.

The more beauty my father found in these trips of reconciliation, the more insane his staunch refusal of the divine seemed to me.

I would give him shit about his penchant for covering up the divinity in all his wild reconciliation stories. His birds, his new German friends, knee-healing Tai Chi, the alchemical Star of David ritual—it seemed to me that there was this mystical force moving over and through him, made even more clear to me by how heartbreaking my own life felt.

Now, I have more compassion for my father's "spiritual teacher" reluctance. I've realized that it's hard to know God when you cannot trust your parents.

Parents are our first gods. They are our stand-ins for the *Great All That Isn't Me* when we're young, and they are our guides for an intact relationship with higher powers as we grow. Given his early life, it's no wonder my father has only ever been able to see the Universe as Unfriendly. What a gift Auschwitz and Buchenwald were and are, because he can go to the most abjectly Unfriendly places on Earth, where the ground is stained with depravity, and then find love, and forgiveness, and friendships, and a wedding.

"You want to face the Unfriendly Universe, Peter? We'll show you Unfriendly," I can imagine these sites of atrocity saying to him. And let the miracles begin.

I've become somewhat of a spiritual pest to my father. The man came to me asking for help writing a book about the story of reckoning and reconciliation he's been on, quite an odyssey in its own right. And here I've been, hounding him about birds and parallel tracks, naming the unseen hand I can see moving him toward healing.

The truth is that this story didn't begin in 2013 at that PTSD conference. This story began much earlier, when he defied his parents' preferences to marry the woman he loved, my mother, an Irish-Catholic woman of faith. *It* persisted in moments of wild serendipity. The Friendly Universe he had been so reluctant to acknowledge had been with him all along.

It was there a couple of decades ago while he was skiing through his favorite Utah forest when the distinctive, deep, gravelly voice of a dear deceased friend came from out of nowhere and blasted him with: "You don't know *Who* you are!"—leaving him sobbing while stopped in knee-deep powder with the sun filtering through the bare Aspen trees. It turns out it was true: he didn't know who he was. But he was about to find out.

It was there a few years before this big reconciliation journey, during a spirit visitation from my dead grandfather at my sister Ellie's acupuncture appointment. Peter was alone in the waiting room, doing standing meditation, when his dead father appeared ten feet away from him. As Peter describes it, he looked exactly as he did in 1975, fit and healthy, dressed in a recognizable overcoat and hat. Peter kept telling himself through his freaking out, not to break contact. Peter says his father had a pleasant look on his face. They said nothing. After a while, his father dipped his head, tipped his hat to him, turned, and disappeared.

The shock of that deepened when the Friendly Universe *confirmed that wild waiting-room experience* eleven years later, when my parents decided—in the spur of the moment—to each get a reading from an intuitive medium while they were in Ireland. The medium told Peter his father was present and spoke about how my grandfather was expressing regret for being frightening and hurtful to my father in his childhood. The medium said, "Peter, your father is coming forward; he's saying, 'You broke the mold.' The mistreatment of children in the generational line stopped with you. He's . . . he's showing me that he's tipping his hat to you." There *It* was again, this time leaving Peter wobbly in his chair.

Over and over, the Friendly Universe, the power of *It*, has been weaving through Peter's life, winding around the tracks that placed him at that PTSD conference all those years ago. He somehow managed (by the skin of his teeth) to have enough grace to keep saying, *"Yes"* when presented with another and then another experience that challenged his view of himself and the world.

The night this story landed firmly and loudly into all of our lives, underneath the pergola many years ago now, I signed on to be a living witness to the courage of my father's *Yes*-saying. When I asked him why he never told me to shut up about all the "spiritual teacher smoking too much weed" stuff I pointed out to him, he said, "I didn't like the medicine, Maura; it brought me back to pain, but I knew I had to take it."

Now, when we point out the hummingbird that buzzes excitedly around us when we're sitting in the backyard under the pergola, my Dad smiles softly. He seems glad. That's the real miracle here.

All these years later, after a divorce, a change of career, *and* a surmounting of obstacles harder than I knew I was capable of, my dad and I took a trip to Yellowstone. I wanted to escape the long-standing reminders of the life I had lost in the divorce by running away from the place I grew up in. He wanted many hours—uninterrupted—of us strapped into a moving vehicle, no escape in sight, so that the book would finally be finished. Neither of us got exactly what we came for.

The vistas had me speechless, and the altitude had me wheezing, barely keeping up with my 70-something-year-old father, who seemed to be living contentedly off of black coffee and Universal Source Qi.

"The trip of a lifetime," the hostess at Old Faithful Geyser Grill commented with full eyes, when we told her what we were up to. "What a gift to get to be with your father like this."

"Yes," I agreed, and then we were all teary-eyed. "Yes, an enormous gift."

We drove around the park leisurely, stopping at lookouts, climbing gingerly down rocky façades (don't tell my mother). Occasionally, the sun would penetrate the pine needles, and the Earth seemed to ask us for some Tai Chi, and so, we willingly complied. Winding our way on a mountain, we spoke of the book:

"I can feel the beginning is a bit flat, Maurz; it—it needs, it needs more story," my Dad commented, looping lazily around the switchbacks. "I guess I have to tell the stories, the ones I said I would never share." He paused. "From my childhood."

The words echoed inside the stillness. I had a sneaking suspicion that if it weren't for the depth of the quiet up here on the mountain, I might not have ever heard this from him. It's the full-circle moment, his readiness to be vulnerable enough to share the depth of the healing he's been doing on this wild journey of reconciliation.

"Now, Dad. Now, you're ready." I smiled cautiously. "You're ready for the book to be finished."

"*Now*?! What do you mean *now*? I've been ready for years!" he yelped incredulously, driving us around the hairpin turns and sharp drop-offs into pine tree and rock.

"Yes, now," I replied with a wry grin. "Now you are ready to lay the truth bare. Now it's time to honor the people who moved you along this path: Louie, and Father Mike, and Reiner, and Dorle . . ."

". . . and Harold, Bernie, Kathleen, Vicki, Salomea, Daniel, and George."

"Yes, they're alongside us. Mom, and us three. Your parents . . . even the boys at military school and the Germans and Nazis and Jews . . ."

". . . my fourth therapist, and Lenny, and Casey-the-tether-dog," he spoke softly and reverently.

"And your monkeys, Dad! Your monkeys! Naming them as your dead, you closed the circle of Reckoning and Reconciliation on that selection platform at Auschwitz—you as victim *and* perpetrator. No, we can't forget your monkeys. Now, we get to see all of you, and the power of the catapult—the miracle of the full transformation."

I paused and glanced at him. We weren't flying off the mountain, so that was a good sign.

"Huh," he pondered. "You really think it's all that?"

"Yes, yes I do. And you're right. The beginning—right now? It's boring as hell. Why not tell the full truth? If we're going to do it, might as well . . ."

". . . Do it." He finished for me, with a bemused, crinkly-eyed smile. "All right. All right. That is what I will do."

We drove on; the mountains did the rest of the talking for us.

It was some deep relief that I could feel his concluding moves here, in this dance he and I and this damn book have been doing for all of these years. He won't have his trip wish—to have the book completed by the time we leave Yellowstone—but I could feel the ending arriving, like I could feel his heart softening.

A miracle.

And then, as we do, we found a spot to sit by the water. The sunlight made the top of the lake look like it was made of diamonds, rippling with a raw power that caught in my throat. And in the stark stillness, amidst the miracle of the beauty there by the rock, I could hear the mountain whispering the words I'm afraid to speak aloud, but, recently, brave enough to claim:

"I've fallen in love again," I murmured, as we looked out at the deep blue of the lake.

He looked up at me with muted surprise. *He's not surprised at what I'm saying,* I thought, *he's just happily startled that I'm saying it aloud.*

I wish so desperately that my confession wasn't true. Falling in love again—it's my own kind of book writing, requiring the hell of walking gingerly through the land mines of the past, in order to make it into the beauty of the future.

"I've fallen in love," I repeated, "and it's—it's—it's such bad news." My voice catches.

A long pause and then, "No, Maurz," my father replied gently, with a hand on my back, "the only bad news would be if you never loved again."

Seeing the Universe as Friendly takes a bravery of spirit that I had lost in the wild hardship of my life in the past few years. I shuddered, put my hands over my face, and shook my head much the way I see him do.

Then, I cried.

All I can do is contemplate the beauty and the power of Auschwitz and Buchenwald, the transformative force of reconciliation work, the purpose behind these very awful, holy places. These things are obvious in my father's story and, of course, in my own. It's undeniable. Sitting on the mountaintop, the power of this is just undeniable. Generations of my family line, and of the future children my sisters and I might have, all seem to gather around us on this mountain. I can finally see my father's story fully.

My grandfather's destructive, violent jealousy and the feeling of deep betrayal in my grandmother's intrusiveness and her subtle, enabling collusion obliterated my father's innate sense of some universal "goodness," or rightness, or safety, or peace. He became hard, unbelieving, wary, and suspicious.

My grandparents took my father's access to faith because, in some way, their parents took it from them, and their parents before that. Because of the injuries to trust and security they sustained in their childhoods, amidst genocide and cultural terror and heartbreak, they were left unable to show their children the possibility of a Friendly Universe. And the big joke is that the catapult-flinging experience of Auschwitz, Buchenwald, those reconciling Germans, and writing this book, returned it—returned *It* to him and returned *It* to me.

It's Parallel Tracks, lifetimes of them, apparently, of hearts and minds and tongues and pens riding opposite trains, capturing the beauty of the intersections, of how we managed to end up as we are, sitting on the mountain, or at the dinner table, or under the pergola, right here, right now.

One time, many years ago, my father wrote his daughters a Father's Day card (as he always does), and, in it, he said that, as far as he could tell, the trick to living free was learning how not to fear death.

And as far as I can tell, it's these deaths that are the trickiest not to fear. It's the inner death that's required for Peter-the-Bombardier to say, *I need to go to Germany.* Or the inner death that's required for Peter to hear his daughter say, *Thank you for letting me work on this with you.* Or the inner death that's required for Maura to let her life burn to the ground, ego slayed, finally finding herself sweaty and singed, and, somehow, willing to build something new, like a book—or even a new marriage.

It's *those* deaths, the dark inner caves of mind and soul, that are asking to be excavated. That's the real boogeyman here. We move through fear into saying "*Yes*" when the Not-So-Friendly Universe tees up the next lesson. Because it's the heartbreak that shows us the truth of who we really are. Peter, a friend to the Germans. Maura, a soon-to-be wife.

Most ironic of all is how almost everything I teach, as the once-secreted "spiritual teacher," I can trace back to something I read in my father's "literary dribble," or something I learned watching him navigate his own flung-off-the-catapult experience, all of which now lives here, in the book.

It's been a *Decade-Long-No-Novocaine-Dentist-Appointment* writing this thing with you, Dad. And apparently, even that kind of torment ends. Miraculous.

I'm glad we wrote the book, Dad. I'm so glad we wrote you a book.

———

Addendum

It was never my intention for this book to address evil in all its current manifestations; such an endeavor would inevitably miss the latest iterations of humanity acting out of savage self-interest. However, this book describes my journey of reckoning with atrocity, religious persecution, responsibility taking, and shame, and those topics compel me to comment on the current crime against humanity being perpetrated by fellow Jews against the Palestinian inhabitants of Gaza and the West Bank.

My people, through their representative government and powerful military, condone brutal, lawless attacks—including wanton murder—by Jewish settlers on Palestinians in the West Bank. And, *my people* are complicit in the starvation of Palestinians in Gaza.

I stand with the many voices in Israel and elsewhere who are horrified by these actions and policies. I denounce the current Israeli leadership and their affiliates. It is particularly depraved that a people who, only two generations ago, suffered starvation as a method of extermination in ghettos and camps are now inflicting similar suffering on others.

Moreover, for the rest of their lives, the Israeli Defense Forces will be carrying a profound *Moral Injury* for their involvement in these actions. That is a contemptible betrayal of them. Turning them into perpetrators is a crime against *their* humanity.

I am filled with revulsion and desperation as I seek ways to help delegitimize and unseat the tyrannical forces in Israel that claim their actions and policies are aligned with the Hebrew Scriptures and thus blessed by the Holy One. These dark forces are a blight on Judaism, the State of Israel, and all of us who share this lineage.

PETER STERNBERG
Chicago, August 5, 2025

Works Cited

Almaas, A.H., *The Diamond Approach,* https://www.diamondap-proach.org/glossary/refinery_phrases/inquiry

Arendt, Hannah, Ph.D., *Eichmann on Trial: A Report on the Banality of Evil,* 2006, New York, Penguin Group, page 252

Battke, Kathleen, Hühner, Reiner, Lommatzsch, Dorle, and Beermann-Zeligson, Judith, Credo of *The Days of Peace* for the 2022 Buchenwald Retreat. Used with permission.

Battke, Kathleen, Ed., *Pearls of Ash and Awe: 20 Years of Bearing Witness in Auschwitz with Bernie Glassman and Zen Peacemakers* (Berlin: edition-Steinrich, 2015), page 64.

Beata-Michlic, Joanna *Poland's Threatening Other: The Image of the Jew from 1880 to the Present* (Lincoln: University of Nebraska, 2006), pp. 122–123.

Becker, Ernest, PhD., *The Denial of Death,* New York: The Free Press, 1973, pp. 123, 127–139, 284, 285

Behrendsen, Susanne, *Maledict Place,* an unpublished poem, used with permission in 2022

Carroll, James, *Constantine's Sword: The Church and the Jews, A History*, Boston, Mariner Books, 2001, pp. 58–59, 134

Chabad.org, 2024, *The Complete Jewish Bible*, Chabad, September 2016 {https://www.chabad.org/library/bible_cdo/aid/15844 /jewish/Chapter-15.htm} *https://en.wikipedia.org/wiki/Yehiel De-Nur*

Elderwarriors, 2015, *Welcome to Elderwarriors: Transformation Happens*, Michael Cicinato and Peter Sternberg, 2024 {*https://www .elderwarriors.org/*}

Elkins, Michael, *Forged in Fury*, London: Piatkus Books, 1996

Gabis, Rita, *A Guest at the Shooter's Banquet: My Grandfather's SS Past, My Jewish Family, A Search for the Truth*, 2015, New York, Bloomsbury Publishing, page 298

Glassman, Bernie, *Bearing Witness: A Zen Master's Lessons in Making Peace*, New York: Bell Tower, 1998, page 214

Gross, Jan, Ph.D., *Neighbors: The Destruction of the Jewish Community in Jedwabne, Poland* (Princeton: Princeton University Press, 2001), pp. 106–110

Hannah Arendt, Directed by Margarethe von Trotta (2012; Toronto, Canada: Zeitgeist Films (US), 2013, Motion Picture

Hitler, Adolf, *Mein Kampf*, 1939, Reynal and Hitchcock, Chapter 1

Hütz, Eugene, "Start Wearing Purple." Voi-La Intruder, Gogol Bordello, 1999

Immerwahr, Daniel, *How to Hide an Empire*, 2019. New York, Random House

Jacobsen, Annie, *Operation Paperclip*, 2014, New York, Little, Brown and Company, page 423

Kakel, III, Carroll, Ph.D., *The American West and the Nazi East: A Comparative and Interpretive Perspective*, New York: Palgrave McMillian, 2011, pp. 2, 17, 30, 45

Works Cited

Kakel, III, Carroll, Ph.D., *The Holocaust as Colonial Genocide: Hitler's "Indian Wars in the Wild East,"* New York: Palgrave McMillian, 2013, page 51

Langer, PhD. Walter, Murray, PhD. Henry, Kris, PhD. Ernst, Lewin, M.D. Betram, "The Psychological Analysis of Adolf Hitler: His Life and Legend," https://archive.org/details /A Psychological Analysis of Adolf Hitler, Office of the OSS (later the CIA), 1943, republished July 29, 2020, pp. 22, 24, 99, 145

Miller, Ron, Ph.D., *recorded lecture series on* Constantine's Sword, presented at Common Ground, Deerfield, IL in September/ October 2001

Ohler, Norman, *Blitzed: Drugs in the Third Reich*, New York, New York: Mariner Books, 2018, pp. 8, 104

Ohlere, David, *Crematorium III,* 2018, Auschwitz-Birkenau State Museum in Oswiecim

Reagan, Ronald, *An American Life,* 1990, New York, Simon and Schuster, page 409

Shay, Jonathan, M.D. *Achilles in Vietnam: Combat Trauma and the Undoing of Character*, New York: Scribner, 1994, page 151

Shirer, William, *Berlin Diary: The Journal of a Foreign Correspondent 1934–1941*, 1941, New York, Alfred Knopf, page 10

Tick, Ph.D., Edward, *War and the Soul*, 2005, Wheaton, IL, Quest Books

The Truth and Reconciliation Commission, April 16, 2024, *Welcome to the official Truth and Reconciliation Commission Website,* The Truth and Reconciliation Commission of South Africa {*https://www.justice.gov.za/trc/index.html*}

The United States Holocaust Memorial Museum, established in 1993, *Euthanasia Program—Photograph* {*https://encyclopedia.ushmm .org/content/en/gallery/euthanasia-program-photographs*}

The United States Holocaust Memorial Museum, opened in 1993, *The Holocaust Encyclopedia*, "Kielce Pogrom," January 2013 {https://encyclopedia.ushmm.org/content/en/timeline-event/holocaust/after-1945/kielce-pogrom}

Uris, Leon, *Exodus.* 1958, New York, Doubleday & Company

Wiesel, Elie, *Night.* 1982, New York, Bantam Books, pp. 61–62

Wiesenthal, Simon, *The Sunflower,* 1976, Schocken Books, New York, Books One and Two

The Zen Peacemakers Order, 2023, *What Is Z.P.O?* The Zen Peacemakers Order, December 2023 {https://zenpeacemakers.org/about/zen-peacemaker-order/}

Peter's Acknowledgments and Gratitudes

As a reader, I have often had the experience of looking at authors' *Acknowledgments* pages. And every time I did, I was re-surprised at how many people were named as having made necessary contributions to the development and production of the book. I am no longer surprised.

To the guy who initially and persistently said, "You have to write a book," my late, dear friend Lou Stoetzer, I offer my humble thanks. I regard him, in life and in death, as the Irritating Monk in my life—saying and doing things that in the moment made my life more difficult, but consistently brought opportunity, richness, and depth. No one read my journals as carefully as he and then sat with me in the blistering emotion that often appeared there. And then, because he is the Irritating Monk, he pointed out the potential for the book he insisted I write. It seems in this, as in many things, you were right, Louie. I hope you like the book.

From her first reading of my journals, my wife told me I'd be writing a book. To my steadfast partner in it all, a woman who unhesitantly supported the long years of effort at producing this book, Maggie McCarthy, I am deeply grateful. She endured my many hours in research, writing endless drafts, and swearing in frustration. In the early days, I foolishly laughed at how preposterous her prophecy of publishing was, aaaaand, here we are. Maggie, more than anyone, saw firsthand and endured firsthand the unusual—and, at times, soul-shredding and soul-reconfiguring—experience I was having. She never wavered. She never doubted what I was doing and the meaning that would be discovered. She consistently supported my travel into challenging experiences. She saw and trusted the larger purpose, when all I could do was plod and stumble along an uncharted path. Without her unwavering support, this book would not have come to fruition.

My daughters—Maura, Ellianna, and Leah—knew from the beginning of all of this in 2013 that their father had become possessed. They saw me plunge into study, self-reflection, and my various practices. They openly expressed their faith and support in me and have been my strongest promoters—including getting me speaking gigs at their high schools and colleges back in the day. You three are my great teachers; I am always amazed by your innate perspective and wisdom about spirituality, life, and death. And I try to follow as best I can . . .

I am very grateful for the input and guidance of my clear-sighted and patient editors: Nina Catanese, Stuart Horwitz, the folks at 1106 Design, and legal guidance from Carolyn Levin. The generous input from readers along the way was necessary both for their encouragement and to nudge the book toward its final form. Thank you all.

I have been blessed with many friends who have encouraged me, stood by me, challenged me, and taught me: Kathleen Battke, Richard Campbell, Ph.D., Vivienne Cardin, Fr. Michael Cicinato, Judy Farrow, Ann Ehringhaus, Judy Feinberg, Ellen Goode, Edward Hamlin, Laurie Hunken, Reiner Hühner, the late Janice Jacobson, the late Michael Johnson, Gerry Lane, Leslie Levin, Dorle Lommatzsch, the late Luther, Gabbi Miller, Joe Monahan, Joni Reed, Jo Ann Seager, the late Bill Smith, LCSW, Ginni Stern, M.S.W., Larry Stoler, Ph.D., Robert Schwarz, Ph.D., Viktoria von Schirach, Chris Turley, and my late, relentless, and beloved tether-dog Casey.

Can we adequately thank our teachers? The ones who, often without ever realizing what they have done, set something loose—planted a seed that perhaps after many years, developed? With my deepest gratitude for: Sensei John Barr, Professor James Carrol, the late Roshi Bernie Glassman, Professor Peter Hayes, the late, the relentless, Lenny Hochman, Ph.D., Professor Judith Levi, the late Professor Ron Miller, the relentless Marge Minervini, MA, Master Peter Moy, Jonathan Shay, M.D., Edward Tick, Ph.D., and Reluctant-Master Lou Ucha. And, of course, there are my patients with whom I get to do performance art and learn by witnessing what emerges from the dance of psychotherapy. What an honor.

This book would never have come into existence without my former-English-teacher daughter Maura devoting hours poring over my misshapen productions until, with gentle questioning and note-taking, she forced me to distill a thread she saw, or a thought that came out of an explanation I offered—all to enrich the story. She bravely presented me with feedback that my work was far from acceptable for presentation and endured my frustration and exasperation. She was *almost* always correct. She is a gifted, patient, and deeply insightful guide and teacher. What meant the world to me were the times she told me *she* was learning a lot. Well, that, and the hysterical laughter . . . What a trip, Maura—what a trip.

The witnesses and allies of my childhood years were my sister and brother, as I was for them. They have been a lifeline of humor and understanding. My mother, in her unique way, and my father in his, kept pushing me toward the truth, requiring me to hone myself and then invariably testing me so I could hone myself some more. . . .

Oh, and one more mention. When my dead father tipped his hat to me at the reading I had with the medium in Ireland, he asked if he could be part of the effort to get this book done. In that moment, I paused and then said, "Sure, if you want to." I cannot tell you with certainty what contributions he made, if any, but on the off-chance he did, "Thanks, Dad."

Maura's Gratitudes

The *project of writing a book* is much like starting a family; it takes a village—and more than a few dark nights of the soul.

My foremost gratitude I must offer to my father, for being brave enough to go on this healing journey of reconciliation, and for being brave enough to live that experience out loud. I learned more working on this project with him than I could have obtained from any degree or training. It was like I was *apprenticing* to his experience of transformation. As I mentioned in the text, almost all of what I do now as a spiritual counselor and medical intuitive has been touched, shaped, honed, or inspired by a teaching I received from his story, and from the process of putting the book together.

There are a great many memories I have that I will cherish for the rest of my life: his gentle swaying in the wooden rocking chair while we wrote, dancing around the kitchen counters laying *each page in order* during our outlining process, emails with updated drafts containing subject lines like: *"brand new Auschwitz updated! yay!"* or *"Buchenwald restructure finally complete."* And I wouldn't have come out the other side of my personal transformation without having witnessed him on the journey we've put to these pages here, in *Tai Chi at Auschwitz*. As we say, ten thousand bows to you, Peter. May my life be an honoring of what I've learned here.

And, of course, deep gratitude to my mother, for saying, "Maura, are you actually interested in helping Dad with his writing? If so . . . he's out on the pergola, and he could use a hand." Almost all of the major life stepping stones that I've traversed, she pointed me toward. So, this project, as with many aspects of my life, I owe to her. I will also cherish our laughter, eyeing each other from across the living room as we grammar-ized poor Dad before dinner. In our family, I learned that hard work could be joyous, that the beauty of collaboration lives in how we sit down to *be* with each other. So much of that comes from you, Mom. Thank you. (Also, thank you for combing through all of my middle- and high-school essays so painstakingly that I was confident/audacious enough to help Dad write a book. That's pretty cool.)

Thank you to my sisters, Ellie and Leah. Nothing I have done or will do would be possible without you. There's nowhere I go where I don't feel you with me. I'd choose you for sisters again and again.

Thank you to my dear sister in life and business Qiddist, and her wife, Olivia. They watched me from afar work tirelessly on this book project, not knowing what the hell was so special about it or why I was so driven to help my father complete it. After our fateful Yellowstone trip, my Dad and I arrived on their land in Oregon and read some excerpts out loud. As they listened, they became solemn, their faces in a half smile of quiet wonder. Their reaction—"Oh, Maura, *this* is what you've been working on? We get it now."—bolstered our energy to see the project through to its completion. I'll never forget the look on my father's face hearing Olivia say, "This *has* to be published." I've never known friendship like ours, Q. The only words I have are: thank God.

I owe much gratitude and acknowledgment to the people who have hurt my heart and to the people whose hearts I've hurt. May what I learned in those hard times be honored in my contribution to this work.

Lastly, to The Chef. Thank you for putting my heart back together, for teaching me to love and write and eat and dance again. I had an inkling I might be yours that first week we met, when you adjusted my syntax better than I could have myself. We're all glad that you're into writers. Thank you for finding me after all this time.

Peter's Bio

Peter Sternberg is a psycho-therapist living with his wife, Maggie, in a suburb of Chicago. They have three grown daughters with partners/spouses. His interests include co-running Elderwarriors Retreats with Fr. Michael Cicinato, helping organize healing retreats at sites of atrocity in the world, and teaching people how to use *Council* for peer support in troubled times.  Peter enjoys hiking, travel, skiing, and pursuing his various practices—most notably, Tai Chi.

Maura's Bio

Maura Sternberg is a Zen Shiatsu practitioner and the co-facilitator of *The Holy Well*, a women's health organization. She lives with her beloved and her dear friends on a farm outside of Portland, Oregon. She writes, teaches, practices herbalism, offers bodywork, and facilitates healing ceremony—in between running after chickens and goats.